Electronic Signatures in International Contracts

European University Studies

Europäische Hochschulschriften
Publications Universitaires Européennes

Series II
Law

Reihe II Série II
Rechtswissenschaft
Law

Vol./Bd. 4982

PETER LANG

Frankfurt am Main · Berlin · Bern · Bruxelles · New York · Oxford · Wien

Carolina M. Laborde

Electronic Signatures
in International Contracts

PETER LANG
Internationaler Verlag der Wissenschaften

Bibliographic Information published by the Deutsche Nationalbibliothek
The Deutsche Nationalbibliothek lists this publication in the Deutsche Nationalbibliografie; detailed bibliographic data is available in the internet at http://dnb.d-nb.de.

Zugl.: Freiburg (Breisgau), Univ., Diss., 2008

D 25
ISSN 0531-7312
ISBN 978-3-631-59536-7

© Peter Lang GmbH
Internationaler Verlag der Wissenschaften
Frankfurt am Main 2010
All rights reserved.

www.peterlang.de

A mis padres, Lilian y Jorge, de quienes aprendí el amor y la dedicación por el trabajo.

A mis hermanos, Lucas, Marcela y Gustavo, por el cariño y las vivencias que nos unen.

A mi esposo, Sven, con quien hacemos camino al andar.

Preface

This work was developed at the Information Management and Market Engineering (IME) Graduate School of the University of Karlsruhe (TH), Germany, directed by Prof. Dr. Christof Weinhardt. It was presented as a doctoral thesis at the Albert Ludwig University of Freiburg School of Law, Germany, in May 2008. The references contained in this work have been updated as of September 2009.

This work could not have been accomplished without the financial support of the German Research Foundation (DFG) nor without the assistance of the IME Graduate School, which provided me with all the means to undertake a genuinely interdisciplinary research. To them, my heartfelt appreciation.

I would especially like to thank my doctoral thesis advisor, Prof. Dr. Peter Sester, for according me the intellectual freedom to approach the topic under study as I thought fit. Similarly, I would like to express my gratitude to Prof. Dr. Maximilian Haedicke for preparing the second doctoral opinion.

Frankfurt, October 2009   Carolina M. Laborde

Table of Contents

Abbreviations

ABA .... American Bar Association
Argentine Digital Signature Act .... Ley de Firma Digital No. 25.506
Begr. RegE .... Gesetzentwurf der Bundesregierung BGB
    Bürgerliches Gesetzbuch
BGBl. .... Bundesgesetzblatt
BGH .... Bundesgerichtshof
BT-Drucks. .... Bundestags-Drucksache
Buenos Aires Protocol .... Protocol of Buenos Aires on International
    Jurisdiction in Contractual Matters
CISG .... Convention on Contracts for the
    International Sale of Goods
DJ .... Doctrina Judicial
DStR .... Deutsches Steuerrecht
DstRE .... DStR-Entscheidungsdienst
E-Sign .... Electronic Signatures in Global and
    National Commerce Act
Ed. / Eds. .... Editor / Editors
EDI .... Electronic Data Interchange
EGBGB .... Einführungsgesetz zum Bürgerlichen
    Gesetzbuch
Electronic Commerce Directive .... Directive 2000/31/EC of the European
    Parliament and of the Council of 8 June
    2000 on certain legal aspects of
    information society services, in particular
    electronic commerce, in the Internal
    Market (Directive on Electronic
    Commerce)
Electronic Signatures Directive .... Directive 1999/93/EC of the European
    Parliament and of the Council on a
    Community framework for electronic
    signatures
Form Adaptation Act .... Gesetz zur Anpassung der
    Formvorschriften des Privatrechts und
    anderer Vorschriften an den modernen
    Rechtsgeschäftsverkehr
German Digital Signature Act .... Gesetz zur digitalen Signatur
German Electronic Signatures Act .... Gesetz über Rahmenbedingungen für
    elektronische Signaturen und zur
    Änderung weiterer Vorschriften
GUIDEC .... General Usage for International Digitally
    Ensured Commerce
ICC .... International Chamber of Commerce
ILPF .... Internet Law & Policy Forum

Mercosur .... Mercado Común del Sur
MMR .... MultiMedia und Recht
NCCUSL .... National Conference of Commissioners of
                                                 Uniform State Law
NJW .... Neue Juristische Wochenschrift
NJW-RR .... NJW-Rechtsprechungs-Report Zivilrecht
No. .... Number
p. / pp. .... Page / Pages
para. .... Paragraph(s)
PIN/PINs .... Personal Identification Number(s)
PKI... Public Key Infrastructure
RCyS .... Responsabilidad Civil y Seguros
RNotZ .... Rheinische Notar-Zeitschrift
Rome Convention .... Convention on the Law Applicable to
                                                 Contractual Obligations
Rome I Regulation............................ Regulation 593/2008 of the European
                                                 Parliament and the Council of 17 June
                                                 2008 on the law applicable to contractual
                                                 obligations (Rome I)
TAN / TANs .... Transaction number(s)
UCC .... Uniform Commercial Code
UETA .... Uniform Electronic Transactions Act
UNCITRAL .... United Nations Commission on
                                                 International Trade Law
UNIDROIT .... International Institute for the Unification
                                                 of Private Law
UNIDROIT Principles .... UNIDROIT Principles of International
                                                 Commercial Contracts
US .... United States of America

Introduction

The purpose of this work is to analyze electronic signatures in the context of international contracts. More precisely, the goal is to study the impact of electronic signature legislation on the legal validity of electronic signatures when used in transactions that bring together different legal systems.

Electronic means of communication such as the Internet and e-mail open the possibility for the execution of contracts. However, some types of contracts must fulfill certain formal requirements to be valid or enforceable. One such formal requirement is the signature; then, contracts that require a signature should be capable of being signed electronically.

The irruption of electronic signatures raised questions in the legal field, mainly as to their validity. Since the mid 1990s the law has addressed those issues and, as a result, legislation on the topic has proliferated at a steady pace but not always in the same direction. Electronic signature legislation seeks to ensure the legal validity of electronic signatures. Nevertheless, the question is whether this goal has been achieved in the international sphere. Contracts entered into electronically are likely to be international and to bear contacts with more than one legal system; however, due to divergent electronic signatures statutes, an electronic signature may be regarded as valid under one law but not under another one.

In order to answer the question as to the legal value of electronic signatures in international contracts different topics have to be analyzed. The work is divided into three parts and ten chapters. Part one presents an introduction to the subject of electronic signatures and its legal regulation because the first topic that needs to be addressed concerns the basics of electronic signatures. To this end, the first chapter is devoted to explaining the nature of electronic signatures. This is a topic where law and technology are deeply intertwined; therefore, in order to comprehend the legal issues surrounding electronic signatures it is necessary to understand the technological background. The second chapter deals with the legal issues triggered by electronic signatures as well as the main solutions adopted by different legal systems.

In order to analyze the legal aspects of electronic signatures in international contracts it is necessary to know what the different legal systems understand by electronic signatures and how they regulate them. Therefore, the second part analyzes the current electronic signatures regulation in the United States of America (Chapter 3), the European Union with special attention to Germany (Chapter 4), and Argentina (Chapter 5). Moreover, the work of organizations active in this field will be covered (Chapter 6).

Finally, the third part focuses on how electronic signatures statutes interrelate in international electronic contracts. Parties to an international electronic contract are interested in knowing which electronic signature legislation will apply to their contract and the consequences of having one electronic signature statute or another governing the electronic signature requirements. Therefore, in an international contract it is necessary to know which one of the different laws with which a contract has contacts may be the one governing the form. For that purpose, chapter seven introduces the issues of the determination of the law governing the formal validity of an international contract; that means, establishing which law will be the one setting forth the electronic signature requirements. For a complete analysis of the topic the concept of international contract as well as the determination of the law applicable to the contract will be addressed. In turn, chapters eight and nine address those issues from the perspective of international conventions and domestic law (Argentina, Germany and the United States of America), respectively. Finally, the interrelation of different electronic signature legislation is examined (Chapter 10). The analysis will be conducted from the perspective of national legislation in three different jurisdictions: Argentina, the United States of America and Germany. Nevertheless, the reference point will always remain the Argentine law.

Part I: Electronic signatures, from technology to law

Chapter 1: Signatures

A. The electronic environment

In order to understand electronic signatures it is first necessary to understand the medium in which they function. Electronic signatures are used in electronic communications, electronic documents and electronic transactions, which take place in channels that are not always secure, either because they are open networks to which everyone has access, like the Internet, or because, in the case of closed networks, unauthorized persons may gain access to them through attacks.[1] Insecurity may arise with regard to three spheres: insecurity as to the identity of persons, insecurity as to the integrity of information and insecurity as to the privacy of information.[2] These risks are common to all types of communications but present new angles when in connection with the electronic medium.

I. Identity of the person

Proper identification of a person is necessary to ensure secure online transactions.[3] This is especially true for transactions with legal relevance, such as when purchasing goods or contracting services, where it is important to know with whom a contract is being entered into.[4] However, when entering into a contract via electronic means the other party is sometimes unknown and there is no certainty as to his or her identity.[5] Even in electronic transactions where contracting parties know and trust each other, there is always the risk that the

---

[1]   *Ferguson / Schneier*, Practical Cryptography, 2003, pp. 21-22.

[2]   *Boyd / Mathuria*, Protocols for Authentication and Key Establishment, 2003, pp. 4-12; *Bruen / Forcinito*, Cryptography, Information Theory, and Error-Correction, 2005, pp. 151-152.

[3]   *Reed*, Internet Law, 2004, pp. 140-141; *Smedinghoff*, The Legal Requirements for Creating Secure and Enforceable Electronic Transactions, 2002, pp. 17-18; UNCITRAL, Thirty-first session, Report of the Working Group on Electronic Commerce on the Work of its Thirty-second Session, 1998, (A/CN.9/446), p. 28, para. 89.

[4]   *Geis*, Die elektronische Signatur: Eine internationale Architektur der Identifizierung im E-Commerce, MMR 2000, 667; *Reed*, Internet Law, 2004, p. 141; *Kania*, The ABA's Digital Signature Guidelines: An Imperfect Solution to Digital Signatures on the Internet, CommLaw Conspectus: Journal of Communications Law and Policy, Volume 7, 1999, 297, 298-299.

[5]   *Valenzi*, Digital Signatures: An Important "Sign" of the Future of E-Government, virginia.edu, Volume IV, Number 2, 2000; *Reed*, Internet Law, 2004, pp. 140-141.

person at the other end is an impostor. Establishing the identity of a person in electronic transactions is referred to as authentication.[6]

In fact, the problem of establishing somebody's identity is as old as human interaction. How can a person be sure of whom the other person is? This question may arise in any oral, mail, e-mail or online communication. Therefore, each medium has developed its own methods of establishing identity in a secure way. For instance, in person-to-person transactions, identity is evidenced by government-issued identifications, such as national identification documents, drivers' licenses or passports, among others. In telephone transactions (telephone banking, for example), personal data or personal identification numbers (PINs) are required. In written transactions the identity of the signatory is established with a handwritten signature or with the intervention of a notary public.[7] In electronic communications, PINs, passwords, private keys, and fingerprints, to name but a few, may be used.[8] Authentication techniques are based on the premises that what a person uses to prove his or her identity is unique to that person, either because it is inherent to him or her (voice, handwriting, fingerprint), or because it is information (PIN, password, personal data) or a device (a card) that can be kept under his or her sole control.[9]

---

[6]   *Atreya / Hammond / Paine / Starrett / Wu,* Digital Signatures, 2002, pp. 3 and 5. The term authentication may have ambiguous meanings. In the United States of America it is used predominantly in reference to the identification of the signer and this is the meaning which has prevailed. In Europe, however, the term has been used in relation to the verification of the signature. See International Chamber of Commerce, GUIDEC II – General Usage for International Digitally Ensured Commerce (version II), 2001, p. 31; *Schellekens,* Electronic signatures – Authentication Technology from a legal perspective, Information Technology & Law Series, Number 5, 2004, p. 15.

[7]   *Reed,* Internet Law, 2004, pp. 141-142; *Lorenzetti,* Comercio Electrónico, 2001, pp. 58-59; *Kania,* The ABA's Digital Signature Guidelines: An Imperfect Solution to Digital Signatures on the Internet, CommLaw Conspectus: Journal of Communications Law and Policy, Volume 7, 1999, 297, 298-299.

[8]   *Atreya / Hammond / Paine / Starrett / Wu,* Digital Signatures, 2002, pp. 142-145.

[9]   The different methods to establish the identity of a person are normally classified into three categories: something the person is (fingerprint, iris or voice identification), something the person knows (PINs, passwords) or something the person has (a token or card), see UNCITRAL, Thirty-first session, Report of the Working Group on Electronic Commerce on the Work of its Thirty-second Session, 1998, (A/CN.9/446), pp. 29-33, para. 87-106; *Kaufman / Perlman / Speciner,* Network Security, 2002, p. 237; *Baker / Hurst,* The Limits of Trust – Cryptography, Governments, and Electronic Commerce, 1998, pp. 247-248; *Vacca,* Practical Internet Security, 2007, pp. 31-33; *Schellekens,* Electronic signatures – Authentication Technology from a legal perspective, Information Technology & Law Series, Number 5, 2004, pp. 15-20.

Thus, as an example, when someone goes in person to the bank to make a transaction using his or her bank account, he or she has to show proof of being the bank account holder. In case of telephone banking, a PIN number previously supplied by the bank is needed or personal information may be requested. In the case of transactions made in an ATM machine or on the Internet, identity is normally established by means of PINs or passwords.

II. Integrity of the document

A second problem in electronic transactions is the integrity of the electronic document.[10] Electronic documents are easy to create, to modify, to send, to store. Yet, these praiseworthy characteristics may explain why security is a main concern when using electronic documents.[11] During its transmission, the document can be modified or replaced; therefore, the recipient may receive an altered document or even a different document than the one sent by the sender.[12]

Unlike paper documents where changes to the document leave a trace, it might not be possible to detect an alteration in an electronic document. Nevertheless, the integrity of a document is also a concern in paper documents. It is possible to intercept mail and to change or alter a paper document. Even though these facts may be easier to prove in paper documents, it may take a considerable amount of time and money in litigation. Therefore, in order to protect the integrity of paper documents during transmission, they are delivered personally or through trusted persons. However, the integrity of a document is a concern not only during its transmission but during the whole time period of the contractual relationship. A contractual party can change a page of the document or alter some of its main provisions. The insertion of initials on every page of the document and the practice of signing any change introduced in the document helps to ensure the integrity of paper documents. In turn, in order to protect the integrity of electronic documents, both during their transmission and thereafter, hash functions are used.

Hash functions are algorithms that reduce the size of an electronic document producing a hash result (also called message digest or hash value) of a fixed size

---

[10] *Atreya / Hammond / Paine / Starrett / Wu,* Digital Signatures, 2002, p. 3.

[11] *Bettendorf,* Elektronische Dokumente und Formqualität, RNotZ 2005, 277, 278; *Smedinghoff,* The Legal Requirements for Creating Secure and Enforceable Electronic Transactions, 2002, p. 18; *Atreya / Hammond / Paine / Starrett / Wu,* Digital Signatures, 2002, pp. 2 and 4.

[12] *Ferguson / Schneier,* Practical Cryptography, 2003, pp. 23-26; *Atreya / Hammond / Paine / Starrett / Wu,* Digital Signatures, 2002, pp. 16-17; *Hall,* El rol de la encriptación de datos en la despapelización, in: Palazzi (Ed.), Derecho y nuevas tecnologías, Year 1, No. 0, 2000, pp. 22-23.

and unique to that specific electronic document.[13] The particularity of hash functions is that given a certain input, the result is always the same; then if the input changes, so does the result.[14] Consequently, the hash result is uniquely linked to the message because if the message (input) changes, so will the hash result.[15] This means that by applying a hash function to a same document, the hash result shall always be identical.[16] On the contrary, if the document changes even a bit (for example, by adding a comma or eliminating a space), the hash result will be different.[17] In other words, if a hash result turns out to be different from the previous one, then, it is certain that the document has been modified. Moreover, one-way hash functions are used to ensure that the message cannot be inferred from the hash result, which means it is not possible to deduce the content of the message from the hash result.[18]

III. Confidentiality of communications

In general, there seems to be an interest in keeping written communications private and unknown to third parties.[19] This concern has existed for centuries.[20] Even Roman emperor Julius Caesar had to find a way to send messages so that only the recipient could understand them.[21] Cryptography has provided the answer to this problem by developing means of sending information written in a

---

[13] American Bar Association, Digital Signature Guidelines, 1996, pp. 52-53; *Ferguson / Schneier*, Practical Cryptography, 2003, pp. 83-84; *Atreya / Hammond / Paine / Starrett / Wu,* Digital Signatures, 2002, p. 88. Common hash algorithms are SHA-1 and MD5, see *Ferguson / Schneier*, Practical Cryptography, 2003, pp. 86-88.

[14] American Bar Association, Digital Signature Guidelines, 1996, pp. 52-53; *Atreya / Hammond / Paine / Starrett / Wu,* Digital Signatures, 2002, p. 88.

[15] *Atreya / Hammond / Paine / Starrett / Wu,* Digital Signatures, 2002, p. 88.

[16] *Atreya / Hammond / Paine / Starrett / Wu,* Digital Signatures, 2002, p. 88.

[17] *Atreya / Hammond / Paine / Starrett / Wu,* Digital Signatures, 2002, p. 88.

[18] *Ferguson / Schneier*, Practical Cryptography, 2003, p. 84; *Atreya / Hammond / Paine / Starrett / Wu,* Digital Signatures, 2002, p. 88; *Kaufman / Perlman / Speciner*, Network Security, 2002, p. 117; American Bar Association, Digital Signature Guidelines, 1996, p. 39.

[19] *Ferguson / Schneier*, Practical Cryptography, 2003, pp. 21-22; *Smedinghoff*, The Legal Requirements for Creating Secure and Enforceable Electronic Transactions, 2002, pp. 18-19; *Atreya / Hammond / Paine / Starrett / Wu,* Digital Signatures, 2002, p. 3.

[20] *Atreya / Hammond / Paine / Starrett / Wu,* Digital Signatures, 2002, p. 15.

[21] He did so by replacing each letter of the alphabet by the third subsequent letter, see *Bruen / Forcinito*, Cryptography, Information Theory, and Error-Correction, 2005, pp. 18-19; *Atreya / Hammond / Paine / Starrett / Wu,* Digital Signatures, 2002, pp. 18-19.

secret manner and, consequently, only readable to those persons having the key to decrypt it.[22]

It should be noted that electronic signatures are not precisely concerned with the issue of confidentiality, but rather focus on the identity of the signer. Besides, in some cases, electronic signatures may also guarantee the integrity of the electronic document. Nevertheless, as this chapter will discuss later, the relevance of cryptography relies on the fact that it can achieve those two purposes, namely ensure identity and integrity.

B.   Electronic signatures

Electronic means of communication, in particular the Internet, have revolutionized our daily life.[23] Thanks to the e-mail it is possible to communicate with and send documents to people all over the world in a speedy and inexpensive manner. Moreover, several operations that used to be carried out in person or by post may now be performed online, like paying bills. Furthermore, electronic communications have opened a new channel for commerce. Electronic commerce makes it possible to purchase goods and services online; therefore, contracts can be executed simply with Internet access.[24] Of lately, electronic commerce transactions have become more frequent and involve larger amounts of money.[25]

In some cases, the law may require a certain transaction to be in writing and signed or evidenced by a written and signed document. While we use handwritten signatures to sign paper documents, it is not possible to sign in this manner a document which only exists in electronic form.[26] This is why, the techniques used in order to ensure identity, integrity and confidentiality in

---

[22]   For the history of cryptography see *Bruen / Forcinito*, Cryptography, Information Theory, and Error-Correction, 2005, pp. 3-15.

[23]   *Atreya / Hammond / Paine / Starrett / Wu*, Digital Signatures, 2002, p. 7.

[24]   However, electronic commerce does not refer only to transactions over the Internet but includes also the e-mail and Electronic Data Interchange (EDI). EDI allows companies counting with the relevant technology to exchange standardized messages and documents from computer to computer without human intervention. See *Mann / Winn*, Electronic Commerce, 2005, pp. 332-343; *Ford / Baum*, Secure Electronic Commerce, 1997, pp. 1-2, and 27-29; *Vacca*, Practical Internet Security, 2007, pp. 71-72; *Rosner* International Jurisdiction in European Union E-Commerce Contracts, in: Kisella / Simpson (Eds.), Online Contract Formation, 2004, pp. 482-483.

[25]   La Nación, May 28, 2007, Fuerte expansión del comercio electrónico, <http://ww w.lanacion.com.ar/archivo/Nota.asp?nota_id=912352>; La Nación, November 14, 2006, Las compras on-line crecen un 60%, <http://www.lanacion.com.ar/archivo/ Nota.asp?nota_id=858554>.

[26]   *Reed*, Internet Law, 2004, p. 180.

electronic transactions started to gain importance in the legal world.[27] These technologies may not only be employed for those purposes but could also perform the same functions as handwritten signatures though in the electronic arena. All of these authentication techniques are known in the legal literature as electronic signatures.

However, it should be noted that these techniques were not developed with the purpose of finding a counterpart of handwritten signatures. The initial goal of electronic signatures was to establish identity in electronic transactions. Therefore, not every time that an electronic signature is used, a signature in the legal sense is being created. These techniques are frequently used just for the purpose of ensuring the identity of a person, the integrity of a document or the privacy of information.[28]

In order to present a clear scheme of the topic, the *signature* aspect of electronic signatures shall be developed in the first place and then, the *electronic* aspect.

I.   Signatures

1.   Concept of signature

Electronic signatures seek to imitate handwritten signatures in the electronic world. The term signature is traditionally associated with a holographic signature, that is, the signature written by a person with his or her own hands with a pen on paper; consequently, the concept of signature is linked to the concept of paper.[29] Therefore, when the law or parties require that a document be signed, the plain understanding – at least until not long ago – was and is that of a signature written by the signatory with his or her own hands on a paper document.

When referring to electronic signatures a certain detachment from this traditional concept is required. More often than not, electronic signatures do not

---

[27] *Reed*, Internet Law, 2004, pp. 142-143.

[28] International Chamber of Commerce, Electronic invoicing in and with the European Union, 2005, pp. 8 and 10 (It distinguishes between the use of electronic signatures for security and for legal purposes.).

[29] Black's Law Dictionary, 2004, s.v. "Signature" ("A person's name or mark written by that person or at the person's direction."); Webster's II New College Dictionary, 2005, s.v. "Signature" ("The name of one as written by oneself."); Diccionario de la lengua española, Real Academia Española, s.v. "Firma" ("Nombre y apellido, o título, que una persona escribe de su propia mano en un documento, para darle autenticidad o para expresar que aprueba su contenido."); Deutsches Rechts-Lexikon, 2001, s.v. "Unterschrift" ("Unterschrift ist der zum Zeichen der Anerkennung des Inhaltes unter einer Urkunde gesetzte, eigenhändig geschrieben – Name einer Person.").

look like a handwritten signature and have nothing to do with writing down a name.[30] There are exceptions, such as the digitalized handwritten signature (a scanned handwritten signature pasted on an electronic document), the signing on a computer pad or the typing of the name at the end of a document. Nevertheless, the departure from the traditional concept of signature is only partial because electronic signatures seek to fulfill the same functions as handwritten signatures.

2. Functions of signatures

Handwritten signatures accomplish several functions.[31] In the first place, handwritten signatures serve to identify the signatory and, consequently, to link a document to a person.[32] A signature on a check serves to identify the issuer; a signature on a drawing identifies the artist. Identification is possible because handwritten signatures are particular to a person. On the one hand, each person freely and creatively decides the characteristic way in which to write down his or her name, and on the other hand, and most importantly, the handwriting is a feature unique to each person, which makes it possible to identify accurately the author of the signature and to distinguish an original signature from a forged one.

Additionally, a signature evidences the signer's will and intention to be bound by the written document, the *animus signandi*.[33] By signing a document the

---

[30] *Hertel*, in: Staudinger, Kommentar zum Bürgerlichen Gesetzbuch, New Edition, 2004, Section 126a, marginal number 4. The lack of similarity of electronic authentication techniques with handwritten signatures is the cause why some authors do not find that the term electronic or digital signature is the most appropriate one, see *Kuechler / Grupe*, Digital Signatures: A Business View, Information Systems Management, 2003, 19, 20.

[31] *Schellekens*, Electronic Signatures – Authentication Technology from a Legal Perspective, Information Technology & Law Series, No. 5, 2004, pp. 59-71; *Reed*, Internet Law, 2004, p. 182; *Atreya / Hammond / Paine / Wu*, Digital Signatures, 2002, pp. 3-4; UNCITRAL, Model Law on Electronic Signatures with Guide to Enactment (2001), 2002, pp. 19-20; American Bar Association, Digital Signature Guidelines, 1996, pp. 4-7; *Cabanellas*, Diccionario Enciclopédico de Derecho Usual, Volume IV (F-I), 1998, s.v. "Firma"; *Einsele*, in: Münchener Kommentar zum Bürgerlichen Gesetzbuch, 5th Edition, 2006, Section 126a, marginal numbers 22-25; *Hertel*, in: Staudinger, Kommentar zum Bürgerlichen Gesetzbuch, New Edition, 2004, Section 126, marginal numbers 125-126; Begr. RegE zu §126a BGB, BT-Drucks. 14/4987, p. 16.

[32] *Hertel*, in: Staudinger, Kommentar zum Bürgerlichen Gesetzbuch, New Edition, 2004, Section 126, marginal number 125; *Atreya / Hammond / Paine / Starrett / Wu*, Digital Signatures, 2002, p. 3.

[33] *Reyes Krafft*, La firma electrónica y las entidades de certificación, 2003, p. 105; *Smedinghoff*, The Legal Requirements for Creating Secure and Enforceable

signer expresses his or her agreement with the content of the document. Therefore, for instance, when a document does not accurately represent the statement of a person, or a contract does not faithfully reproduce the agreement of the parties, a person will normally refuse to sign it because doing so would be an external sign of agreement with its content.

The above-mentioned are the two main functions of signatures: establishing the identity and the intent of the signer.[34] Nevertheless, in legal transactions, signatures also serve other functions; namely, signatures help to ensure the integrity of the document.[35] Signatures are normally written at the end of the document and notations under the signature have no value.[36] The reason is that notations below the signature can be added at any time, by any person and without the knowledge and consent of the signatory. Likewise, writing the initials on every page of a document is a sound legal practice because it serves to ensure that the pages of the document are not replaced.[37]

Electronic Transactions, 2002, pp. 11-12; *Atreya / Hammond / Paine / Starrett / Wu,* Digital Signatures, 2002, p. 3.

[34]   UNCITRAL, Explanatory note by the UNCITRAL secretariat on the United Nations Convention on the Use of Electronic Communications in International Contracts, in: United Nations Convention on the Use of Electronic Communications in International Contracts, 2007, p. 53, para. 154; Enciclopedia Jurídica Omeba, Volume XII, 1960, s.v. "Firma", p. 292.

[35]   *Atreya / Hammond / Paine / Starrett / Wu,* Digital Signatures, 2002, p. 3.

[36]   Argentine case law has ruled so in: Bongiovanni, Luis vs. Cadamuro, Rubén E., Civil and Commercial Court of Appeals of Cordoba, October 31, 1994, La Ley Córdoba 1995, 420 (The signature is to be at the end of the document and the additions below the signature are of no value.); Lazzari, Rafael vs. Amura, Orio M., National Civil Court of Appeals, March 29, 1996, La Ley 1997-E, 1014 (It is not required that the guarantor signs all the pages of a lease contract as long as his signature is at the end of the document.). See also: *Einsele,* in: Münchener Kommentar zum Bürgerlichen Gesetzbuch, 5th Edition, 2006, Section 126, marginal number 10; *Lagomarsino,* in: Belluscio / Zannoni (Eds.), Código Civil, Volume 4, 2001, Section 1012, pp. 646-647. In German legal literature this function of signatures is referred to as *Abschlussfunktion,* see *Prütting / Wegen / Weinreich,* BGB Kommentar, 4th Edition, 2009, Section 126, marginal number 9; *Palm,* in: Erman, Bürgerliches Gesetzbuch, 12th Edition, 2008, Section 126, marginal number 7; *Heinrichs / Ellenberger,* in: Palandt, Bürgerliches Gesetzbuch, 68th Edition, 2009, Section 126, marginal number 5; *Wendtland,* in: Bamberger / Roth, Bürgerliches Gesetzbuch, 2nd Edition, 2007, Section 126, marginal number 6; BGH, NJW 1991, 487, 488.

[37]   Razzeto, Héctor L. vs. Fiorotto, Humberto P., Second Civil and Commercial Court of Appeals of Parana, July 17, 1997, La Ley Litoral 1999, 124 (The practice of signing each page is advisable to avoid possible conflicts between the signatories.); *Cabanellas,* Diccionario Enciclopédico de Derecho Usual, Volume IV, 1998, s.v. "Firma".

Finally, signatures seek to increase awareness of the act a person is consenting to.[38] The law sets forth the requirement of a signed writing for documents and contracts that are deemed of importance. For this reason, the fact that persons have to write down their agreement and sign it may lead them to pay more attention and to be aware of what they are doing and what they are agreeing to.

The terms used in different languages to denote the concept of signature evidence different features of signatures. In English and in French the word *signature* is used.[39] Signature comes from the Latin *signum*, which means sign. The signature is then a sign that serves to identify a person. In Spanish the word *firma* is used, which comes from the verb *firmar* (to sign) meaning to affirm, to give strength.[40] In this case the intention of the signer is stressed. In German the word *Unterschrift* means "below what is written", which is linked to the integrity function of signatures.[41]

The goal of electronic signatures is to perform the same functions as handwritten signatures though adapted to the particularities of electronic transactions. Handwritten and electronic signatures, despite being clearly different, seek to achieve the same objectives but in different media.[42] The United Nations Commission on International Trade Law (UNCITRAL) has used the expression "functional equivalence" to refer to this characteristic.[43] The focus is not on the form of the signature but on the functions it accomplishes. Thus, also in the case

---

[38] *Atreya / Hammond / Paine / Starrett / Wu*, Digital Signatures, 2002, p. 3. This signature feature is highlighted by German legal literature as the warning function (*Warnfunktion*), see *Einsele*, in: Münchener Kommentar zum Bürgerlichen Gesetzbuch, 5th Edition, 2006, Section 126a, marginal number 25; *Heinrichs / Ellenberger*, in: Palandt, Bürgerliches Gesetzbuch, 68th Edition, 2009, Section 126a, marginal number 5; *Hertel*, in: Staudinger, Kommentar zum Bürgerlichen Gesetzbuch, New Edition, 2004, Section 126, marginal numbers 66-68. *Chissick*, Electronic Commerce: Law and Practice, 1999, marginal number 3.65 (The author discusses the issue of the ceremonial function of signatures in click-wrap agreements.).

[39] Written alike but pronounced differently.

[40] Diccionario de la lengua española, Real Academia Española, s.v. "Firmar".

[41] *Creifelds / Weber* (Ed.), Rechtswörterbuch, 19th Edition, 2007, s.v. "Form(erfordnisse, -vorschriften)"; *Hertel*, in: Staudinger, Kommentar zum Bürgerlichen Gesetzbuch, New Edition, 2004, Section 126, marginal numbers 127-128; *Palm*, in: Erman, Bürgerliches Gesetzbuch, 12th Edition, 2008, Section 126, marginal number 7; *Heinrichs / Ellenberger*, in: Palandt, Bürgerliches Gesetzbuch, 68th Edition, 2009, Section 126, marginal number 5. It should be noted that the term *Unterschrift* is used for handwritten signatures. However, all norms dealing with electronic or digital signatures use the term *Signatur*.

[42] *Ford / Baum*, Secure Electronic Commerce, 1997, pp. 6-7.

[43] UNCITRAL, Model Law on Electronic Signatures with Guide to Enactment (2001), 2002, pp. 10 and 43.

of electronic signatures the main requirements are that they are able to establish the identity and intent of the signatory.[44]

3. Terminology

The methods to sign electronic documents are commonly labeled electronic signatures and digital signatures. However, the meaning of these terms is not always consistent in norms and scholarly studies. Sometimes they are used interchangeably, sometimes to mean different things.

The term electronic signature is sometimes used to embrace all of the methods used to sign electronic documents except for one, based on asymmetric or public key cryptography, which is called digital signature.[45] The first generation of legislation followed this distinction and used the term digital signature to refer to the type of signatures based on asymmetric cryptography. That is the case of the Utah Digital Signature Act (1995), the German Digital Signature Act (1997) (*Gesetz zur digitalen Signatur*) and the Argentine Digital Signature Act (2001) (*Ley de Firma Digital* 25.506).[46]

However, subsequent legislation has preferred to use the generic term electronic signature to refer to all types of signing methods including digital signatures. These norms have abandoned, at least as far as terminology is concerned, the use of the term digital signature. Following this line are the UNCITRAL Model Law on Electronic Signatures (2001), the Uniform Electronic Transactions Act (1999) (UETA) and the Electronic Signatures in Global and National Commerce Act (2000) (E-Sign) of the United States of America, as well as the Directive 1999/93/EC of the European Parliament and of the Council on a Community framework for electronic signatures (Electronic Signatures Directive). These norms use only the term electronic signature and this term shall also include the concept of digital signature. However, a distinction shall be drawn between

---

[44] *Reyes Krafft*, La firma electrónica y las entidades de certificación, 2003, pp. 106-107 (The main function of signatures is to be the means by which the signer expresses his consent and not the identity of the signer.); Uniform Electronic Transactions Act with preparatory note and comments, 1999, pp. 9-10; *Reed*, Internet Law, 2004, pp. 191-193.

[45] In Argentine legal literature it is debated whether electronic signature is the generic term and digital signature a kind or otherwise two different and independent concepts, see *Devoto,* Comercio Electrónico y Firma Digital, 2001, pp. 166 and 168; *Lorenzetti*, Comercio Electrónico, 2001, p. 78; *Luz Clara*, Ley de Firma Digital Comentada, 2006, p. 47; *Hocsman*, Negocios en Internet, 2005, p. 360.

[46] The Argentine Digital Signature Act dates from the year 2001 and, therefore, is not among the first statutes enacted in this field. However, in its legal approach to the issue it resembles the first generation of electronic signature legislation, which focused on digital signatures. See *Farrés*, Firma Digital, 2005, pp. 50-54.

these texts. The UNCITRAL Model Law on Electronic Signatures and the Electronic Signatures Directive are silent as to the term digital signature but were drafted taking into consideration and, to a certain extent, tailored around digital signatures. On the other hand, UETA and E-Sign were drafted without having a particular technology in mind.[47]

The latest legislative approach, however, seems to be that of making no reference to the distinction in terminology between electronic and digital signatures. The Convention on the use of Electronic Communications in International Contracts adopted by UNCITRAL in the year 2005 does not use the term electronic signature or digital signature.

This work will respect the terminology chosen by each guideline, statute, regulation, convention or law and, therefore, when making reference to a particular text will use its respective term. On the other hand, when addressing the issue as a whole, and without reference to a specific document, the term electronic signature will be used in a broad sense embracing all techniques including digital signatures. That was the criterion followed when choosing the title for this work. In contrast, the term digital signature will be used when specific reference to public key cryptography-based signatures is required.

II.   Electronic signature techniques

There exists a great variety of electronic signatures based on different technologies. Electronic signatures range from passwords and personal identification numbers (PINs) to biometric methods such as fingerprint, iris, voice or handwriting identification.[48]

Electronic signatures can be as simple as typing one's name or initials, pasting a scanned handwritten signature on an electronic document or clicking on "I agree". These methods are used every day when writing one's name or initials in an e-mail.[49] Commercial e-mails have sometimes a scanned handwritten

---

[47]   For a comparison between E-Sign and the Electronic Signatures Directive see *Lincoln,* Electronic Signature Laws and the Need for Uniformity in the Global Market, The Journal of Small and Emerging Business Law, Volume 8, 2004, 67, 77-79.

[48]   *Bradgate,* Evidential issues of EDI, in: Walden (Ed.), EDI and the Law, 1989, pp. 34-36; *Blythe,* Digital Signature Law of the United Nations, European Union, United Kingdom and United States: Promotion of Growth in E-Commerce with Enhanced Security, Richmond Journal of Law and Technology, Volume IX, No. 2, 2005, 1, 3-5; *Lincoln,* Electronic Signature Laws and the Need for Uniformity in the Global Market, The Journal of Small and Emerging Business Law, Volume 8, 2004, 67, 69-71.

[49]   A name written in an e-mail was considered a valid signature in England and Wales (Hall v. Gognos Limited, Hull Industrial case No. 1803325/97) as well as in

signature of the sender. When buying online it is required to show agreement to the contractual terms or general conditions by clicking or checking a box that reads "I agree" or a similar expression.

Other types of electronic signatures are PINs and passwords. These types of electronic signatures are based on a shared secret. The two parties know the secret word or number that belongs to and identifies a certain person.[50] A personal identification number is, as its name indicates, a number employed to establish the identity of a person based on the fact that the number was individually assigned to that person and is only known by that person. Passwords are normally alphanumeric codes. PINs and passwords are very easy to use. Each time a person accesses a system, he or she has to prove his or her identity by typing the PIN or password. However, there are certain weaknesses inherent to these methods.[51] In the first place, PINs and passwords – unless created by the user – have to be securely transmitted so that no one else knows them. Besides, PINs and passwords may be easy to guess or to eavesdrop. For this reason, it might be required that PINs and passwords be changed on a regular basis. Moreover, any person having knowledge of the PIN or password can access the system and it is not possible to detect whether an intruder and not the legitimate user is the one accessing it.[52]

Despite the weaknesses of scanned handwritten signatures, PINs, passwords or checking of a box reading "I agree", they work successfully in multiple applications. Therefore, they are good examples that show that even though safer technologies are available, they might not be necessary in certain contexts.

---

the United States of America (Could Corp v. Hasbro, Inc. 314 F.3d 289 (7th Cir., 2002) quoted by *Mason*, Electronic Signatures in Practice, Journal of High Technology Law, Volume VI, No. 2, 2006, 148, 157, 161.

[50] However, it is not necessary that the other party knows the PIN or password. Hash algorithms are also used to verify PINs and passwords. Instead of saving the PIN or password the system saves the hash result of the PIN or password. Every time the PIN or password is entered, it is hashed and compared with the hash result saved. Due to the fact that when given a same data a hash function produces always the same hash result, if the password entered is the correct one, the hash result calculated and the has result already saved will be identical, see *Kaufman / Perlman / Speciner*, Network security, 2002, p. 55.

[51] A deeper analysis of the risks associated with passwords can be found in *Kaufman / Perlman / Speciner*, Network Security, 2002, pp. 238-250.

[52] In Germany, in order to increase security, individual transactions normally require a transaction number (TAN). Therefore, a person first has to access the system (bank account, university account) using his or her PIN or password and for a special transaction (wiring money, paying the university fees) a TAN number is required. This ensures that in case of unauthorized access, no transaction will be able to be conducted if the intruder does not have the TANs.

The human body has certain features that are distinctive and unique to each person such as fingerprint, voice, DNA, or iris. Electronic signatures based on these characteristics are called biometric methods. Biometrics is "the measurement and analysis of unique physical or behavioral characteristics (as fingerprint or voice patterns) especially as a means of verifying personal identity".[53] Another unique characteristic is the handwriting. Therefore, one method sometimes used is the signing with a special pen on a special pad. In this case the signature is handwritten neither on paper nor in ink. Biometric methods are extremely reliable as a means of authentication because they are based on personal features that belong only to a particular individual allowing a person's identification with a high degree of certainty.[54] However, implementing biometric methods requires having a data base with enough personal information to be able to compare the data. This is costly and it might be difficult to implement in open networks.

III. Digital signatures

The term digital signature is generally reserved for the method based on asymmetric or public key cryptography. Currently, the digital signature is the technique which ensures with most certainty the identity of the signer as well as the integrity of the message.[55] A digital signature should not be confused with a digitalized image of a handwritten signature or with a signature written on an electronic pad.[56]

1. Cryptography

Cryptography is the discipline that deals with writing in a secret manner.[57] *Crypto* means secret or hidden and *grafía* means graphy.[58] The aim of cryptography is to render a message confidential so that it cannot be read by persons who are not the intended recipient. In order to make a message

---

[53] Merriam Webster Online, <http://www.m-w.com/dictionary/biometrics>, s.v. "Biometrics".

[54] It was reported that in Japan a company launched a paying system based on fingerprint authentication, see Clarín, August 9, 2007, Una compañía japonesa pone a prueba un sistema de pago a través de las huellas digitales, <http://www.clarin.com/diario/2007/08/09/um/m-01474834.htm>.

[55] *Atreya / Hammond / Paine / Starrett / Wu,* Digital Signatures, 2002, p. 4.

[56] *Devoto,* Comercio Electrónico y Firma Digital, 2001, p. 166. However, it could be possible to combine both things, see <http://www.signature-perfect.com>.

[57] Bibliography on cryptography: *Ferguson / Schneier,* Practical Cryptography, 2003; *Boyd / Mathuria,* Protocols for Authentication and Key Establishment, 2003; *Bruen / Forcinito,* Cryptography, Information Theory, and Error-Correction, 2005; *Kaufman / Perlman / Speciner,* Network Security, 2002.

[58] Merriam Webster Online, <http://www.m-w.com/dictionary/cryptography>, s.v. "Cryptography" and "Crypt".

confidential the sender encrypts the message.[59] This means the message (plaintext) is converted into unreadable form (named ciphertext).[60] In turn, in order to read the message the recipient needs to convert it back into readable form, that is from ciphertext into plaintext.[61] To do so the recipient needs to know how to access the content of the message that presents itself as unreadable. In other words, in order to decrypt the message it is necessary to know how it was encrypted.

Cryptography dates back many centuries. The Roman emperor Julius Caesar encrypted his messages by replacing each letter of the alphabet by the third subsequent letter.[62] Today's cryptography uses mathematical keys to encrypt and decrypt. It is possible that the same key is used both to encrypt and to decrypt (symmetric cryptography) or, alternatively, that two different, although mathematically related, keys are used, one to encrypt and one to decrypt (asymmetric cryptography).

a)   Symmetric cryptography

Symmetric cryptography uses a single key both for encryption and decryption of a message.[63] With the same key the message is encrypted by the sender and decrypted by the recipient.

In certain scenarios the use of a single key may present problems. First, the parties have to find a safe way to transmit the key in order to ensure that no one but the intended parties get to know the key. Second, the existence of only one key both to encrypt and decrypt makes it impracticable that the same key be used if the counter party changes because a message can no longer be kept confidential if different parties have knowledge of the one and only key.

---

[59]   *Bruen / Forcinito*, Cryptography, Information Theory, and Error-Correction, 2005, pp. 41-42.

[60]   *Bruen / Forcinito*, Cryptography, Information Theory, and Error-Correction, 2005, pp. 41-42; *Atreya / Hammond / Paine / Starrett / Wu,* Digital Signatures, 2002, pp. 17-18.

[61]   *Atreya / Hammond / Paine / Starrett / Wu,* Digital Signatures, 2002, pp. 17-18; *Bruen / Forcinito*, Cryptography, Information Theory, and Error-Correction, 2005, pp. 41-42.

[62]   *Bruen / Forcinito*, Cryptography, Information Theory, and Error-Correction, 2005, pp. 18-19; *Atreya / Hammond / Paine / Starrett / Wu*, Digital Signatures, 2002, pp. 18-19.

[63]   Examples of symmetric cryptography algorithms are Data Encryption Standards (DES), International Data Encryption Algorithms (IDEA) and Advanced Encryption Standard (AES). For details on their functioning and application, see *Atreya / Hammond / Paine / Starrett / Wu,* Digital Signatures, 2002, pp. 32-35; *Kaufman / Perlman / Speciner*, Network security, 2002, pp. 59-91.

Therefore, the use of a single key for encrypting and decrypting also means that a person needs to have as many keys as persons he or she deals with.[64]

b)   Asymmetric or public key cryptography

Another type of cryptography uses two keys - actually one pair of related keys. Each person holds two keys. One key is the so-called public key, which is made available to everyone and is used to encrypt the message.[65] The other key, the so-called private key, on the contrary, is only known to its holder and is used to decrypt the message.[66] This type of cryptography is known as asymmetric or public key cryptography.

In asymmetric or public key cryptography an algorithm creates two different but mathematically related keys. The key holder discloses the public key but keeps the private key confidential. The special quality of these keys is that making the public key available does not jeopardize the private key as it is arguably not possible to derive the private key from the public key.[67]

When one person sends an encrypted text to somebody else, he or she makes use of the public key of the recipient; that means, the sender encrypts the text with the public key of the recipient. In this way the sender is certain that only the recipient is able to read the message since the recipient has the sole control of the corresponding private key. On the other hand, if a person wants to save a document in his or her computer and keep it confidential, the document has to be encrypted with that person's public key so that he or she is the only one able to decrypt it – hence to read it – using the corresponding private key.

---

[64] *Ferguson / Schneier*, Practical Cryptography, 2003, p. 26.

[65] International Chamber of Commerce, GUIDEC II – General Usage for International Digitally Ensured Commerce (version II), 2001, p. 48; *Ford / Baum*, Secure Electronic Commerce, 1997, p. 107.

[66] International Chamber of Commerce, GUIDEC II – General Usage for International Digitally Ensured Commerce (version II), 2001, p. 48; *Ford / Baum*, Secure Electronic Commerce, 1997, p. 107. Concerning knowledge of the private key, it is unlikely that the holder of a digital certificate actually knows his or her private key. See *Ferguson / Schneier*, Practical Cryptography, 2003, p. 17 ("A good key is too long to remember."). A private key is not a password which a person is able to memorize but instead a complex mathematical method of hashing and encrypting information. A private key may, however, be protected with a password and, therefore, before applying the private key a password is required to activate it.

[67] *Ford / Baum*, Secure Electronic Commerce, 1997, p. 107; van Tilborg (Ed.), Encyclopedia of Cryptography and Security, 2005, s.v. "Public key cryptography", p. 488.

Public-key cryptography solves the problem of the key transmission posed by symmetric cryptography.[68] It is no longer necessary for the parties to exchange the one and only key. In public key cryptography the private key remains under the control of one party and the public key is disclosed.[69] Besides, the fact that the private key is only known to the signer and under his or her sole control means that the same pair of keys can be used with as many parties as desired. Thus, public key cryptography renders it unnecessary for a party to have more than one pair of keys.

2.   Cryptography applied to digital signatures

Public key cryptography may not only be used for confidentiality purposes but also for authentication.[70] Digital signatures are based on asymmetric or public key cryptography; however, the use of cryptography for digital signatures differs from the use of cryptography for confidentiality purposes. When signing a message with a digital signature it is not the aim to protect the message from third-party access and, therefore, a digitally signed message is not confidential.[71]

The use of cryptography in digital signatures aims at ensuring the identity of the signer and the integrity of the message. This is achieved by using the private and public key in the reverse order as they are employed to turn a message confidential. In order to digitally sign a message the signer uses his or her private key. The private key of the signer is used in order to show that the signature belongs to the private key holder because he or she should be the only one with access to the private key. Besides, by using the private key, any person can verify the signature by means of the signer's public key. Therefore, in the case of digital signatures the keys of the signatory are used in the following manner: the private key to create the signature and the public key to verify the signature. In turn, for confidentiality purposes the keys of the recipient[72] are used in the following order: the public key, to encrypt and the private key, to decrypt. However, a message can be both encrypted for confidentiality purposes and digitally signed. With his or her private key, the sender signs the message so

---

[68]   *Ferguson / Schneier*, Practical Cryptography, 2003, p. 27; *Atreya / Hammond / Paine / Starrett / Wu,* Digital Signatures, 2002, pp. 51-52.

[69]   However, in the case of public key cryptography applied to digital signatures, when the key pair is not generated by the signer but by a third party (a certification authority for example) the transmission of the private key is once more a concern.

[70]   *Baker / Hurst*, The Limits of Trust – Cryptography, Governments, and Electronic Commerce, 1998, pp. 2-5.

[71]   *Ferguson / Schneier*, Practical Cryptography, 2003, p. 26.

[72]   The keys of the recipient are used as long as the document which is being encrypted is intended to be read by another person, what is the case of documents to be sent to other persons. Of course, the signer can encrypt the document for his own privacy and in this case the keys of the signer, in the manner indicated above, are used to encrypt and decrypt the document.

that any person can verify the signature; with the public key of the recipient the signer encrypts the message so that only the recipient using his or her private key can decrypt it.[73] In this case, the message is digitally signed and confidential.[74]

The 1976 paper "New Directions in Cryptography" by *Whitfield Diffie* and *Martin Hellman*[75] was a breakthrough in the field of authenticity for electronic communications and the implementation of a functional equivalent to handwritten signatures.[76] This paper presents the solution to two of the main problems concerning electronic communications: privacy and authentication. With respect to the first issue, public key cryptosystems solve the problem of the key distribution and, therefore, enhance the confidentiality level of the message.[77] Concerning authentication, public key cryptosystems can also be used as a means of authentication in electronic communications. A public key cryptosystem makes it possible for anyone to verify whether a signature was created by the holder of the pr ivate key.[78]

---

[73] International Chamber of Commerce, GUIDEC II – General Usage for International Digitally Ensured Commerce (version II), 2001, p. 48.

[74] It is advisable to encrypt first and then to sign, see *Ferguson / Schneier*, Practical Cryptography, 2003, pp. 115-117.

[75] *Diffie / Hellman*, New Directions in Cryptography, IEEE Transactions on Information Theory, 1976.

[76] For more on Diffie Hellman algorithms, see *Ferguson / Schneier*, Practical Cryptography, 2003, pp. 207-222; *Atreya / Hammond / Paine / Starrett / Wu*, Digital Signatures, 2002, pp. 39-44.

[77] "A cryptosystem (or cipher system) is a system consisting of an encryption algorithm, a decryption algorithm, and a well-defined triple of text spaces: plaintexts, ciphertexts and keytexts. For a given keytext the encryption algorithm will map a plaintext to a (usually uniquely determined) ciphertext. For the corresponding keytext, the decryption algorithm will map the ciphertext to the (usually uniquely determined) plaintext", see *van Tilborg* (Ed.), Encyclopedia of Cryptography and Security, s.v. "Cryptosystem", p. 119.

[78] Examples of public key algorithms are RSA (stands for the names of its inventors Ron Rivest, Adi Shamir and Leonard Adleman), ElGamal and DSS (Digital Signature System), see *Kaufman / Perlman / Speciner*, Network Security, 2002, p. 147. For more on RSA, see *Ferguson / Schneier*, Practical Cryptography, 2003, pp. 223-243; *Bruen / Forcinito*, Cryptography, Information Theory, and Error-Correction, 2005, pp. 45-51.

3.   Functioning of digital signatures

Digital signatures involve basically two stages: the creation of the digital
signature by the signer with his or her private key and the verification of the
digital signature by the recipient with the signer's public key.[79]

a)   Creation of the digital signature

The signing of the message is a two-step process. The first step is the reduction
of the size of the message by means of a hash function.[80] The second one is the
application of the signer's private key to the hash result.[81] The private key with
which the signer signs the message is not applied directly to the message but to
the hash result of the message.[82] If the private key were applied to the whole
message, it would be computationally expensive; that means, it would be time-
consuming and would reduce the accuracy of the process.[83] Besides, by using a
hash function the signature has a smaller size and, therefore, the size of the data
to be transmitted to the recipient is reduced.[84]

---

[79]   Literature that covers in detail digital signature and PKI: *Ford / Baum*, Secure
Electronic Commerce, 1997; *Atreya / Hammond / Paine / Starret / Wu*, Digital
Signatures, 2002. For short references: *Kiran / Lareau / Lloyd*, PKI Basics – A
Technical Perspective, PKI Forum, November 2002; *Mendez*, Adopting the Digital
Signature Guidelines in Implementing Public Key Infrastructure for Federal
Procurement of Electronic Commerce, Public Contract Law Journal, 2000,
Volume 29, 285-295; *Valenzi*, Digital Signatures: An Important "Sign" of the
Future of E-Government, virginia.edu, Volume IV, No. 2, 2000; *Devoto, Comercio
Electrónico y Firma Digital*, 2001, pp. 168-176; *Hocsman*, Negocios en Internet,
2005, pp. 362-398; UNCITRAL, Model Law on Electronic Signatures with Guide
to Enactment (2001), 2002, pp. 22-31; *Miedbrodt*, Signaturregulierung im
Rechtsvergleich, 2000, pp. 25-35; *Marly*, in: Soergel, Bürgerliches Gesetzbuch,
13th Edition, 2002, Section 126a, marginal numbers 8-9.
[80]   *Marly*, in: Soergel, Bürgerliches Gesetzbuch, 13th Edition, 2002, Section 126a,
marginal number 9; *Einsele*, in: Münchener Kommentar zum Bürgerlichen
Gesetzbuch, 5th Edition, 2006, Section 126a, marginal number 10.
[81]   It should be noted that the steps described for creating the digital signature are all
part of a same process. Once the signer decides to sign a document the calculation
of the hash result and application of the private key is a single process conducted
automatically. The same applies when verifying the digital signature.
[82]   *Marly*, in: Soergel, Bürgerliches Gesetzbuch, 13th Edition, 2002, Section 126a,
marginal number 9; *Einsele*, in: Münchener Kommentar zum Bürgerlichen
Gesetzbuch, 5th Edition, 2006, Section 126a, marginal number 10; *Wendtland*, in:
Bamberger / Roth, Bürgerliches Gesetzbuch, 2nd Edition, 2007, Section 126a,
marginal number 6.
[83]   *Ferguson / Schneier*, Practical Cryptography, 2003, p. 83.
[84]   Otherwise, "[e]s muss nun ungefähr die doppelte Datenmenge übertragen werden,
nämlich die gleiche Nachricht einmal im Klartext und einmal chiffriert.", see
Sorge, Softwareagenten – Vertragsschluss, Vertragsstrafe, Reugeld, 2006, p. 14.

The digital signature is created as a result of applying the private key of the signer to the hash result. The signer signs using his or her private key for two reasons: on the one hand, it serves as a proof of identity because only the signer knows and has access to his or her private key; on the other hand, what is signed with a private key may be verified with the corresponding public key.

The process of creation of a digital signature clarifies why a message that is digitally signed is not confidential. In the first place, because the private key is not applied directly to the message but to the hash result; thus, what is encrypted with the private key is the hash result. The message itself is transmitted in plaintext.[85] Secondly, even if the private key were applied to the message, everyone could read the message signed with a private key because public keys are disclosed.

b)   Verification of the digital signature

The verification process of digital signatures aims at ensuring that the message has been signed by the sender and that the message has not been altered or replaced during its transmission. Because of these features, digital signatures are currently considered the safest technique to sign electronic documents.[86]

The recipient uses the public key of the signatory to verify that the signature was created using the corresponding private key. The public key can only verify a signature created by the corresponding private key. If the sender's private key was not used, the public key of the sender would not be able to verify the message. In other words, if another private key was used, the public key of the sender would not be able to undo what had been done with the private key that signed the message.[87] In contrast, if the message is verified with the public key of the sender, it means that it was signed with the private key of the sender.

In order to verify whether a message has suffered any changes, a hash function calculates a new hash result of the message as received. The hash result obtained will be compared with the hash result contained in the digital signature, which

---

[85]   *Hertel*, in: Staudinger, Kommentar zum Bürgerlichen Gesetzbuch, New Edition, 2004, Section 126a, marginal number 5; *Einsele*, in: Münchener Kommentar zum Bürgerlichen Gesetzbuch, 5th Edition, 2006, Section 126a, marginal number 10.

[86]   *Einsele*, in: Münchener Kommentar zum Bürgerlichen Gesetzbuch, 5th Edition, 2006, Section 126a, marginal number 23.

[87]   The same is the case when encryption is used for confidentiality purposes. The private key may only decrypt what was encrypted with the corresponding public key. The Resolution 45/1997 of the Secretary of the Public Function (Argentina), Annex – Digital Signature – Relevant Technical Aspects, states this clearly: *"sólo una clave puede "deshacer" lo que su par ha "hecho"'"* (only one key can undo what its pair has done). See also International Chamber of Commerce, GUIDEC II – General Usage for International Digitally Ensured Commerce (version II), 2001, p. 48.

was calculated at the moment of signing. A same message may not produce two different hash results but always the same one and it is practically impossible that two different messages will produce the same hash result.[88] This means that if the two hash results – the one calculated by the recipient when receiving the message and the one calculated and sent by the signatory in the digital signature – are identical, the message has not been altered since it was signed. In contrast, had the message been altered since its signing, the hash result calculated by the recipient would not match the hash result to which the private key was applied to and sent by the sender.

If a message is successfully verified, the recipient has certainty that the signature was created with the corresponding private key and that the document has not been modified since signed.

4.   Public Key Infrastructure

Unlike handwritten signatures, public keys are only a group of numbers and symbols which are not unique to a certain person. A given public key could perfectly belong to one person or another.[89] Therefore, what is missing is a link between the key pair and a person. Likewise, the unique number that identifies a person in a passport or a national identification card is not inherent in a person because it could, in principle, belong to any person. What makes such a number unique to a certain person is the fact that it has been attributed to that person by a reliable authority as well as the fact that the link between the person and the number can be verified by means of a document (passport, identity card) deemed reliable because of the source issuing it.

If the digital signature verification process is correct, then the recipient is ensured that the message was signed by the sender and that the message has not been altered. What the recipient cannot know is whether the private key actually belongs to the sender and whether the person identified as the holder of the keys is the one he or she claims to be.[90] The linking of a set of keys to a person is made through a trusted third party, normally referred to as certification authority or simply as CA.[91] It is the same principle as in notarized handwritten signatures

---

[88]   It is theoretically possible to find two messages that produce the same hash result but in practice it should be extremely difficult to do so. This property of hash functions is referred to as collision-resistance, see *Ferguson / Schneier*, Practical Cryptography, 2003, pp. 84-85; *Atreya / Hammond / Paine / Starrett / Wu*, Digital Signatures, 2002, p. 89; *Kaufman / Perlman / Speciner*, Network Security, 2002, pp. 117-121.

[89]   UNCITRAL, Model Law on Electronic Signatures with Guide to Enactment (2001), 2002, p. 25.

[90]   *Ferguson / Schneier*, Practical Cryptography, 2003, pp. 28-29.

[91]   UNCITRAL, Model Law on Electronic Signatures with Guide to Enactment (2001), 2002, pp. 25-26. It should be noted that in norms, case law and scholarly

where a notary public attests to the identity of the signer. The intervention of a third party requires an infrastructure controlling its functioning, establishing technological requirements and issuing regulation, which is known as Public Key Infrastructure or PKI.[92]

The certification authorities verify the identity of the holder of the public key and issue a certificate attesting that a public key belongs to a certain person.[93] Therefore, certificates contain the name and public key of their holders. The recipient of a digital signature can then verify whether the public key belongs to the signer by checking the certificate. Certificates are contained in public repositories normally available online.[94] Therein, the status of the certificate is provided, that is, whether the certificate is still valid or otherwise has been revoked or has expired.

Public-key certificates are themselves digitally signed by the certification authority.[95] This means that the public key certificate is an electronic document that bears a digital signature. Certification authorities are also holders of a private key and have a corresponding public key contained in a public key certificate. The recipient of a digitally signed message verifies in the first place that the public key certificate of the signer is valid. However, as the certificate also bears a digital signature, the public key certificate of that signature can and is to be verified. In this manner all the chain of digital signatures and public key certificates is verified. The certification authority obtains its public key from a higher authority that is normally the root authority. The root authority issues and

---

works of different countries the terminology has not always been uniform. Under Argentine law they are referred to as certifiers (*certificadores*). The Electronic Signatures Directive and the UNCITRAL Model Law on Electronic Signatures use the term certification service provider.

[92] The public key infrastructure is a complex structure and the way it is structured may vary from one jurisdiction to another. Certification authorities may be independent units or be subject to a higher authority in a hierarchical structure. The hierarchical structure may in turn follow different models, see *Ford / Baum*, Secure Electronic Commerce, 1997, pp. 265-275; *Atreya / Hammond / Paine / Starrett / Wu*, Digital Signatures, 2002, pp. 75-78 and 163-182; UNCITRAL, Model Law on Electronic Signatures with Guide to Enactment (2001), 2002, pp. 26-27 and 29.

[93] *Ferguson / Schneier*, Practical Cryptography, 2003, pp. 29 and 315-316; *Atreya / Hammond / Paine / Starrett / Wu*, Digital Signatures, 2002, pp. 52-53; *Vacca*, Practical Internet Security, 2007, pp. 349-351; *Dickie*, Internet and Electronic Commerce Law in the European Union, 1999, p. 36.

[94] UNCITRAL, Model Law on Electronic Signatures with Guide to Enactment (2001), 2002, p. 28; American Bar Association, Digital Signature Guidelines, 1996, p. 15.

[95] UNCITRAL, Model Law on Electronic Signatures with Guide to Enactment (2001), 2002, p. 28.

signs the public key certificates of the certification authority.[96] However, the chain of digital signature verification has to end at some point and it ends in the root authority. The root authority validates its own public key.[97]

The intervention of a trusted third party serves also to ensure that the sender cannot deny having sent the digitally signed message. This feature is called non-repudiation, which means that the originator of the message cannot successfully claim not having sent the message.[98] However, the non-repudiation feature of digital signatures does not bar the sender from alleging not sending the message, but protects the recipient in case that the allegation is made.[99] It is presumed that a digital signature created with a private key was made by the holder of the private key and in case the holder denies it – claiming, for example, that the private key has been used without authorization – he or she bears the burden of proof.[100]

5.   Strengths and weaknesses of digital signatures

The digital signature scheme with trusted third parties provides certainty and solves the authenticity and integrity problem existing in electronic transactions. However, the system has one main drawback: its complexity.[101] The more secure the system, the more complex it becomes.[102] The complexity of public key infrastructure clashes with the simplicity common in electronic transactions.[103] This reason may explain why digital signatures have not developed as expected despite their high security standards.

---

[96]   American Bar Association, Digital Signature Guidelines, 1996, pp. 15-16.
[97]   American Bar Association, Digital Signature Guidelines, 1996, p. 16.
[98]   *Atreya / Hammond / Paine / Starrett / Wu,* Digital Signatures, 2002, p. 3.
[99]   *Ford / Baum,* Secure Electronic Commerce, 1997, pp. 99-101.
[100] In this line is the Argentine Digital Signature Act, Section 7.
[101] *Atreya / Hammond / Paine / Starrett / Wu,* Digital Signatures, 2002, p. 5; *Biddle,* Legislating Market Winners: Digital Signature Laws and the Electronic Commerce Market Place, San Diego Law Review, Volume 34, No. 3, 1125-1246 (The author discusses another problem present in PKI models, namely liability allocation.).
[102] American Bar Association, Digital Signature Guidelines, 1996, pp. 64-65 ("Computer security is a matter of degree rather than an absolute". It goes on to say that in most cases it would be possible to have a higher degree of security but that that determination shall be done taking into account all the circumstances. Also, according to the guideline it might not be prudent to request the highest degree of security available.).
[103] In Europe, complexity was one of the reasons mentioned for the lack of use of signatures based on public key cryptography, see Commission of the European Communities, Report from the Commission to the European Parliament and Council, Report of the operation of Directive 1999/93/EC on a Community framework for electronic signatures, 2006, p. 7. Also highlighted in *Nödler,* Legal Framework of Electronic Signatures in the European Union and Germany, Seminar

Digital signatures ensure with high level of certainty both the identity of the signer and the integrity of the electronic document; consequently, digital signatures provide further reliability than simple handwritten signatures.[104] In paper-based transactions the only way to have undisputed certainty as to the identity of the parties and as to the integrity of the document as well as to be protected from allegations of the other party denying having signed the document is through the intervention of a notary public. Therefore, in terms of security, digital signatures seem to be one step ahead than plain handwritten signatures. As far as ensuring identity and integrity is concerned, digital signatures may be compared to notarized signatures. However, in paper transactions the utmost level of security is not always required. Rather, it is only reserved for contracts or acts which the law deems worth enveloping with additional formal requirements; most written contracts and documents bear simple handwritten signatures. The same happens with digital signatures, the security they provide may be excessive for certain acts but justifiable for others. And also there is a matter of cost. The parties are willing to pay the expenses of a notarized contract for relevant transactions but not for those where it is cheaper to bear the risks. The same occurs with digital signatures.

Since digital signatures offer a high level of security, they have often been preferred by legislators. The digital signature is the method recognized in several statutes as the only one having the same legal value as handwritten signatures. Some laws expressly state so as is the case of the Argentine Digital Signature Act. Others require this type of technology only implicitly by establishing requirements that, so far, can only be fulfilled by using digital signatures. The Electronic Signatures Directive falls within this latter category.[105]

---

in Network Security, Institute of Computer Science, Georg-August-Universität Göttingen, 2006, p. 18. Technical difficulties in implementing PKI can be found in *Ferguson / Schneider,* Practical Cryptography, 2003, pp. 323-338 (The authors state that "PKIs simply don´t work in the real world like they do in the dream. This is why the PKI hype of a few years ago never matched the reality", p. 323).

[104] *Farrés,* Firma Digital, 2005, p. 120 (The author finds that a digital signature protects the electronic document in a safer way than handwritten signatures protect paper documents.).

[105] Commission of the European Communities, Report from the Commission to the European Parliament and Council, Report of the operation of Directive 1999/93/EC on a Community framework for electronic signatures, 2006, p. 4; *Blythe,* Digital Signature Law of the United Nations, European Union, United Kingdom and United States: Promotion of Growth in E-Commerce with Enhanced Security, Richmond Journal of Law and Technology, Volume IX, No. 2, 2005, 1, 9; International Chamber of Commerce, Electronic invoicing in and with the European Union, 2005, p. 9.

Paper transactions are neither perfect nor exempted from risks. Nevertheless, whenever the electronic sphere is compared with the paper sphere it is done as if in the latter nothing could go wrong and no risks existed. However, paper documents can be altered, signatures can be forged and parties to a contract can deny having signed it. Despite these flaws, handwritten signatures have been the quintessential means of identifying parties, of showing consent and of safeguarding the integrity of a document.

The tradition of using handwritten signatures is the reason why people are more familiar with paper documents and are willing to run the risks that result from them or, otherwise, know what measures to take to reduce those risks. The risks of using an electronic document may seem higher than they really are because of lack of familiarity with it.[106] That is why it is sometimes expected from electronic signatures to offer a level of security and reliability that is far higher than those offered by handwritten signatures.[107] Yet, these high standards might render the system so complex that even if it is secure, it is not attractive to business and users.

C. Conclusions

Electronic signatures respond to the needs of the electronic environment. Specifically, they seek to present a solution to the identity and integrity problem. Just as there are different levels of security in handwritten signatures, in like form there are also different types of electronic signatures and with different

---

[106] *Bradgate*, Evidential issues of EDI, in: Walden (Ed.), EDI and the Law, 1989, p. 42 ("Perhaps the biggest obstacles to the legal recognition of telematic transmissions as evidence is the public perception of computers. Commerce and the computer world must convince the public and the judiciary that their systems are accurate, secure and reliable.").

[107] UNCITRAL, Model Law on Electronic Commerce with Guide to Enactment (1996), 1999, p. 21 ("... the adoption of the functional-equivalent approach should not result in imposing on users of electronic commerce more stringent standards of security (and the related costs) than in a paper-based environment."); *Baum*, Electronic Contracting in the US: The Legal and Control Context, in: Walden (Ed.), EDI and the Law, 1989, p. 127 ("... conventional signatures are legally sanctioned despite their susceptibility to fraud and forgery [...] the same standards (shall) be applied to electronic signatures." *Baum* also shows a comparison between the different methods available to sign documents including handwritten signatures. The comparison is in terms of their level of difficulty to be defrauded. Interestingly handwritten signatures are in the lowest category, as the easiest to defraud. Digital signatures are the safest ones and are labeled as virtually impossible to defraud. It should be noted that the table focuses on how easy or how difficult it is to defraud a signing technique and not on how easy or difficult it is to prove the fraud. Handwritten signatures might be easy to forge but it might not be difficult to prove a forgery.).

levels of safety. The best-known types of electronic signatures are the simplest ones: PINs, passwords, typing of one´s name, digitalized handwritten signatures, checking of a box saying "I agree". The most sophisticated types of electronic signatures based on biometric methods or public key cryptography are still not frequently used even though they provide a high level of security.

Chapter 2: The legal approach to electronic signatures

A. The legal question

The use of electronic signatures raises the question of their legal validity. The issue is whether electronic signatures comply with the legal requirement of a signature. In some cases the law requires certain acts to be in writing and to bear a signature. For example, the Uniform Commercial Code (UCC), Section 2-201, requires a signed writing for a sale of goods contract equal or above USD $500 to be enforceable. Therefore, the question arises as to whether an electronic document bearing an electronic signature fulfills the UCC requirement.[108] Under Argentine law a private instrument needs to be signed (Section 1012 Argentine Civil Code). Is this formal requirement fulfilled with an electronic signature? These questions are common to all electronic transactions, including those conducted over the Internet, through e-mail, or EDI.

The issue of the validity of electronic signatures is directly related to the validity of electronic documents and the electronic form in general. The legal validity of electronic signatures and electronic documents is sometimes addressed in one legal instrument (E-Sign, UETA and the Argentine Digital Signature Act), while sometimes electronic signature norms focus exclusively on electronic signatures (Electronic Signatures Directive).

I. The need to regulate

In general, national law has responded to the legal questions raised by electronic signatures by means of statutes. However, the question of the validity of electronic signatures could have been tackled by the application and adaptation of existing legal principles. Judges on a case by case basis have the power to decide whether an electronic signature fulfills the legal requirement of a signature.

As a matter of fact, the issue of the legal validity of signature methods other than handwritten signatures is not new to the appearance of electronic signatures; on the contrary, electronic signatures pose again an old question. Nowadays, the handwritten signature is the usual way a person validates his or her identity and expresses consent to written transactions. However, it has not always been like that. In earlier times when the majority of persons did not know how to read and

---

[108] *Bradgate*, Evidential issues of EDI, in: Walden (Ed.), EDI and the Law, 1989, pp. 30-31; *Smedinghoff*, The Legal Requirements for Creating Secure and Enforceable Electronic Transactions, 2002, pp. 2-3; *Scoville*, Clear Signatures, Obscure Signs, Cardozo Arts & Entertainment Law Journal, Volume 17, 1999, 345, 370-372.

write, seals or other marks were used.[109] Still nowadays, sometimes marks, seals or fingerprints are used instead of a handwritten signature. In these cases courts have to analyze the equivalence of these methods with a handwritten signature. The same issue was at stake when the first technologies, such as the telegraph[110] and later the fax[111] appeared. The focus has been on the identity of the signer and, specially, the voluntary nature of the act.[112] Therefore, since long courts have been faced with the decision to assess whether the method used instead of a handwritten signature fulfills the same functions as handwritten signatures and, consequently, meet the legal requirement of a signature.

Nevertheless, as from the mid 1990s national legislative bodies in different countries as well as international and domestic organizations started to notice that legal rules were needed to provide a clear legal framework for electronic signatures.[113] The lack of a legal regime was seen as an obstacle to the use and furtherance of electronic signatures.[114] Accordingly, electronic signature legislation was enacted.

II.   The goal of legal regulation

In the first place, statutes concerning electronic signatures have concentrated on the legal recognition of electronic signatures. The goal of the regulation has been twofold. First, to determine the legal value of electronic signatures and as a result to eliminate the existing doubts about their validity. Second, electronic signature legislation has sought to encourage the use of electronic signatures. Without a legal framework, contracting parties considering the use of electronic means for the execution of contracts may opt for the traditional paper in order to avoid a possible legal fight with regard to the validity of the electronically signed document. Also for the contracting parties already executing contracts

---

[109] Enciclopedia Jurídica Omeba, Volume XII, 1960, s.v. "Firma"; *Lorenzetti*, Comercio Electrónico, 2001, pp. 55-56.

[110] *Lui-Kwan*, Recent Developments in Digital Signature Legislation and Electronic Commerce, Berkeley Technology Law Journal, Volume 14, 1999, 469 footnote 40.

[111] In the United States of America courts have recognized the validity of signs other than signatures, such as names on telegrams, letterheads or telexes. See the case law quoted in *Smedinghoff / Bro*, Electronic Signature Legislation, 1999, footnotes 48 to 53.

[112] *Chissick*, Electronic Commerce: Law and Practice, 1999, marginal number 3.62; *Scoville*, Clear Signatures, Obscure Signs, Cardozo Arts & Entertainment Law Journal, Volume 17, 1999, 345, 369 ("The cases, however, generally hinge on the question of the signer's intent.").

[113] *Dickie*, Internet and Electronic Commerce Law in the European Union, 1999, p. 35; *Smedinghoff*, The Legal Requirements for Creating Secure and Enforceable Electronic Transactions, 2002, pp. 3-5.

[114] Uniform Electronic Transactions Act with preparatory note and comments, 1999, p. 1; Antecedentes Parlamentarios, 2002, 843.

electronically, a legal framework eliminates the uncertainties as to the validity and enforceability of an electronic document bearing an electronic signature.

In the late nineties and beginning of the new millennium the trend to legislate proliferated leading to a vast number of statutes.[115] Although national laws have addressed the same issues – the legal validity of electronic signatures – and have had the same goals – the elimination of the legal obstacles to the use of the electronic signatures, the approach in the different jurisdictions has not always been uniform.[116] Thus, from a state of lack of legislation concerning the value of electronic signatures, the situation rapidly became the opposite. In less than a decade, several countries (and among those, the majority of the most powerful nations) adopted electronic signature regulations with different approaches.

It was soon clear that for a tool aimed at an international medium like the Internet, the existence of divergent legislation was a risk as dangerous as the lack of legislation.[117] While in electronic transactions the concept of boundaries blurs,[118] electronic signature requirements and their effects are subject to national law. Therefore, the issue as to the validity of electronic signatures appears again but, instead of domestically, in the international sphere. The question now is whether the signature that complies with the law of one country will be recognized in another one. Different approaches in the drafting of legislation led to legal insecurity as to the value of electronic signatures in international transactions. Nowadays the legal framework exists;[119] however, in

---

[115] *Fischer*, Saving Rosencrantz and Guildenstern in a Virtual World? A Comparative Look at Recent Global Electronic Signature Legislation, Boston University Journal of Science & Technology Law, Volume 7, 2001, 229, 237; *Smedinghoff*, The Legal Requirements for Creating Secure and Enforceable Electronic Transactions, 2002, pp. 4-5. The following website shows the results of a country-by-country legislation research, see Tilburg University, Digital Signature Law Survey, <https://dsls.rechten.uvt.nl/>.

[116] *Breslin*, Electronic Commerce: Will it ever truly realize its Global Potential?, Penn State International Law Review, Volume 20, No. 1, 2001-2002, 275-300.

[117] *Lincoln,* Electronic Signature Laws and the Need for Uniformity in the Global Market, The Journal of Small and Emerging Business Law, Volume 8, 2004, 67, 79-84.

[118] *Burnstein,* A Global Network in a Compartmentalised Legal Environment, in: Boele-Woelki / Kessedjian (Eds.), Internet, Which Court Decides? Which Law Applies?, Law and Electronic Commerce, Volume 5, 1998, p. 24; *Miedbrodt*, Signaturregulierung im Rechtsvergleich, 2000, p. 38. For the impact of globalization in private international law see *Basedow,* The Effects of Globalization on Private International Law, in: Basedow / Kono (Eds.), Legal aspects of globalization, 2000, pp. 6-7.

[119] *Nimmer*, The legal landscape of E-Commerce: Redefining Contract Law in an Information Era, Journal of Contract Law, Volume 23, 2007, 10, 24.

international contracts, the legal validity of electronic signatures is again a concern due to non-uniform criteria on regulation.

Thus, a second type of legislation appeared trying to harmonize national norms.[120] This task has been tackled from different angles. In the international sphere, UNCITRAL has taken the leading role because the lack of uniform electronic signature legislation has been regarded as an obstacle to international trade and, therefore, falls within UNCITRAL's goal of bringing uniformity to trade law.[121] UNCITRAL first issued the UNCITRAL Model Law on Electronic Commerce (1996), then the UNCITRAL Model Law Electronic Signatures (2001) and most recently the Convention on the Use of Electronic Communication in International Contracts (2005). But also harmonization has been sought within the European Union through the Electronic Signatures Directive and in the United States of America by means of UETA and E-Sign.[122]

B.   The different legal approaches

The approaches adopted by the different legal texts may be classified under different criteria. Traditionally, legal norms regulating electronic signatures have been grouped based on their openness to the recognition of the different technologies.[123]

---

[120] UNCITRAL, Explanatory note by the UNCITRAL secretariat on the United Nations Convention on the Use of Electronic Communications in International Contracts, in: United Nations Convention on the Use of Electronic Communications in International Contracts, 2007, p. 52, para. 147. On the topic of harmonization of legislation concerning the Internet, see *Benabou*, Should there be a minimum harmonization of the law?, in: Internet – International Law, 2005, pp. 167-178.

[121] UNCITRAL, Legal Aspects of automatic trade data interchange, in: Note by the secretariat: legal aspects of automatic data processing (A/CN.9/238), Yearbook of the United Nations Commission on International Trade Law, Volume XIV, 1983, (TRADE/WP.4/R.185/Rev.1), pp. 176-188.

[122] *Smedinghoff / Bro*, Electronic Signature Legislation, 1999.

[123] *Schellekens*, Electronic Signatures – Authentication Technology from a Legal Perspective, Information Technology & Law Series, No. 5, 2004, pp. 56-57; *Smedinghoff / Bro*, Electronic Signature Legislation, 1999; *Aalberts / van der Hof*, Digital Signature Blindness, 1999, pp. 24-42; *Shenk / Baker / Chang*, Cryptography and Electronic Signatures, in: Campbell / Bán (Eds.), Legal Issues in the Global Information Society, 2005, pp. 390-391; *Blythe*, Digital Signature Law of the United Nations, European Union, United Kingdom and United States: Promotion of Growth in E-Commerce with Enhanced Security, Richmond Journal of Law and Technology, Volume IX, No. 2, 2005, 1, 17-18; *Fischer*, Saving Rosencrantz and Guildenstern in a Virtual World? A Comparative Look at Recent Global Electronic Signature Legislation, Boston University Journal of Science & Technology Law, Volume 7, 2001, 229-230 and 234-237.

I.   The digital signature, mandatory or prescriptive approach

One approach is known as the digital signature, mandatory or prescriptive approach and recognizes only digital signatures.[124] Therefore, solely signatures based on public key cryptography are considered to be the counterpart of handwritten signatures. This approach was characteristic of the first electronic signature statutes.[125] Examples of this type of legislation are the Utah Digital Signature Act and the German Digital Signature Act.

II.   The minimalist or enabling approach

The minimalist or enabling approach, on the contrary, recognizes and grants legal value to all types of electronic signatures.[126] This type of regulation is very flexible and the concept of electronic signature is defined broadly. Only some minimum requirements are imposed and, therefore, all types of electronic signatures have the capacity of having the same value as handwritten signatures.

---

[124] *Schellekens*, Electronic Signatures – Authentication Technology from a Legal Perspective, Information Technology & Law Series, No. 5, 2004, pp. 56-57; *Smedinghoff / Bro*, Electronic Signature Legislation, 1999; *Aalberts / van der Hof*, Digital Signature Blindness, 1999, pp. 25-29; *Shenk / Baker / Chang*, Cryptography and Electronic Signatures, in: Campbell / Bán (Eds.), Legal Issues in the Global Information Society, 2005, p. 390; *Blythe*, Digital Signature Law of the United Nations, European Union, United Kingdom and United States: Promotion of Growth in E-Commerce with Enhanced Security, Richmond Journal of Law and Technology, Volume IX, No. 2, 2005, 1, 17; *Fischer*, Saving Rosencrantz and Guildenstern in a Virtual World? A Comparative Look at Recent Global Electronic Signature Legislation, Boston University Journal of Science & Technology Law, Volume 7, 2001, 234-235.

[125] *Stern*, The Electronic Signatures in Global and National Commerce Act, Berkeley Technology Law Journal, Volume 16, 2001, 391, 394.

[126] *Schellekens*, Electronic Signatures – Authentication Technology from a Legal Perspective, Information Technology & Law Series, No. 5, 2004, p. 57; *Smedinghoff / Bro*, Electronic Signature Legislation, 1999; *Aalberts / van der Hof*, Digital Signature Blindness, 1999, pp. 35-40; *Shenk / Baker / Chang*, Cryptography and Electronic Signatures, in: Campbell / Bán (Eds.), Legal Issues in the Global Information Society, 2005, pp. 390-391; *Blythe*, Digital Signature Law of the United Nations, European Union, United Kingdom and United States: Promotion of Growth in E-Commerce with Enhanced Security, Richmond Journal of Law and Technology, Volume IX, No. 2, 2005, 1, 18; *Fischer*, Saving Rosencrantz and Guildenstern in a Virtual World? A Comparative Look at Recent Global Electronic Signature Legislation, Boston University Journal of Science & Technology Law, Volume □, 2001, 236-237.

This type of legislation is common in the United States of America (UETA and E-Sign).[127]

III. The hybrid or two-tier approach

A third approach is labeled the hybrid or two-tier approach because it combines aspects of the two other approaches.[128] On the one hand, it imposes stringent requirements for the recognition of electronic signatures as equivalent to handwritten signatures but, on the other, it recognizes the validity of other types of electronic signatures.

The Electronic Signatures Directive and the UNCITRAL Model Law on Electronic Signatures are examples of this type of legislation. These two pieces of legislation recognize the legal validity of all types of electronic signatures. Nevertheless, one type of electronic signature – normally with high security requirements – fulfills the legal requirements of a signature. It is sustained that nowadays those requirements may only be met by using public key cryptography.[129] However, unlike in the digital signature approach, the public key cryptography is not expressly required, leaving the path open for other technologies.

Sometimes, as it happens with classifications it is not easy to categorize a statute within one or another category. That is specially the case of the Argentine Digital Signature Act, which recognizes all types of electronic signatures but only attaches to digital signatures the same value as handwritten signatures. On

---

[127] Internet Law & Policy Forum (ILPF), An Analysis of International Electronic and Digital Signature Implementation Initiatives, 2000, pp. 6-7 (It is noted that countries based on common law have normally followed the minimalist approach while countries based on civil law follow the prescriptive approach.).

[128] *Schellekens*, Electronic Signatures – Authentication Technology from a Legal Perspective, Information Technology & Law Series, No. 5, 2004, p. 57; *Smedinghoff / Bro*, Electronic Signature Legislation, 1999; *Aalberts / van der Hof*, Digital Signature Blindness, 1999, pp. 29-35; *Shenk / Baker / Chang*, Cryptography and Electronic Signatures, in: Campbell / Bán (Eds.), Legal Issues in the Global Information Society, 2005, p. 391; *Blythe*, Digital Signature Law of the United Nations, European Union, United Kingdom and United States: Promotion of Growth in E-Commerce with Enhanced Security, Richmond Journal of Law and Technology, Volume IX, No. 2, 2005, 1, 17-18; *Fischer*, Saving Rosencrantz and Guildenstern in a Virtual World? A Comparative Look at Recent Global Electronic Signature Legislation, Boston University Journal of Science & Technology Law, Volume 7, 2001, 235-236.

[129] *Schellekens*, Electronic Signatures – Authentication Technology from a Legal Perspective, Information Technology & Law Series, No. 5, 2004, p. 57; International Chamber of Commerce, Electronic invoicing in and with the European Union, 2005, p. 9.

the one hand, it could be argued that it follows the two-tier approach admitting in the prescriptive prong only digital signatures as equivalents to handwritten signatures. On the other hand, it could also be argued that the Argentine Digital Signature Act falls within the prescriptive approach because it focuses almost entirely on digital signatures and PKI.[130]

Some Argentine scholarly studies consider that the Argentine Digital Signature Act is a technologically neutral statute because no specific technique is required.[131] However, the Argentine Digital Signature Act does not fall within the concept of technology neutral statutes because it favors digital signatures over other types of electronic signatures. The regulation on digital certificates and the structuring of a public key infrastructure attest to it. Also the government website relating to this topic goes with the name PKI, <www.pki.gov.ar>. Although it has been argued that other types of technologies may meet the requirements to be considered a digital signature, at this point in time only public key cryptography can achieve this.[132]

C. Technology neutrality in electronic signature statutes

Legislation can certainly promote the use of electronic signatures by providing an appropriate legal framework. In this regard clear-cut legislation providing answers to the validity of electronic signatures and electronic documents is desirable.[133] Yet, legislation can have the opposite effect and undermine an institution by means of excessive or defective regulation. This is true in every field but in statutes relating to electronic commerce it is easily verifiable.[134]

The law must accompany the technological developments and not try to – directly or indirectly – impose or favor a certain type of technology over another. Ultimately, whether a particular technology will be used, is going to be decided by the market and not by legislators.[135] Moreover, this approach might result in the exclusion of other techniques equally or better fitted for achieving the desired goals. Finally, legislation based on a specific technique runs the risk

---

[130] *Mason* considers that the Argentine Digital Signature Act follows what he calls the functional equivalent approach. However, the distinction the author makes between this approach and the two-tier approach is not clear, see *Mason, Electronic Signatures in Practice*, Journal of High Technology Law, Volume VI, No. 2, 2006, 148, 151-152 and 154-156.

[131] *Fernández Delpech*, Internet: Su Problemática Jurídica, 2004, p. 366; *Luz Clara*, Ley de Firma Digital Comentada, 2006, p. 30.

[132] *Devoto*, Comercio Electrónico y Firma Digital, 2001, p. 230. With a different view: *Hocsman*, Negocios en Internet, 2005, pp. 503-504.

[133] *Smedinghoff / Bro*, Electronic Signature Legislation, 1999.

[134] *Nimmer*, The legal landscape of E-Commerce: Redefining Contract Law in an Information Era, Journal of Contract Law, Volume 23, 2007, 10, 13.

[135] *Marquess*, Sign on the Dot-Com Line, ABA Journal, October 2000, 74-76.

of becoming obsolete.[136] Statutes are drafted with the goal that they last in time. If legislation attempts to crystallize a certain signing method, law and technology might end up running along separate tracks.

Early statutes only recognized signatures based on public key cryptography, which is claimed to be the most secure type of signature for electronic transactions.[137] Also more recent statutes assign to digital signatures a preponderant role as is the case of the Electronic Signatures Directive or of the Argentine Digital Signature Act. By recognizing the safer technology the aim was to defeat the fear and mistrust to the new medium. However, the use of digital signatures as a substitute for handwritten signatures was and continues to be relatively low. Thus, even though furthered or required by the legislation, signatures based on public key cryptography are not used as widely as expected.

Of course it does not mean that the law cannot encourage the use of a certain technology; however, there are other ways of achieving this goal other than basing a whole statute on a certain technology. For example, it could be established in the law or a lower rank regulation, that a particular technology fulfills the legal requirements. In this way it is ensured that the technique considered suitable is promoted but that the law remains open to other techniques that might be unknown or unthinkable of today. Another way is for the governments themselves to start using the technique they want to foster so as to gradually let the public become familiar with and trust this technology.[138]

Nevertheless, it cannot be denied that, to a certain extent, technology-specific statutes provide legal certainty. Contracting parties will know in advance what requirements the electronic signature has to comply with and which electronic signature will be recognized. In contrast, technology-neutral statutes remain silent as to the type of technology. They are based on the principle that the choice of the most suitable technology shall be market-driven and that statutes must be capable of surviving successive technological changes.[139] A technology-neutral statute admits the use of all possible techniques; however, it does not determine in advance whether the technique actually used will be considered sufficient to prove the identity of the signer. In this sense, technology-neutral statutes do not provide such a high level of certainty as statutes based on a

---

[136] *Breslin*, Electronic Commerce: Will it ever truly realize its Global Potential?, Penn State International Law Review, Volume 20, No. 1, 2001-2002, 275, 289.

[137] *Scoville*, Clear Signatures, Obscure Signs, Cardozo Arts & Entertainment Law Journal, Volume 17, 1999, 345, 373-374.

[138] Further on the roles of governments for the promotion of electronic commerce, see Organization for economic co-operation and development, Electronic Commerce – Opportunities and Challenges for Government, 1997, pp. 64-69.

[139] *Aalberts / van der Hof*, Digital Signature Blindness, 1999, pp. 40-42.

particular technology where the parties know before concluding a contract that by using a certain technology the signature will be valid.[140]

D. Conclusions

Electronic signatures may in electronic transactions perform what handwritten signatures do in paper transactions. This is the reason why the regulation of electronic signatures has attracted the attention of legislators worldwide. However, not all technologies ensure the same level of security. Some legal systems have recognized as valid for the conclusion of legal acts only techniques that ensure a high level of reliability with respect to the identity of the person and integrity of the document, while others have adopted a more flexible approach. Nevertheless, the legal trend seems to be that of avoiding statutes based on a particular technology.

---

[140] *Lincoln,* Electronic Signature Laws and the Need for Uniformity in the Global Market, The Journal of Small and Emerging Business Law, Volume 8, 2004, 67, 78.

Part II: Electronic signature legislation

Electronic signatures have been the object of attention by lawmakers starting from the second half of the nineteen nineties. The regulation and legal approach taken towards the recognition of electronic signatures will be analyzed with regard to the legislation passed in the United States of America, the European Union with particular reference to Germany, and Argentina. This section will also cover the work of UNCITRAL as well as other organizations.

Chapter 3: The United States of America

A. UETA and E-Sign

Since 1995 the states of the United States of America have been very active in facilitating and promoting the electronic form.[141] In that year the state of Utah enacted the Utah Digital Signature Act,[142] the first statute on the matter in the United States of America and, arguably, also worldwide.[143] The statute focused on digital signatures and did not recognize types of signatures other than those based on asymmetric cryptography. Moreover, it established a licensing scheme for certifiers. Although the licensing scheme was not mandatory, the signatures based on certificates issued by licensed certifiers enjoyed higher legal protection due to the application of legal presumptions (Section 46-3-401).

After the Utah Digital Signature Act was enacted most of the state legislatures passed laws on the issue of electronic signatures; however, they did not always follow the same legal approach.[144] The enactment of state statutes in an individual, isolated manner resulted in a vast amount of legislation and different legal rules. In view of this situation two institutions took steps towards the harmonization of domestic law: the National Conference of Commissioners of Uniform State Law (NCCUSL) and the United States Congress.

---

[141] In the United States of America, as a federal state, there is federal and state legislation. The US states have a greater degree of autonomy than in other federal countries such as, for example, Argentina where civil and commercial legislation is within the sphere of the national congress. See Section 75, paragraph 12 of the Argentine Constitution. In turn, Section 8 of the US Constitution does not confer those powers to the US Congress.

[142] The Utah Digital Signature Act has been repealed and replaced by the Uniform Electronic Transactions Act, Utah Code, Title 46, Chapter 3.

[143] *Smedinghoff / Bro*, Electronic Signature Legislation, 1999; *Stern*, The Electronic Signatures in Global and National Commerce Act, Berkeley Technology Law Journal, Volume 16, 2001, 391, 394.

[144] *Smedinghoff / Bro*, Electronic Signature Legislation, 1999.

The NCCUSL works towards the uniformity of state legislation within the United States of America.[145] Within this scope, the NCCUSL prepared the Uniform Electronic Transactions Act (UETA) in 1999. One of the sources of UETA was the UNCITRAL Model Law on Electronic Commerce (1996).[146] It should be noted that the UNCITRAL Model Law on Electronic Signatures was not ready until 2001.

UETA is not an act which is directly applicable but model legislation; thus, UETA has to be adopted by state legislatures in order to be effective law. The states are free to adopt or not to adopt UETA as well as to amend its text. As a consequence, some states adopted a modified version of UETA[147] whereas other states did not adopt UETA.[148] These diverging approaches prompted the enactment by the United States Congress –within its constitutional power to regulate commerce with foreign nations and within the US states[149] – of the Electronic Signatures in Global and National Commerce Act (E-Sign)[150] on June 30, 2000.[151] The Act is effective since October 1, 2000.[152]

The goal of E-Sign is that the states adopt the original text of UETA in order to ensure uniform legislation within the United States of America.[153] Normally federal law preempts state law;[154] nevertheless, in order to promote the adoption

---

[145] NCCUSL, <http://www.nccusl.org/Update/>. The NCCUSL prepared also the well-known Uniform Commercial Code (UCC).

[146] The UNCITRAL Model Law on Electronic Commerce is indicated as the source of Sections 2, 7, 12, 13, 14 and 15, see Uniform Electronic Transactions Act with preparatory note and comments, 1999, pp. 6, 27, 42-43 and 46.

[147] *Lillie*, Will E-Sign force states to adopt UETA?, Jurimetrics, The Journal of Law, Science, and Technology, Volume 42, 2001, 21-22.

[148] By the time E-Sign was adopted eighteen states had legislation following UETA, see *Stern*, The Electronic Signatures in Global and National Commerce Act, Berkeley Technology Law Journal, Volume 16, 2001, 391, 394; *Lillie*, Will E-Sign force states to adopt UETA?, Jurimetrics, The Journal of Law, Science, and Technology, Volume 42, 2001, 21-22.

[149] Constitution of the United States of America, Article I, Section 8.

[150] The Act is divided into four titles: Electronic Records and Signatures in Commerce, which contains the core provisions of the act, Transferable Records, Promotion of International Electronic Commerce, and Commission on Online Child Protection.

[151] *Lincoln,* Electronic Signature Laws and the Need for Uniformity in the Global Market, The Journal of Small and Emerging Business Law, Volume 8, 2004, 67, 73-74.

[152] In certain cases, however, effectiveness was delayed to a later point in time (Section 107 E-Sign).

[153] *Lillie*, Will E-Sign force states to adopt UETA?, Jurimetrics, The Journal of Law, Science, and Technology, Volume 42, 2001, 21, 30.

[154] *Rainey,* United States, in: Kinsella / Simpson (Eds.), Online Contract Formation, 2004, pp. 309-313.

of the original version of UETA, state legislation following UETA supersedes the application of E-Sign in interstate and international commercial transactions.[155] Preemption also takes place if the state law is compatible with E-Sign or if the state law makes express reference to E-Sign (Section 102(2)).[156] So far most of the states in the United States of America have adopted legislation based on UETA.[157]

E-Sign facilitates the use of electronic records and signatures in national and international (or global, according to the name of the act) commerce, and aims at achieving uniformity in electronic signature legislation. E-Sign is, to a large extent, based on UETA and, therefore, both texts have several points in common.[158] As a matter of fact there are not substantial differences between the principles governing UETA and the principles governing E-Sign. There are differences, though, in the issues covered.[159] Namely, E-Sign contains provisions addressing consumer protection.[160] Also, E-Sign authorizes the use of electronic agents so long as the action of the electronic agent can be legally attributable to the person to be bound by it (Section 101(h)).[161] On the other hand, UETA contains provisions concerning attribution of electronic signatures

---

[155] *Weiser*, United States, in: Campbell (Ed.), E-Commerce and the Law of Digital Signatures, 2005, pp. 698-700 and 730 (UETA may, nonetheless, apply to transactions governed by E-Sign when issues not covered in E-Sign are involved); *Lillie*, Will E-Sign force states to adopt UETA?, Jurimetrics, The Journal of Law, Science, and Technology, Volume 42, 2001, 21, 30.

[156] However, the relationship between E-Sign and state legislation and establishing when preemption operates is not so clear-cut. See *Smart*, E-Sign Versus State Electronic Signature Laws: The Electronic Statutory Battleground, North Carolina Banking Institute, Volume 5, 2001, 485, 496-499 and 501-522; *Weiser*, United States, in: Campbell (Ed.), E-Commerce and the Law of Digital Signatures, 2005, pp. 698-700; *Smedinghoff*, The Legal Requirements for Creating Secure and Enforceable Electronic Transactions, 2002, p. 7.

[157] Forty-six of the fifty US states, the District of Columbia and the Virgin Islands enacted legislation following UETA, see National Conference of State Legislators, Uniform Electronic Transactions Act, <http://ncsl.org/programs/lis/CIP/ueta-statutes.htm>. The remaining four states (Georgia, Illinois, New York and Washington) also have electronic signature legislation, see McBride, Baker & Coles, Legislative Analysis Database for E-Commerce and Digital Signatures, <http://www.mbc.com/ ecommerce/legislative.asp>.

[158] *Lincoln,* Electronic Signature Laws and the Need for Uniformity in the Global Market, The Journal of Small and Emerging Business Law, Volume 8, 2004, 67, 74.

[159] *Smedinghoff*, The Legal Requirements for Creating Secure and Enforceable Electronic Transactions, 2002, p. 7.

[160] Section 101(c) E-Sign.

[161] E-Sign defines electronic agent as the automated medium that acts without review by an individual at the time of the action or response (Section 106(3)).

(Section 9) and the time and place an electronic record is deemed sent and received (Section 15).[162]

B.   Validity of electronic signatures

UETA and E-Sign do not present divergences in the concept and recognition of electronic signatures. For this reason, these aspects are going to be dealt with simultaneously for both legal instruments.

I.   Recognition of electronic signatures

Both statutes recognize the validity of electronic signatures and electronic records.[163] The prevailing principle is the non-discrimination against the electronic form. This means that the legal value of writings or signatures cannot be exclusively based on whether they are on paper or on electronic form.

The non-discrimination principle is materialized through different provisions. A signature, contract or record cannot be denied legal value solely because it is in electronic form (Section 101 (a)(1) E-Sign; Section 7(a) UETA). Therefore, norms which contain the terms writing and signature shall be construed to encompass documents and signatures in electronic form (Section 101(b)(1) E-Sign; Section 7(c) and 7(d) UETA). In other words, when the law requires a writing or a signature, that requirement may be complied with an electronic record and an electronic signature. Also, according to the acts, the use of electronic records or signatures in the formation of contracts cannot be the sole ground on which the legal effect, validity or enforceability of contracts is based (Section 101(a)(2) E-Sign; Section 7(b) UETA).

The use of the electronic form is voluntary. The fact that the writing and signature requirement can be met by electronic means shall not be construed to signify that the use and acceptance of electronic records and signatures is imposed by law. The law favors their use, does not mandate it. Therefore, a person may not be forced to use or to accept an electronic record or an electronic signature. Parties have to freely agree on the use and acceptance of the electronic form (Section 101(b)(2) E-Sign; Section 5(a) UETA).[164]

---

[162] *Fry*, Why Enact UETA? The Role of UETA After E-Sign, 2002.

[163] Examples of the implementation of electronic signatures can be found in: *Marquess,* Sign on the Dot-Com Line, ABA Journal, October 2000, 74-76; *Valenzi*, Digital Signatures: An Important "Sign" of the Future of E-Government, virginia.edu, Volume IV, No. 2, 2000.

[164] According to Section 5(b) of UETA whether an agreement for the use of the electronic form exists or not "is determined from the context and surrounding circumstances, including the parties' conduct". E-Sign has special consent provisions for consumers (Section 101(c)(C)(ii) E-Sign). E-Sign contains an

II. Concept of electronic signature

Electronic signature is defined as an electronic sound, symbol or process attached to or logically associated with a record and executed or adopted by a person with the intent to sign the record (Section 106(5) E-Sign; Section 2(7) UETA).

The electronic signature definition consists of an objective and a subjective component. The objective component is the technological one which, in turn, consists of two elements: on the one hand, the record and, on the other hand, the electronic sound, symbol or process. The electronic signature definition does not require the record to be an electronic one; however, the term record encompasses electronic records. A record is defined as information retrievable in electronic means (Section 106(9) E-Sign; Section 2(13) UETA). In turn, an electronic record is a record created, sent, received or stored by electronic means (Section 106(4) E-Sign; Section 2(8) UETA). The concept of electronic record is broad and includes different electronic media such as voice recording, audio and video.[165] An electronic record fulfills the legal requirement of a writing.[166]

---

exception to the voluntary use of the electronic form for governmental agencies in non-contractual relations (Section 101(b)(2) E-Sign). In these cases, E-Sign does not require a governmental agency to previously agree to the use of electronic records. This means that in non-contractual transactions with governmental agencies the use of the electronic medium is possible without their agreement. Contrarily, when the governmental agency is a contracting party the consent of the governmental agency to use the electronic form is required as with any other party. See *Smedinghoff*, The Legal Requirements for Creating Secure and Enforceable Electronic Transactions, 2002, pp. 9-10.

[165] The comment to UETA lists several types of records that fall within the concept of electronic record, see Uniform Electronic Transactions Act with preparatory note and comments, 1999, p. 9. The term record is preferred to the term document because it encompasses information in non-written form such as video recordings and voice messages.

[166] However, there are further requirements. When the law requires a document to be in writing the electronic record shall be capable of being retained (Section 101(e) E-Sign; Section 8 UETA). E-Sign further requires that the document be accurately reproducible. Besides, sometimes the law requires that a document is retained for a certain period of time or that the original version of the document is retained. In these cases those requirements are met with the retention of an electronic record that accurately reflects the information in the record and that remains accessible for later reference (Section 101(d)(1) E-Sign; Section 12(a) UETA). Note that the provision refers to the retention of information contained in a record and not in an electronic record. This means that the provision is applicable to both paper and electronic documents. Therefore, a paper document may be retained by electronic means. Furthermore, the retention of the record itself is not necessary; it is enough

The means to produce the signature are wide; they can be a sound, a symbol or process, which have to be attached to the record. A mouse click, a PIN, a scanned handwritten signature or a digital signature are deemed to comply with that requirement.[167] Thus, the concept of electronic signature is broad and not bound to a certain technology. For this reason both E-Sign and UETA are regarded as technology neutral statutes.[168]

The signing method has to be accompanied by the intent to sign the record, which is the subjective element. The intent has to exist at the moment the signature is executed or adopted. The intention is the key element of a signature. As a consequence, a mouse click, a voice message and a person's name in an e-mail may be considered an electronic signature as long as the intention to sign is present.[169]

Therefore, there is a three-part test to determine whether the signature is an electronic one: Is there a record? If so, is there a symbol, sound or process attached to it? If so, did the signer execute or adopt them with the intent to sign the record? If these three elements are present, there is an electronic signature according to UETA and E-Sign.[170]

III.   Exclusion of electronic signatures

UETA and E-Sign apply to commercial transactions (Sections 101(a) and 106(13) E-Sign; Sections 3(a) and 2(16) UETA).[171] Consequently, they are not applicable to transactions subject to the law governing the creation and

---

that an electronic record of the information is retained. The retained electronic document has to be accurate, accessible and reproducible.

[167] *Smedinghoff*, The Legal Requirements for Creating Secure and Enforceable Electronic Transactions, 2002, pp. 12-13.

[168] On the benefits and drawbacks of technology neutrality in US legislation, see *Stern*, The Electronic Signatures in Global and National Commerce Act, Berkeley Technology Law Journal, Volume 16, 2001, 406-411; *Smedinghoff*, The Legal Requirements for Creating Secure and Enforceable Electronic Transactions, 2002, pp. 21-23.

[169] Uniform Electronic Transactions Act with preparatory note and comments, 1999, pp. 9-10.

[170] However, the fact that a certain type of electronic signature is legally valid does not mean that the electronic signature ensures reliability and trust in the electronic transaction. In other words, an electronic signature may be valid but it may not serve to ensure the identity and integrity functions, see *Smedinghoff*, The Legal Requirements for Creating Secure and Enforceable Electronic Transactions, 2002, pp. 13-16.

[171] Uniform Electronic Transactions Act with preparatory note and comments, 1999, p. 14 (UETA was conceived to apply to "business, commercial (including consumers) and governmental" transactions.).

execution of wills, codicils and testamentary trusts (Section 103(a)(1) E-Sign; Section 3(b)(1) UETA).[172] Transactions governed by the Uniform Commercial Code are also excluded with the exception of Sections 1-107, 1-206 and Articles 2 (Sales) and 2A (Leases) to which the electronic signature statutes apply (Section 103(a)(3) E-Sign; Section 3(b)(2) UETA).[173] In addition to these common exceptions each statute contains its own.

1. UETA

UETA excludes its application in case of transactions governed by the Uniform Computer Information Transactions Act (UCITA) and by any other law that a state may identify as outside its scope (Section 3(b)(3) and 3(b)(4) UETA).

2. E-Sign

In the case of E-Sign the list of exceptions is longer. E-Sign does not apply if the record is governed by state family law. Furthermore, the use of electronic means is excluded for certain court documents. Nevertheless, several courts in the US have implemented online filing systems as well as online consultation systems. It is construed that the exclusion contained in E-Sign does not impinge on the power of courts to adopt their own procedural rules and organize the filing and docketing of court documents in the way they deem most appropriate.[174] Thus, some federal courts are equipped with an electronic filing system named Case Management / Electronic Case Files (CM/EFC), which allows online filing of court documents.[175] In order to file documents a lawyer (or "pro se" litigant) requires a login name and a password, which are both provided by the court. The use of the login name and password amounts to the signature of the attorney (Section 103(b)(2) and (3) E-Sign).[176] The integrity of the filed documents is achieved by verifying that the documents have not changed since the filing.[177]

---

[172] It should be noted that in the case of E-Sign only one section, Section 101, which is nonetheless the main section dealing with electronic signatures, is excluded. In the case of UETA the whole act is excluded.

[173] Accordingly, Section 1-108 of the Uniform Commercial Code establishes that Article 1 modifies, limits, and supersedes the federal Electronic Signatures in Global and National Commerce Act except for the sections dealing with consumer disclosure and the additional exceptions contained in Section 103(b).

[174] U.S. Department of Commerce, National Telecommunications and Information Administration, Electronic Signatures, A Review of the Exceptions to the Electronic Signature in Global and National Commerce Act, 2003, pp. 35-40.

[175] <http://www.uscourts.gov/cmecf/cmecf_about.html>.

[176] <http://pacer.psc.uscourts.gov/cmecf/ecffaq.html#CR70>.

[177] <http://www.uscourts.gov/cmecf/cmecf_faqs.html>.

Also the Public Access to Court Electronic Records (PACER) is available, which allows online consultation of files.[178]

For consumer protection purposes, E-Sign prohibits certain notifications to be served using electronic means of communication.[179] Finally, the use of electronic documents is also excluded for transport documents or handling instructions of toxic or dangerous products (Section 103(b)(3) E-Sign).

The underlying idea in all exceptions is that the use of the electronic form might be premature and prejudicial. Therefore, the exceptions have a protective goal and when the exceptions no longer fulfill that goal they have no reason to be. That is why a review shall be conducted by the Secretary of Commerce to assess whether the exceptions are still required (Section 103(c) E-Sign). In the report "Electronic Signatures: A Review of the Exceptions to Electronic Signatures in Global and National Commerce Act"[180] the U.S. Department of Commerce concludes that it is in the consumers' best interest that the exceptions in E-Sign be retained.[181] When balancing the elimination of the exception and the effect of such removal on consumers, consumers´ interests prevail.

C. Conclusions

In the United States of America, electronic signatures have been regulated both by state legislatures and the US Congress. Therefore, in order to avoid divergent legislation within the United States of America, UETA and E-Sign were adopted.

---

[178] <http://pacer.psc.uscourts.gov/>.

[179] The notices excluded are: notices of cancellation or termination of utility services, notices related to the lease of a primary residence or of a credit agreement secured by an individual´s primary residence – the exception is limited to notices related to default, acceleration, repossession, foreclosure, eviction or the right to cure –, notices related to the cancellation or termination of health insurance, product recall notices or notices of products containing a material failure, see U.S. Department of Commerce, National Telecommunications and Information Administration, Electronic Signatures: A Review of the Exceptions to the Electronic Signature in Global and National Commerce Act, 2003, pp. 40-67.

[180] The report is available at <http://www.usinfo.org/enus/economy/technology/docs/e signfinal.pdf>.

[181] Yet, some amendments were suggested. Utility companies shall be allowed to send cancellation and termination notices to consumers voluntarily accepting online notification. Also, it was suggested eliminating from the UCC exception the electronic letter of credit transactional records of Article 5 and the electronic notices of Article 6 of the UCC, see U.S. Department of Commerce, National Telecommunications and Information Administration, Electronic Signatures: A Review of the Exceptions to the Electronic Signature in Global and National Commerce Act, 2003, p. 76.

Concerning the legal approach to electronic signatures, electronic signature legislation in the United States of America recognizes all types of electronic signatures. Both UETA and E-Sign remain neutral with respect to the technology requirements of electronic signatures. Consequently, a special type of technique or process is not required for a signature to have the same value as a handwritten signature.

Chapter 4: The European Union and Germany

A. Electronic Signatures Directive

The Electronic Signatures Directive seeks to prevent the possible or remove the existing legal barriers posed by divergent legislation in the European Union.[182] When the Electronic Signatures Directive was adopted, only some of the fifteen member states composing the European Union at that time had electronic signature legislation in place.[183] That means that the existence of diverging legislation was only at its inception; the lack of legislation on electronic signatures was the prevailing situation in most jurisdictions. Therefore, the Electronic Signatures Directive served two purposes: to direct member states to adopt legislation governing electronic signatures and to ensure uniform legislation in that field within the European Union.[184]

The uniformity sought by the Electronic Signature Directive is limited to the recognition of different types of electronic signatures (Article 1) and the granting the same legal effects as handwritten signatures to one type of electronic signature (Article 5.1). The Electronic Signatures Directive does not seek harmonization of national law relating to form requirements (Article 1 and whereas clause 17). Therefore, which type of signature is required, for example, whether a notarized signature or a simple handwritten signature, or whether a signature is required at all, is decided by national law.[185]

---

[182] *Miedbrodt*, Signaturregulierung im Rechtsvergleich, 2000, pp. 84-86; *Schlechter*, Ein europäischer Rahmen für elektronische Signaturen, in: Geis (Ed.), Rechtsaspekte des elektronischen Geschäftsverkehrs, 1999, pp. 110-112.

[183] Nevertheless, most of the member states had either adopted some type of regulation or were discussing the issue of enacting legislation on the topic, see *Schlechter*, Ein europäischer Rahmen für elektronische Signaturen, in: Geis (Ed.), Rechtsaspekte des elektronischen Geschäftsverkehrs, 1999, p. 109; *Dickie*, Internet and Electronic Commerce Law in the European Union, 1999, pp. 37-39 (The author shows the stage of the work on electronic signature national legislation within the European Union before the enactment of the Electronic Signatures Directive.).

[184] The whereas clauses of the Electronic Signatures Directive highlight the importance and convenience of a uniform electronic signature framework for the electronic commerce (whereas clause 4 Electronic Signatures Directive). Moreover, in the current unified and free-mobility Europe where citizens of one country relocate to another, unified electronic signature legislation would be helpful in the communication of citizens with public foreign authorities (whereas clause 7 Electronic Signatures Directive).

[185] *Schaub*, European Legal Aspects of E-Commerce, 2004, p. 139; *Roßnagel*, Die europäische Richtlinie für elektronische Signaturen und ihre Umsetzung im neuen Signaturgesetz, in: Lehman (Ed.), Electronic Business in Europa – Internationales, europäisches und deutsches Online-Recht, 2002, marginal number 24; *Dumortier*,

The Electronic Signatures Directive was adopted on December 13, 1999 and entered into force on January 19, 2000, day of its publication in the Official Journal of the European Union (Article 14 Electronic Signatures Directive). Directives are not directly applicable; therefore, the member states have to transpose them into national law. The EU member states had until July 18, 2001 to do so (Article 13 Electronic Signatures Directive).[186]

I.   Concept of electronic signature

The Electronic Signatures Directive establishes three types of electronic signatures: (i) the electronic signature (Article 2.1), (ii) the advanced electronic signature (Article 2.2), and (iii) the advanced electronic signature based on a qualified certificate created by a secure-signature-creation device (Article 5.1). The EU member states must ensure through national legislation that this third type of electronic signature satisfies the legal requirement of a signature (Article 5.1(a)).[187] That is, out of three types of electronic signatures only one must be granted the same treatment as handwritten signatures. This does not mean that states do not have the power to recognize other types of electronic signatures as equivalent to handwritten signatures but that at least one type must enjoy that benefit.

1.   Electronic signatures

Electronic signatures are the simplest type of signature included in the Electronic Signatures Directive. An electronic signature is defined as "data in

---

The European Regulatory Framework for Electronic Signatures: A Critical Evaluation, in: Nielson / Jakobsen / Trzaskowski (Eds.), EU Electronic Commerce Law, 2004, pp. 78 and 85-87.

[186] According to the report of the Commission of the European Communities as of March 2006 all 25 member states had transposed the Electronic Signatures Directive into national law, see Commission of the European Communities, Report from the Commission to the European Parliament and Council, Report of the operation of Directive 1999/93/EC on a Community framework for electronic signatures, 2006, p. 4. Besides, based on the information provided by the European Union in its website six countries (Belgium, Denmark, Germany, Greece, Italy and Austria) of the 15 members at the time the Electronic Signatures Directive was adopted transposed it within the allocated time period; other four (France, Netherlands, Portugal and United Kingdom) did it at a later point in time, see <http://eurlex.europa.eu/LexUriServ/LexUriServ.do?uri=CELEX:71999L0093:EN :NO>. Information as to the legislation adopted in each country may be found at: Tilburg University, Digital Signature Law Survey, <https://dsls.rechten.uvt.nl/>.

[187] According to Section 5.1(b), EU member states shall also ensure that advanced electronic signatures based on a qualified certificate and created by a secure-signature-creation device are admissible into evidence in legal proceedings.

electronic form which are attached to or logically associated with other electronic data and which serve as a method of authentication" (Article 2.1).

The analysis of the definition leads to the following remarks. An electronic signature is electronic data which has to be attached or associated to another electronic data. This other electronic data is an electronic record, such as an e-mail or a document drafted in a computer. This means that the electronic signature is always used in relation to an electronic document; however, as will later be analyzed, the Electronic Signatures Directive does not include the concept of electronic document or record. Finally, the electronic signature is an authentication method; that is to say, it serves to identify the signatory. In other words, an electronic signature is electronic data affixed or linked to an electronic document which serves to establish identity. Examples of electronic signatures are PINs, a typed name or a scanned handwritten signature.[188]

The definition of electronic signature bears resemblance to the definition adopted by E-Sign, UETA and the UNCITRAL Model Law on Electronic Signatures. However, there is an important difference. In the Electronic Signatures Directive the intent to sign is not part of the concept of electronic signature; that is, there is no subjective element in its definition. On the contrary, in E-Sign and UETA the intent to sign is the core concept of the definition while in the UNCITRAL Model Law on Electronic Signatures electronic signatures may be used to establish the intent to sign.

It should be noted that the Electronic Signatures Directive preceded E-Sign, adopted in 2000, and the UNCITRAL Model Law on Electronic Signatures adopted in 2001. The Electronic Signatures Directive was issued the same year as UETA, 1999, but UETA is a model statute. Thus, the Electronic Signatures Directive was the first type of legislation addressed to different international jurisdictions since E-Sign governs the issue in a federal state. The Electronic Signatures Directive had to be transposed into national law by mid-July 2001, more or less the same time the UNICTRAL Model Law on Electronic Signatures was adopted. This means that for the EU member states that complied with the implementation period the UNCITRAL Model Law on Electronic Signatures, at least its final version, came too late.[189]

---

[188] Commission of the European Communities, Report from the Commission to the European Parliament and Council, Report of the operation of Directive 1999/93/EC on a Community framework for electronic signatures, 2006, p. 4; *Roßnagel*, Die fortgeschrittene elektronische Signatur, MMR 2003, 164.

[189] For example, in the case of Germany, *Heydn* holds that, what electronic commerce legislation concerns, "...the German legislation on e-commerce was developed independently from the 1996 Model Law and the 2001 Model Law. However, the objectives of the 1996 Model Law and the 2001 Model Law are quite similar to those of the German legislation", see *Heydn*, Germany, in: Campbell (Ed.), E-

2. Advanced electronic signatures

An advanced electronic signature is an electronic signature that can determine with precision the identity of the signatory and the integrity of a document. The Electronic Signatures Directives establishes four requirements for an electronic signature to be considered an advanced electronic signature (Article 2.2), namely that:

• there is a unique link between the signatory and the signature,
• the signature is capable of identifying the signatory,
• the signature is created by means that the signatory can maintain under his or her sole control, and
• any change to the signed data is detectable.

Examples of advanced electronic signatures are public key cryptography signatures.[190] The Electronic Signatures Directive does not indicate digital signatures as a preferred technique; however, the requirements of an advanced electronic signature can arguably so far only be met by digital signatures.[191]

3. Advanced electronic signatures based on qualified certificates created using a secure-signature-creation device

This type of signature is an advanced electronic signature with two additional requirements: a qualified certificate and a secure-signature-creation device (Article 5.1). Since these signatures are based on qualified certificates under some national laws (Germany, for example), they are referred to as *qualified electronic signatures*.

a) Qualified certificate

A qualified electronic signature has to be based on a qualified certificate. A certificate links the data used to verify the signature to a certain person (Article 2.9). The data used to create and verify a signature is not directly attributable to a certain person because it is normally not unique to a person but consists of

---

Commerce and the Law of Digital Signatures, 2005, p. 224. For a comparison between the validity of electronic signatures under the UNCITRAL Model Law on Electronic Signatures and the Electronic Signatures Directive, see *Griffiths / Harrison*, European Union, in: Campbell (Ed.), E-Commerce and the Law of Digital Signatures, 2005, pp. 744-745.

[190] Commission of the European Communities, Report from the Commission to the European Parliament and Council, Report of the operation of Directive 1999/93/EC on a Community framework for electronic signatures, 2006, p. 4.

[191] International Chamber of Commerce, Electronic invoicing in and with the European Union, 2005, p. 9; Commission of the European Communities, Report from the Commission to the European Parliament and Council, Report of the operation of Directive 1999/93/EC on a Community framework for electronic signatures, 2006, p. 4.

numbers or mathematical processes. Therefore, a certificate establishes the link between a person and the signature-verification-data. Moreover, the certificate warrants the identity of the certificate holder (Article 2.9).

A qualified certificate has to contain certain information and has to be issued by a certification-service-provider. The information that a certificate must contain in order to be a qualified certificate is specified in Annex I of the Electronic Signatures Directive and is the following:

- the indication that it is a qualified certificate,
- the identification of the certification-service-provider and the state in which it is established,
- the name of the signatory. It can also contain a pseudonym but in that case it should be indicated as such,
- the signature-verification-data (the signature-creation-data remains confidential),
- the validity period stating its beginning and end,
- the identity code of the certificate, and
- the advanced electronic signature of the certification-service-provider.

These seven requirements must be present in all qualified certificates. Other three may be present depending on the type of certificate:

- a specific attribute of the signatory,
- limitations to the scope of the certificate, or
- limits on the value of the transactions.[192]

The qualified certificate has to be issued by a certification-service-provider. An entity, a natural person or legal person may be certification-service- providers. Annex II of the Electronic Signatures Directive establishes the requirements that a certification-service-provider must comply with concerning personnel, operating systems, financial resources, and management of certificates. Certification-service-providers may be domiciled in one EU member state and offer their products and services in other EU member states (Article 4 and whereas clause 10).

It is not required that certification-service-providers obtain prior authorization to operate – meaning a license or any other measure to that effect (Article 3.1 and

---

[192] In Germany, the Federal Financial Court (*Bundesfinanzhof*) held that a monetary limit on a certificate is relevant only in case of direct financial transactions (for example, wire transfers and other monetary transactions such as purchases); however, in other cases such as writs by an attorney the existence of such a limitation does not hinder the effectiveness of a qualified electronic signature (BFH, DStRE 2007, 515, 516). See also *Fischer-Dieskau / Hornung*, Erste höchstrichterliche Entscheidung zur elektronischen Signatur, NJW 2007, 2897-2899.

whereas clause 10).[193] The goal is to have a competitive and open market. Yet, the member states may establish voluntary accreditation schemes aiming at promoting a high-quality level of services (Article 3.2 and whereas clause 11). The voluntary accreditation scheme has to be based on objective, transparent, proportionate and non-discriminatory requirements (Article 3.2). In order to reinforce the voluntary nature of certification-service-providers' accreditation, the Electronic Signatures Directive expressly states that an electronic signature cannot be denied validity solely because the qualified certificate on which it is based was not issued by an accredited certification-service-provider (Article 5.2).

b)   Secure-signature-creation device

Qualified electronic signatures have to be created by a secure-signature-creation device. The term signature-creation device means simply the program or process that creates the signature (Article 2.5). The signature-creation device is deemed secure if it meets the requirements set out in Annex III of the Electronic Signatures Directive (Article 2.6). The first requirement is that the signature-creation data[194] "can practically occur only once". In other words, that it is almost impossible that the same signature-creation data is generated twice. In the case of public key cryptography it means that the chances of generating the same key pair twice shall be very low. The second requirement for a secure-signature-creation device is that it be possible to keep the signature-creation data secret and protected from unauthorized third-party use. In the third place, it must be reasonably ensured that the signature-creation data cannot be derived or forged. Finally, the signed data shall remain unaltered and accessible.

Whether a signature-creation device meets these requirements is to be determined by public or private bodies (Article 3.4). If the bodies of one member state find the requirements are met, such decision is binding on other member states (Article 3.4). In addition, if a signature-creation device complies with the standards published by the Commission, there is a presumption that the requirements of Annex III are met (Article 3.5).

---

[193] The states have nonetheless the obligation to supervise the certification-service-providers which are established within their territory (Article 3.3 and whereas clause 13 Electronic Signatures Directive). Moreover, the state supervision does not prevent the existence of private sector based supervision systems (whereas clause 13 Electronic Signatures Directive).

[194] The term signature-creation data encompasses all types of information employed to create the signature, such as passwords or the private key in asymmetric cryptography based signatures (Article 2.4 Electronic Signatures Directive).

II. Value of electronic signatures

The Electronic Signature Directives regulates the legal effects of qualified electronic signatures. According to Article 5.1(a) it is mandatory that one type of signature, the electronic signature based on a qualified certificate and created by a secure-signature-creation device, satisfy the legal requirement of a signature "in the same manner as a handwritten signature satisfies those requirements in relation to paper-based data". Therefore, for the equivalence between handwritten and qualified electronic signatures to operate, the conditions imposed for handwritten signatures have to be met by the qualified electronic signatures. In this same line, whereas clause 20 states that qualified electronic signatures have the same value as handwritten signatures "only if the requirements for handwritten signatures are fulfilled".[195]

In order to ensure that qualified electronic signatures are considered to be at the same level as handwritten signatures the Electronic Signatures Directive establishes high security standards. It is clear from the requirements and terminology set forth by the Electronic Signatures Directives that public key cryptography is the predominant technique for legally valid qualified electronic signatures. Nevertheless, the Electronic Signatures Directive grants the value of handwritten signatures to one type of electronic signature but not to one specific technique. Even though digital signatures are currently the only type of signature that can meet these requirements,[196] in theory any technique could be used to comply with the requirements established by the Electronic Signatures Directive. Therefore, it can be argued that the Electronic Signatures Directive remains open to future techniques that may fulfill the qualified electronic signature requirements. Nevertheless, the fact that the Electronic Signatures Directive was issued taking into account public key cryptography may hinder that a new technology complies with requirements tailored made for another one.

The goal of the Electronic Signatures Directive is to have a single, unified type of electronic signature that can be used whenever the law requires a handwritten signature.[197] It is important to note, however, that the Electronic Signatures Directive does not cover aspects of national law as to when or which type of

---

[195] *Dumortier*, The European Regulatory Framework for Electronic Signatures: A Critical Evaluation, in: Nielson / Jakobsen / Trzaskowski (Eds.), EU Electronic Commerce Law, 2004, p. 86.

[196] International Chamber of Commerce, Electronic invoicing in and with the European Union, 2005, p. 9; Commission of the European Communities, Report from the Commission to the European Parliament and Council, Report of the operation of Directive 1999/93/EC on a Community framework for electronic signatures, 2006, p. 4.

[197] *Geis*, Die elektronische Signatur: Eine internationale Architektur der Identifizierung im E-Commerce, MMR 2000, 667, 668.

signature is required. Therefore, member states have the power to decide whether electronic signatures may be used instead of handwritten signatures. The Electronic Signatures Directive expressly clarifies that the harmonization sought in the field of electronic signatures does not impinge on contract law and the formal requirements of contracts. These aspects are governed by national law and outside the scope of the Electronic Signatures Directive (Article 1 and whereas clause 17).[198]

Even though the Electronic Signatures Directive grants the most relevant effects to qualified electronic signatures, it also ensures protection to the other two types of electronic signatures.[199] To this end, national legislation shall not discriminate against non-qualified electronic signatures; more precisely, national legislation cannot deprive electronic signatures of legal value solely because the signature: (i) is in electronic form, (ii) is not based on a qualified certificate, (iii) is not created by a secure-signature-creation device, or (iv) is not based on a qualified certificate issued by an accredited certification-service-provider (Article 5.2). Subparagraph (i) conveys the principle of media neutrality and subparagraphs (ii) and (iii), the principle of technology neutrality. The Electronic Signatures Directive does not name these two principles; however, this terminology used by UNCITRAL is appropriate to illustrate the goal of the provision. Subparagraph (iv) reinforces the voluntary nature of the certification-service-provider's accreditation.[200]

---

[198] *Geis*, Die elektronische Signatur: Eine internationale Architektur der Identifizierung im E-Commerce, MMR 2000, 667, 669; *Dumortier*, The European Regulatory Framework for Electronic Signatures: A Critical Evaluation, in: Nielson / Jakobsen / Trzaskowski (Eds.), EU Electronic Commerce Law, 2004, pp. 85-86.

[199] *Geis*, Die elektronische Signatur: Eine internationale Architektur der Identifizierung im E-Commerce, MMR 2000, 667, 669.

[200] Nevertheless, the use of electronic signatures in the public sector may be subject to additional requirements but these should not "constitute an obstacle to cross-border services for citizens" (Article 3.7 Electronic Signatures Directive). The additional requirements have to be objective, transparent, proportionate, and non-discriminatory (Article 3.7 Electronic Signatures Directive). On March 31, 2004 two directives were adopted, Directive 2004/17/EC regulating the procurement procedures of entities operating in the water, energy, transport and postal services sectors, and Directive 2004/18/EC coordinating the procedures for the award of public works contracts, public supply contracts and public service contracts. Both directives authorize the use of electronic signatures, and taking into account the importance of transparency and security in public contracts, the use of advanced electronic signatures is contemplated (Whereas clause 48 and Article 48.5 Directive 2004/17/EC; whereas clause 37 and Article 42.5(b) Directive 2004/18/EC).

The media-neutrality principle ensures the non-discrimination against the electronic form. Electronic signatures shall not be denied legal effect or admissibility into evidence solely because the signature is in electronic form (Article 5.2). In other words, the form shall not be the only element to weigh when deciding on the effectiveness or admissibility of a signature.

The technology-neutrality principle guarantees the non-discrimination between different electronic signature techniques. In the Electronic Signatures Directive the technology-neutrality principle aims at ensuring the non-discrimination against non-qualified electronic signatures, that is, signatures that are not based on a qualified certificate or created using a secure-signature-creation device. In concrete this is the case of advanced electronic signatures, which share some of the requirements with the qualified electronic signatures (actually a qualified signature needs to comply with the requirements for advanced electronic signatures) except for the existence of a qualified certificate and a secure-signature-creation device.

III. Recognition of foreign electronic signatures

The use of electronic signatures does not take place only within the European Union but worldwide. Consequently, the Electronic Signatures Directive contains one provision, Article 7, establishing when a qualified certificate issued by a certification-service-provider in a third country shall be recognized. This means, in the first place, that the Electronic Signatures Directive only establishes the recognition of signatures based on qualified certificates. In the second place, that the recognition of foreign certificates is viable if the foreign certificate is a qualified certificate. Thus, in order to be recognized, the foreign certificate has to comply with the requirements of the Electronic Signatures Directive, or more precisely, with the implementation norms of an EU member state.

There are three ways to recognize a foreign qualified certificate as legally equivalent. One option is that the foreign certification-service-provider fulfills the certification requirements established for EU certification-service-providers. This means that the foreign certification-service-provider has to comply with the laws of an EU member state. Additionally, it is required that the certification-service-provider be registered in a voluntary accreditation scheme. Therefore, accreditation schemes are voluntary for EU certification-service-providers but mandatory for foreign ones. Otherwise, another option is that a certification-service-provider established in the European Union guarantees the certificate. It is not necessary that the certification-service-provider be in the state where the certificate is being recognized; the certification-service-provider guaranteeing the foreign certificate can be placed anywhere in the European Union. Finally, a third option is that a treaty recognizes the certificate or the certification-service-provider. The Electronic Signatures Directive in its whereas clause 23 highlights the importance of this type of international agreements and encourages their use in this field.

IV. Review of the implementation of electronic signatures in the EU

The Commission of the European Communities issued, in accordance with Article 12, a report on the operation of the Electronic Signatures Directive on March 15, 2006.[201]

The report concludes that the goal of establishing the legal value of electronic signatures has been accomplished. The use of the simple electronic signature is frequent in two areas: personal e-banking (with the one-time passwords – TANs) and e-government. However, the use of advanced and qualified electronic signatures is low. The reasons mentioned are several. The first one is that PKI requires a vast infrastructure rendering the system complex. Also, companies do not want customers to use their authentication devices for other transactions; therefore, there is no incentive to create advanced and qualified electronic signatures. Another reason is the lack of interoperability between certification-service-providers both at a national and international level. Also, the costs of archiving documents for long periods of time as sometimes required by law may curb the use of electronic signatures because the technology used today has to be continually updated so that an electronically signed document is accessible in the future.

V.   Writing requirement

The Electronic Signatures Directive does not address the topic of the legal validity of electronic records. Actually, it does not even include the term electronic record or alike. Therefore, the Electronic Signatures Directive facilitates the use of electronic signatures but it does not say anything about the element which contains them or which they are linked to.[202] And yet signature and writing are deeply intertwined. When the law requires a signature it has to be contained in or linked to a document.

---

[201] Commission of the European Communities, Report from the Commission to the European Parliament and Council, Report of the operation of Directive 1999/93/EC on a Community framework for electronic signatures, 2006. On November 28, 2008 the Commission of the European Communities issued the Communication from the Commission to the Council, the European Parliament, the European Economic and Social Committee and the Committee of the Regions on the Action Plan on e-signatures and e-identification to facilitate the provision of cross-border public services in the Single Market.

[202] *Schaub*, European Legal Aspects of E-Commerce, 2004, p. 131.

The legal validity of electronic documents is dealt with in relation to contracts entered into through electronic means by the EU Directive 2000/31/EC on electronic commerce (Electronic Commerce Directive).[203] The Electronic Commerce Directive was adopted on June 8, 2000 in Luxembourg and entered into force on July 17, 2000 (day of its publication in the Official Journal, Article 23 of the Electronic Commerce Directive). The goal of the Electronic Commerce Directive is to harmonize divergent legislation in order to ensure a unified framework for the free movement of information society services in the European Union (Article 1).[204] The Electronic Commerce Directive deals with different topics related to the information society services including electronic contracts.

The Electronic Commerce Directive establishes that national law shall authorize the execution of contracts by electronic means as well as guarantee their effectiveness and validity (Article 9).[205] Therefore, the fact that a contract is in electronic form shall not affect its legal effectiveness and validity and all legal obstacles to the execution of contracts by electronic means shall be removed.[206] However, the member states retain the power to exclude a limited number of contracts from being executed electronically (Article 9.2).[207] Contracts related to real estate (except for lease contracts), family and succession law, or requiring the involvement of courts or public authorities as well as suretyship or collateral

---

[203] Directive 2000/31/EC of the European Parliament and of the Council of 8 June 2000 on certain legal aspects of information society services, in particular electronic commerce, in the Internal Market (Directive on Electronic Commerce), published in the Official Journal of the European Communities on July 17, 2000.

[204] Information society service is defined as "any service normally provided for remuneration, at a distance, by electronic means and at the individual request of a recipient of services. For the purposes of this definition: "at a distance" means that the service is provided without the parties being simultaneously present; "by electronic means" means that the service is sent initially and received at its destination by means of electronic equipment for the processing (including digital compression) and storage of data, and entirely transmitted, conveyed and received by wire, by radio, by optical means or by other electromagnetic means; "at the individual request of a recipient of services" means that the service is provided through the transmission of data on individual request.", see Article 2(a) Electronic Commerce Directive and Article 1(2) of Directive 98/34/EC as amended by Directive 98/48/EC.

[205] For the interaction of Article 5.1 of the Electronic Signatures Directive and Article 9 of the Electronic Commerce Directive, see *Roßnagel*, Die europäische Richtlinie für elektronische Signaturen und ihre Umsetzung im neuen Signaturgesetz, in: Lehman (Ed.), Electronic Business in Europa – Internationales, europäisches und deutsches Online-Recht, 2002, marginal numbers 24-27.

[206] In the whereas clause 37 of the Electronic Commerce Directive it is pointed out that the removal of obstacles refers to the legal ones and not to practical obstacles.

[207] *Rehse*, Der Vertragsschluss auf elektronischem Wege in Deutschland und England, 2005, pp. 26-27.

contracts may still require a handwritten signature. In case an EU member state decides to exclude the applicability of the Electronic Commerce Directive to other contracts, it has to submit a report to the European Commission every five years explaining the reasons for maintaining the exclusion (Article 9.3).

B.   Legal framework of electronic signatures in Germany

The transposition of the Electronic Signatures Directive into national law will be analyzed under German law. Germany also had legislation on the topic before the enactment of the Electronic Signatures Directive.

I.   German Digital Signature Act

The German Parliament enacted the German Digital Signature Act[208] on June 13, 1997, which was one of the first statutes addressing the topic of digital signatures. Indeed, this statute dealt only with digital signatures, meaning signatures based on public key cryptography (Section 2.1).[209] Nonetheless, the statute recognized the possibility of using other type of digital signatures (the term electronic signature was not used) unless the law required digital signatures in accordance with the German Digital Signature Act (Section 1.2). The German Digital Signature Act established a mandatory licensing scheme for certification authorities (Section 4); therefore, certification authorities needed to obtain a license to issue certificates (Section 4).[210] The German Digital Signature Act was effective until the German Electronic Signatures Act came into effect.[211]

---

[208] *Gesetz zur digitalen Signatur*, BGBl. I 1997, 1870. The statute was included as Article 3 of the Information and Communication Service Act (*Informations- und Kommunikationsdienste-Gesetz, IuKDG*).

[209] *Bettendorf*, Elektronische Dokumente und Formqualität, RNotZ 2005, 277, 282.

[210] *Geis*, Die elektronische Signatur: Eine internationale Architektur der Identifizierung im E-Commerce, MMR 2000, 667, 668; *Miedbrodt*, Signaturregulierung im Rechtsvergleich, 2000, pp. 63-65.

[211] Section 5 of the German Electronic Signatures Act (*Gesetz über Rahmenbedingungen für elektronische Signaturen und zur Änderung weiterer Vorschriften (Signaturgesetz – SigG)*, BGBl. I 2001, 876). More on the German Digital Signature Act may be found in: *Erber-Faller*, Elektronischer Rechtsverkehr und digitale Signaturen in Deutschland – Bisherige Entwicklung, internationale Bezüge und Zukunftsperspektiven aus notarieller Sicht, in: Geis (Ed.), Rechtsaspekte des elektronischen Geschäftsverkehrs, 1999, pp. 88-94; *Bizer / Miedbrodt*, Die digitale Signatur im elektronischen Rechtsverkehr – Deutsches Signaturgesetz und Entwurf der Europäischen Richtline, in: Kröger / Gimmy (Eds.), Handbuch zum Internetrecht, 2000, pp. 147-151; *Miedbrodt*, Signaturregulierung im Rechtsvergleich, 2000, pp. 52-73.

II. Transposition of the Electronic Signatures Directive

In Germany, the transposition of the Electronic Signatures Directive into national law was done by means of the German Electronic Signatures Act[212] and the Act on Adaptation of Civil Law Form Requirements and Other Statutes to Modern Legal Transactions[213] (Form Adaptation Act).[214] The German Electronic Signatures Act transposes the different types of electronic signatures and the infrastructure required for their implementation. In turn, the Form Adaptation Act deals with the legal equivalence of electronic and handwritten signatures.

1. Concept of electronic signature

Following the Electronic Signatures Directive the German Electronic Signatures Act recognizes three types of signatures: electronic signatures, advanced electronic signatures and qualified electronic signatures. The concept of electronic signature (*elektronische Signatur*) is identical to the one contained in the Electronic Signatures Directive and is defined as data in electronic form attached to or logically connected to other data which serve for authentication purposes (Section 2.1). The definition of advanced electronic signature (*fortgeschrittene elektronische Signatur*) also follows the same definition as the one in the Electronic Signatures Directive.[215] An advanced electronic signature has to be capable of identifying and linking uniquely to the signatory, has to be

---

[212] *Gesetz über Rahmenbedingungen für elektronische Signaturen und zur Änderung weiterer Vorschriften (Signaturgesetz – SigG)*, BGBl. I 2001, 876. The German Electronic Signatures Act was enacted on May 16, 2001 and entered into effect on May 22, 2001. According to the German Electronic Signatures Act the statute comes into effect the day after its publication. The publication date was May 21, 2001. According to Section 5, Section 2 (*Umstellung von Vorschriften auf Euro*) became effective on January 1, 2002. The German Electronic Signatures Act was amended in 2005 by means of the First Act on the Amendment to the Signature Act (*Erste Gesetz zur Änderung des Signaturgesetz* – 1.SigÄndG), BGBl. I 2005, 2. For comments on the amendment act, see *Roßnagel*, Elektronische Signaturen mit der Bankkarte? – Das Erste Gesetz zur Änderung des Signaturgesetzes, NJW 2005, 385-388.

[213] *Gesetz zur Anpassung der Formvorschriften des Privatrechts und anderer Vorschriften an den modernen Rechtsgeschäftsverkehr*, BGBl. 2001 I, 1542. The statute was enacted on July 13, 2001 and entered into force on August 1, 2001.

[214] *Geis,* Die elektronische Signatur: Eine internationale Architektur der Identifizierung im E-Commerce, MMR 2000, 667, 670; *Roßnagel*, Die europäische Richtlinie für elektronische Signaturen und ihre Umsetzung im neuen Signaturgesetz, in: Lehman (Ed.), Electronic Business in Europa – Internationales, europäisches und deutsches Online-Recht, 2002, p. 132; EUR-Lex, National Implementation Measures of the Electronic Signatures Directive, <http://eurlex.europa.eu/LexUriServ/LexUriServ.do?uri=CELEX:71999L0093:EN:NOT>.

[215] For more on the advanced electronic signature under German law, see *Roßnagel*, Die fortgeschrittene elektronische Signatur, MMR 2003, 164-170.

created by means that the signatory can maintain under his or her sole control, and any change to the signed data has to be detectable (Section 2.2).

Concerning the third type of signature, the Electronic Signatures Directive refers to them as advanced electronic signatures which are based on a qualified certificate and created by a secure-signature-creation device.[216] As they are based on a qualified certificate the German Act names them qualified electronic signatures (*qualifizierte elektronische Signatur*) (Section 2.3).

The certification-service-provider issuing the qualified certificate may be accredited to a voluntary accreditation scheme. If so, the signature is named qualified electronic signature with certification-service-provider certification (*qualifizierte elektronische Signaturen mit Anbieter-Akkreditierung*) (Section 15.1). In this way the German Electronic Signatures Act distinguishes a fourth type of electronic signature. [217] Nevertheless, the Electronic Signatures Directive expressly rules that member states may not discriminate against signatures that are based on a qualified certificate issued by a non-accredited certification-service-provider (Article 5.2 Electronic Signatures Directive).[218] However, according to the Electronic Signatures Directive it is possible to impose additional requirements for the implementation of electronic signatures in the public sector (Article 3.7 Electronic Signatures Directive). The additional requirements shall not impinge on cross-border services for citizens (Article 3.7 Electronic Signatures Directive). That is why, it is construed that signatures with certification-service-provider accreditation will apply principally within the public administration.[219]

2.   Legal value of electronic signatures

Article 5.1 of the Electronic Signatures Directive directs member states to ensure that one type of electronic signature, the electronic signature based on a qualified certificate and created by a secure-signature-creation device, satisfy the legal requirement of a signature. The German Electronic Signatures Act regulates different aspects of electronic signatures but does not put handwritten signatures and qualified electronic signatures on the same level. In order to comply with the mandate of the Electronic Signatures Directive, the German

---

[216] Some authors reckon that qualified electronic signatures can be based on secure-signature-creation devices provided by institutions that do not qualify as certification-service-providers under the German Electronic Signatures Act, see *Roßnagel*, Die Ausgabe sicherer Signaturerstellungseinheiten, MMR 2006, 441-446.

[217] For an analysis of the legal consequences of the different types of signatures, see *Roßnagel*, Rechtliche Unterschiede von Signaturverfahren, MMR 2002, 215.

[218] *Bettendorf*, Elektronische Dokumente und Formqualität, RNotZ 2005, 277, 283.

[219] *Roßnagel*, Rechtliche Unterschiede von Signaturverfahren, MMR 2002, 215, 221.

national legislation was amended by means of the Form Adaptation Act. The statute recognizes the validity of qualified electronic signatures to satisfy the legal requirement of a signature. This principle has been materialized in Section 126a of the German Civil Code (*Bürgerliches Gesetzbuch* – BGB) whereby when the law imposes the requirement of a writing and a signature only qualified electronic signatures may be used. However, German law recognizes also the validity of all other types of electronic signatures for acts where the law does not impose the written form and the parties have agreed on the electronic form without specifying the type of signature to be used (Section 127 BGB).[220]

3. Foreign electronic signatures

In accordance with the Electronic Signatures Directive, Section 23 of the German Electronic Signatures Act deals with foreign electronic signatures. Section 23 covers only electronic signatures based on qualified certificates. There are no rules for the recognition of foreign electronic signatures not based on certificates.

The German Electronic Signatures Act differentiates between, on the one hand, certificates from EU member states and affiliated states, and, on the other hand, certificates from third countries. In both cases the foreign electronic signature has to be based on a qualified certificate and meet the requirements of Article 5.1 of the Electronic Signatures Directive. However, when the qualified certificate is issued by a certification-service-provider in an EU member state or by an associate state to the European Union, it is enough for the electronic signature to meet the requirements of Article 5.1 to be considered a qualified electronic signature. On the contrary, with regard to third countries there is one additional condition to be met, which is the compliance with at least one of the following requirements:

- The certification-service-provider fulfils the Electronic Signatures Directive's requirements and is registered in a voluntary accreditation scheme (Article 23(1)1), or
- A certification-service-provider established in the European Union guarantees the foreign qualified certificate (the certification-service-provider guaranteeing the foreign certificate can be placed in Germany or in another EU member state) (Article 21(1)2), or

---

[220] *Heinrichs / Ellenberger*, in: Palandt, Bürgerliches Gesetzbuch, 68th Edition, 2009, Section 127, marginal number 5; *Prütting / Wegen / Weinreich*, BGB Kommentar, 4th Edition, 2009, Section 127, marginal number 5; *Einsele*, in: Münchener Kommentar zum Bürgerlichen Gesetzbuch, 5th Edition, 2006, Section 127, marginal number 13; *Bettendorf*, Elektronische Dokumente und Formqualität, RNotZ 2005, 277, 282; *Hertel*, in: Staudinger, Kommentar zum Bürgerlichen Gesetzbuch, New Edition, 2004, Section 127, marginal number 78.

• A treaty recognizes the foreign certificate or the foreign certification-service-provider (Article 23(1)3).

4. Licensing of certification authorities

An important change introduced by the German Electronic Signatures Act is the abandonment of the licensing requirement for certification-service-providers. The German Digital Signature Act required certification-service-providers to obtain a license (Article 4).[221] Under the German Electronic Signatures Act and in accordance with the Electronic Signatures Directive no license is required for a certification-service-provider to operate. Only voluntary accreditation schemes based on objective, transparent, proportionate and non-discriminatory conditions can be implemented (Article 3.2 Electronic Signatures Directive).

C. Conclusions

The Electronic Signatures Directive distinguishes three types of electronic signatures with different standards of security. Only one type of electronic signature, the qualified electronic signature, which arguably requires to be based on public key cryptography, shall be granted the same value as handwriting signatures. Within the European Union, the use of the simple type of electronic signatures is widespread while advanced and qualified electronic signatures are uncommon.

In Germany, the implementation of the Electronic Signatures Directive by means of the Electronic Signatures Act 2001 meant the repeal of the German Digital Signature Act and the abandonment of a digital signature approach with a mandatory accreditation scheme.

---

[221] *Geis*, Die elektronische Signatur: Eine internationale Architektur der Identifizierung im E-Commerce, MMR 2000, 667, 668; *Miedbrodt*, Signaturregulierung im Rechtsvergleich, 2000, p. 63.

Chapter 5: Argentina

A. Norms before the enactment of the Argentine Digital Signature Act

Since the mid 1990s the Argentine legal system has had norms of different rank dealing with the issue of electronic signatures.[222] These norms paved the way for the enactment of the Argentine Digital Signature Act.[223]

I. Resolution 45/1997 of the Secretary of Public Function[224]

Resolution 45/1997 authorizes the use of digital signatures for the public administration; however, it does not regulate digital signatures but only allows their application within the public sector.

Furthermore, Resolution 45/1997 adopts the conclusions of the Cryptography and Digital Signature Subcommittee on the technical requirements for prospective digital signature regulation. The Cryptography and Digital Signature Subcommittee concluded that legislation shall put digital signatures on the same level as handwritten signatures. Moreover, digital signatures are to be based on asymmetric or public key cryptography organized within a public key infrastructure. Yet, it was advised that digital signature legislation ought not to refer to only one technology. How to conciliate both ideas? The Subcommittee regarded the public key mechanism as a mathematical method and not as a technology. Therefore, it is possible, according to their view, that new efficient algorithms be found but that they continue to be based on a public key mechanism. Resolution 45/1997 is a clear example that, from the beginning, Argentine law has focused on digital signatures and public key infrastructure.

II. Resolution 293/1997 of the Superintendence of Retirement and Pension Fund Administrators[225]

Resolution 293/1997 sets forth a telecommunication system via e-mail between, on the one hand, the Superintendence of Retirement and Pension Fund Administrators (*Superintendencia de Administradoras de Fondos de*

---

[222] The Argentine norms are published in the Official Gazette (*Boletín Oficial*) and are available at the following free-access website <http://infoleg.mecon.gov.ar/>.

[223] A comment on the norms enacted before the Argentine Digital Signature Act may also be found in: *Devoto,* Comercio Electrónico y Firma Digital, 2001, pp. 60-76; *Hocsman,* Negocios en Internet, 2005, pp. 494-499.

[224] Published in the Official Gazette on March 24, 1997. The Secretary of the Public Function (*Secretaría de la Función Pública*) was later replaced by the Under Secretary of Public Management (*Subsecretaría de Gestión Pública*).

[225] Published in the Official Gazette on May 29, 1997.

Jubilaciones y Pensiones) and, on the other hand, the Retirement and Pension Fund Administrators (*Administradoras de Fondos de Jubilaciones y Pensiones*).

In order to access the telecommunication system a password is required. The password has the same value as a handwritten signature and, therefore, electronic communications are deemed signed when the password is used (Sections 10 and 16). Besides, the password is regarded as sufficient to ensure the integrity of the communication and the identity of the sender (Sections 10 and 16). Moreover, electronic communications have the same legal effects as written documents (Sections 9 and 16). This norm is one of the few cases in Argentine law where an electronic signature is given the same value as a handwritten signature without requiring the use of public key cryptography.

III.   Executive Order 427/1998[226]

Executive order 427/1998 introduced the first digital signature regulation for the public administration. Following the guidelines of Resolution 45/1997, the executive order regulated only digital signatures, meaning signatures based on public key cryptography.[227] The goal of the regulation was to create a valid alternative to handwritten signatures; however, digital signatures could only be used in acts without direct individual legal effects. The resolution also established a public key infrastructure with a licensing body, licensed certification authorities and an auditing body. For these reasons Executive Order 427/1998 was a clear precedent of the Argentine Digital Signature Act. Executive Order 427/1998 was later repealed by Executive Order 2628/2002 implementing the Argentine Digital Signature Act (Section 45 Executive Order 2628/2002).

---

[226]   Published in the Official Gazette on April 21, 1998.
[227]   *Lorenzetti*, Comercio Electrónico, 2001, p. 91. The Executive Order granted the authorization to use digital signatures within the Public Administration for an initial period of two years so as to assess the functioning, reliability and security of the system. The two-year period started running from the approval of the technological standards and the proceeding manuals for the licensing body, auditing body and licensed certification authorities. The Secretary of Public Function approved the technological standards on November 27, 1998 (Resolution 194/1998 of the Secretary of Public Function published in the Official Gazette on December 4, 1998) and the Certification Policy on November 30, 1998 (Resolution 212/1998 of the Secretary of Public Function published in the Official Gazette on January 6, 1999). Therefore, the two-year period was to expire on December 2000. The authorization can be renewed once for another two-year period. This was done by means of Administrative Decision 102/2000 published in the Official Gazette on January 25, 2001.

IV. Resolution 4536/1999 of the Secretary of Communications[228]

In order to promote the access to the Internet, the National Government launched a program named argentin@internet.todos.[229] Within the framework of said program, each person, physical or legal, has the right to a free e-mail account.[230] According to Resolution 4536/1999 of the Secretary of Communications (*Secretaría de Comunicaciones*) the holder of such an e-mail account has the right to request the use of a digital signature (although in this case subject to a fee). The Argentine Postal Service was appointed as the certification authority.

Only ten days after its publication the application of Resolution 4536/1999 was suspended due to a change of government.[231] Resolution 4536/1999 was issued two days before the expiration of Carlos Menem's second presidential term and published during the presidency of Fernando de la Rúa.

V. Executive Order 1023/2001[232]

Executive Order 1023/2001 as amended establishes the contracting regime for the Public Administration.[233] One of the goals of the new regulation was to incorporate the use of electronic technologies to procurement contracts. To that end, Executive Order 1023/2001 devotes Chapter II of Title I to electronic public contracting.

Contracts which fall within the regime of the Executive Order 1023/2001 as well as certain administrative contracts outside its scope may be executed in digital format and signed using a digital signature (Section 21). Documents digitally signed have the same value as paper documents bearing handwritten signatures and can be introduced in court as evidence (Section 21). Besides, notifications within the public contracting process are valid if made in digital format and digitally signed, including those having direct individual effects (Section 21). In this regard Executive Order 1023/2001 differentiates from Executive Order

---

[228] Published in the Official Gazette on December 21, 1999.

[229] Executive Order 1018/1999 published in the Official Gazette on September 1, 1999.

[230] Executive Order 1335/1999, published in the Official Gazette on November 19, 1999, Section 1.

[231] Joint Resolution 3/1999 of the Secretary of Science, Technology and Innovative Production (*Secretaría de Ciencia, Tecnología e Innovación Productiva*) and of the Secretary of Communications, published in the Official Gazette on December 31, 1999.

[232] Published in the Official Gazette on August 16, 2001.

[233] The contracting regime is applicable to purchase, service, provision, lease, concession, licence and public works contracts, among others (Section 4). Employment contracts are excluded according to Section 5.

427/1998 that excluded the use of the digital form for that type of acts. The new contracting process also contemplates the use of the Internet for the publication of invitations to bid as well as other relevant information during the contracting period (Section 32).[234] As the Internet is a tool that makes information available at all times it serves the purposes of transparency and publicity, which are principles that shall govern the contracting process (Section 3).

The use of the electronic form is not imposed but just given as an option. However, the public administration is obliged to receive documents relating to the contracting process which are in digital format and digitally signed (Section 21).

The concrete implementation of the public electronic contracting was deferred to its regulation by each branch of the Federal Government. The Executive branch fixed a time period of 60 days in which to issue the relevant regulation and invited the Judicial and Legislative branches to enact the relevant regulation (Section 39).[235] Consequently, the Senate introduced a computerized purchase system for the acquisition of homogeneous, low-cost, consumable products used regularly in large amounts.[236]

B.   Argentine Digital Signature Act

I.   Legislative process of the Argentine Digital Signature Act

1.   Congressional debate

a)   House of Representatives

The digital signature bill originated in the House of Representatives (*Cámara de Diputados*). According to the Argentine National Constitution bills can either

---

[234] When for reasons of national defense the contracting process is secret, the publication requirement is waived (Executive Order 1023/2001, Section 32).

[235] However, nineteenths months later and still without having enacted the regulation the Executive branch extended the time period for its enactment to 360 business days (Section 10 Executive Order 666/2003, published in the Official Gazette on March 25, 2003). It should be noted that after the enactment of the Argentine Digital Signature Act digital signatures have to be in compliance with it.

[236] Executive Order 632/2002 published in the Official Gazette on June 25, 2002. See Section 7 and Title IX, Chapter 2 of the Annex to Executive Order 632/2002. In the version published in the Official Gazette, Section 7 makes mistakenly reference to Chapter 2 of Title X instead of Title IX.

originate in the House of Representatives or in the Senate (*Senado*) unless otherwise provided.[237]

The bill was introduced by Congressmen Fontdevila, Parentella and Nicrota in the 118th Session of the Congress in the year 2000.[238] In the report submitted with the bill, Congressman Fontdevila highlighted the importance of a legal framework for digital signatures for the development of electronic commerce and the reduction in paper and storage costs.[239]

The bill on digital signatures was referred to the Commission on Communications and Informatics (*Comisión de Comunicaciones e Informática*) and to the Commission on General Legislation (*Comisión de Legislación General*).[240] Congressman Fontdevila was the reporting member of the commissions.[241] The commissions took into consideration the bills of Congressman Fontdevila as well as four other bills: the bill of Corchuelo Blasco and other Representatives (4175-D.-00), the bill of Representative Puiggrós (5460-D.-00), the bill of Representative Cardesa and other Representatives (7099-D.-00), and the bill of Representatives Atanasof and Camaño (7331-D.-00).[242] Despite some differences, all bills focused on signatures based on asymmetric or public key cryptography. However, the most important bill – not often mentioned in the reports of the House of Representatives – was the bill of Senator Del Piero introduced to the Senate on June 20, 2000 (file number S.-

---

[237] For example, Section 52 of the Argentine National Constitution establishes that the bills referring to taxes and troop recruitment shall originate in the House of Representatives.

[238] The bill was assigned the file number 3534-D-00.The first number is the correlative number assigned to a bill according to the order in which it is introduced. The letter D stands for *Diputados* (Representatives) and the last two numbers refer to the year when the bill is introduced.

[239] Every bill presented to the House of Representatives shall include a written explanation of the reasons for its introduction (Section 123 Rules of the House of Representatives).The report of Congressman Fontdevilla may be found in: Antecedentes Parlamentarios, 2002, 740-741. The Rules of the House of Representatives may be found at: <http://www.diputados.gov.ar/>.

[240] According to the Rules of the House of Representatives the bills are announced in the session they are introduced and referred to the relevant commission. It is possible that a same bill is referred to several commissions when it addresses topics of a mixed nature (Section 102 of the Rules of the House of Representatives). Besides, each bill before being considered by the House of Representatives must have a report from an assessing commission unless the House waives such requirement by two-thirds of the votes (Section 147 Rules of the House of Representatives).

[241] Antecedentes Parlamentarios, 2002, 727.

[242] The bills can be found in: Antecedentes Parlamentarios, 2002, 742-790. For more details on these bills, see *Devoto,* Comercio Electrónico y Firma Digital, 2001, pp. 219-227; *Hocsman*, Negocios en Internet, 2005, pp. 499-503.

1155/00).[243] This project is a clear precedent of the Argentine Digital Signature Act especially in its firsts and most important provisions.[244]

The amended bill was approved by the commissions on July 24, 2001.[245] The commissions' report highlights the benefits of having legislation on digital signatures mainly in order to avoid a gap between developed and developing countries.[246] Moreover, the lack of a national law was regarded as an obstacle to the development of a new way of communication and trade. Article 7 of the UNCITRAL Model Law on Electronic Commerce is mentioned as a reference in the drafting of the bill.

The bill prepared by the commissions was presented to the House of Representatives, which passed it on August 15, 2001.[247] Actually, the bill as drafted by the commissions was the text that became law because neither the House of Representatives nor the Senate introduced further amendments.

---

[243] Antecedentes Parlamentarios, 2002, 834-841. In his speech to the Senate when the Argentine Digital Signature Act was passed Senator Del Piero explained the reasons why his project could not advance in the Senate. The year 2000 was a hectic year for the Senate when numerous accusations of bribes involved several of its members. Senator Del Piero was among the accusing members and, therefore, he believed the Senate was not going to endorse his project. Thus, he decided to collaborate with the House of Representatives. See Antecedentes Parlamentarios, 2002, 843-844.

[244] *Farrés*, Firma Digital, 2005, p. 54.

[245] Antecedentes Parlamentarios, 2002, 729-739. The commissions had previously held an open hearing with persons from different disciplines and entities (among others, public, private and professional entities and universities) to exchange opinions about digital signatures and their regulation. The debate may be found in: Antecedentes Parlamentarios, 2002, 791-818.

[246] The report of the commissions has to be printed and presented to the secretary where it is assigned a number. The report of the Commissions was printed on August 3rd, 2001 and contained in the Agenda No. 2651/2001. The report is available at <http://www.diputados.gov.ar/dependencias/dcomisiones/periodo-118/118-2651.pdf> or in Antecedentes Parlamentarios, 2002, 729-741. Every commission's report shall be open for observation for seven business days and then it is submitted to the House of Representatives (Section 113 Rules of the House of Representatives).

[247] Antecedentes Parlamentarios, 2002, 727. Actually the bill was not debated by the House of Representatives. According to the House of Representatives' Rules, a bill on which a report has been issued, has no dissenting opinion and no observations can be approved in bulk with other bills (Section 152 Rules of the House of Representatives).

b)   Senate

After the House of Representatives passed the bill it was referred to the Senate on August 23, 2001.[248] In the Senate the bill was assigned to the Commission on General Legislation (*Comisión de Legislación General*), the Commission on Administrative and County Matters (*Comisión de Asuntos Administrativos y Municipales*) and the Commission on Criminal Matters and Jail Regime (*Comisión de Asuntos Penales y Regímenes Carcelarios*).[249] The Senate passed the bill on November 14, 2001 without introducing any amendments to the House's bill.[250] Once approved, the Senate sent the bill to the Executive power.

2.   Promulgation

The Executive branch has the power to approve or veto a bill.[251] The Executive power tacitly approved the digital signature bill because the president did not return the bill within 10 working days (Section 80 Argentine National Constitution).[252] Thereafter, the Argentine Digital Signature Act 25.506 was published in the Official Gazette on December 14, 2001 and entered into force on December 23, 2001.[253]

II.   Scope

Despite its name the Argentine Digital Signature Act recognizes the use and effectiveness of both electronic and digital signatures. [254] However, and that

---

[248]   Senate, <http://www.senado.gov.ar/web/proyectos/verExpe.php?origen=CD&num exp=71/01&tipo=PL&tConsulta=1>.

[249]   These commissions, without modifying the bill, issued Opinion 1033 contained in the Agenda bearing the same number.

[250]   Previously, in the Senate's Session on September 18, 2001, a motion for preference had been requested and granted, <http://www.senado.gov.ar/web/taqui/t aqui_op_adjunto.php?clave=F7467/180901.htm>, para. 7.

[251]   Argentine National Constitution, Section 78 and Section 99 para. 3.

[252]   Actually, the Argentine National Constitution uses in this Section the term useful days (*días útiles*), consistently with the wording of Section 28 of the Argentine Civil Code.

[253]   According to Section 2 of the Argentine Civil Code if statutes do not establish the day on which they enter into force they are valid after eight days following their publication. This means that the period starts running the day following the publication and that the law is effective after the eighth day of its publication, that is, on the ninth day after publication. See *Borda*, Tratado de Derecho Civil - Parte General, Volume I, 1991, p. 166. Disposition 13/2004 of the Coordination and Innovation Secretary mistakenly mentions that the Argentine Digital Signature Act entered into force on December 11, 2001, which would mean that the law entered into force even before it was published.

[254]   The Argentine Digital Signature Act mandates the promotion of digital signature technology as well as its use in legal norms and judicial decisions within five years

explains the name given to the statute, electronic and digital signatures do not have the same value under Argentine law. Additionally, the Argentine Digital Signature Act also governs electronic documents.

The Argentine Digital Signature Act is composed of fifty-three sections. The first sixteen sections contain the core provisions of the statute. The remaining sections are devoted mainly to structuring the public key infrastructure. The statute is regulated by means of Executive Order 2628/2002.[255]

III. Digital signatures

1. Concept of digital signature

The definition of digital signature contained in Section 2 of the Act establishes that a digital signature is the result of applying a mathematical procedure which requires information exclusively known by and under the absolute control of the

---

of the issuance of the Act (Section 48). However, the Argentine Digital Signature Act has been in force since December 2001 and this has not yet occurred. Nevertheless, there are initiatives towards the implementation of digital signatures. Several provinces have taken steps towards the incorporation of digital signatures in their judicial system. That is the case of the Province of Chubut establishing the employment of digital signatures in judicial proceedings, see Chubut's Judicial System, Digital Signature, <http://www.juschubut.gov.ar/firma_digital.htm>. Also digital presentations are allowed in criminal proceedings, see Diario Judicial, Trelew: fiscales y defensores, con presentaciones electrónicas, 29/02/08, <http://w ww.diariojudicial.com/nota.asp?IDNoticia=34715>. In the Province of Mendoza authorization has been granted for the issuance of warrants by means of electronic mail, see Diario Uno, La Corte autorizó librar órdenes de allanamiento mediante mail, 28/08/07, <http://www.diariouno.com.ar/edimpresa/2007/08/28/nota157297. html>. The Province of Salta has also introduced digital signature technology in criminal proceedings, see Salta Noticias, El Poder Judicial de Salta avanza en la digitalización, 2/09/07, <http://www.noticias.iruya.com/content/view/1529/411>. The Province of Santa Fe has introduced the use of digital signatures within the provincial public administration, see El Litoral.com, Primer trámite en el Estado Provincial con firma digital, <http://www.ellitoral.com/accesorios/imprimir.php?id =/diarios/2007/10/23/politica/POLI-04.html>. Moreover, the National Exchange Commission (Comisión Nacional de Valores) has established the financial highway (autopista financiera) for the submission of information in electronic form and digitally signed via the Internet. Electronic documents bearing digital signatures replace the submission of paper documents. Electronic documents have to be encrypted to ensure confidentiality and signed with digital signatures based on public key cryptography technology in order to ensure their authorship and integrity. See Comisión Nacional de Valores (National Exchange Commission), Autopista de la Información Financiera, <http://www.cnv.gov.ar/auto_financiera.a sp?Lang=0>.

[255] Published in the Official Gazette on December 20, 2002.

signatory to a digital document. In addition, a digital signature shall be verifiable by third parties in order to enable the identification of the signatory and the detection of any alteration of the digital document after it was signed.

The definition does not expressly refer to public key cryptography; therefore, some authors reckon that the concept of digital signature is broad enough to encompass other types of technologies.[256] Nevertheless, it is possible to find references to the public key cryptography technique in the digital signature definition.[257] In the first place, the digital signature is defined as a mathematical procedure referring to the use of mathematics for encrypting and decrypting. In the second place, the signature requires information "known only by the signatory and under its exclusive control".[258] That type of information refers to the private key used to create the digital signature. In order to ensure that it is in fact the holder of the private key who signed the document the signatory shall be the only one to know signature creation data. The exclusive control required by the statute excludes the sharing of private keys. Therefore, the holder of the private key may not authorize another person to sign with his or her private key.

The two moments in the life of a digital signature are described in the definition. The first one is the creation of the digital signature that occurs when the signatory signs a document; that is, when the signatory applies the mathematical procedure to the electronic document. The second moment is the verification of the digital signature that takes place when a third party confirms (or not) the identity of the signatory and the integrity of the electronic document. A digital signature aims at establishing the identity of the signatory, or in other words whether the person claiming to have signed the document is the one who actually signed it, as well as the integrity of the electronic document which addresses the issue of whether an electronic document has been modified since

---

[256] *Devoto*, Comercio Electrónico y Firma Digital, 2001, p. 230; *Hocsman*, Negocios en Internet, 2005, p. 503. In any event, even if the definition allows embracing other techniques, it seems that currently public key cryptography is the only technology that can meet the requirements under the Argentine Digital Signature Act. The Digital Signature website of Argentina, <http://www.pki.gov.ar/>, is based exclusively on public key cryptography.

[257] *Fornari / Lavalle Cobo*, in: Belluscio / Zannoni (Eds.), Código Civil, Volume IX, 2007, p. 1329. This comes to no surprise since digital signatures based on public key cryptography have been the technique traditionally recognized under Argentine law. All the bills considered when passing the Argentine Digital Signature Act are primarily based on the concept of digital signature and in most of the cases contain more descriptive definitions than the one finally passed. In addition, the norms previous to the Argentine Digital Signature Act focus also on digital signatures.

[258] Section 25(a) of the Argentine Digital Signature Act, in turn, lists these requirements as duties of the digital certificate holder.

signed. The verification of the signature answers these two questions simultaneously.

2. Validity requirements

In order to have full legal effects, digital signatures need to comply with the validity requirements set forth in Section 9 of the Argentine Digital Signature Act. The requirements for a digital signature to be valid are three: a valid digital certificate, the creation of the digital signature during the validity period of the digital certificate, and the due verification of the digital signature.

a) A valid digital certificate

A digital certificate is an electronic document digitally signed by a certifier which links the signature-verification data to its holder (Section 13). For a digital signature to be valid it has to be based on a valid digital certificate issued (in case of domestic digital certificates) or recognized (in case of foreign digital certificates) by a licensed certifier (Section 9(a) and 9(c)). However, it would have been enough that Section 9 established the requirement of a valid digital certificate. It was not necessary to clarify that the digital certificate had to be issued or recognized by a licensed certifier because that requirement is already encompassed in the notion of a valid digital certificate.

The Argentine Digital Signature Act establishes three requirements for digital certificates to be valid (Section 14). A digital certificate which does not meet these requirements is invalid and, consequently, cannot create valid digital signatures.

One of the requirements is that the digital certificate be issued according to international standards.[259] A second requirement is that the certificate contains certain minimum data such as the identity of the holder and of the licensed certifier who issued it, and information that individualizes the digital certificate (Section 14(b)1). The importance of this last feature is that a digital certificate must be easily and accurately identifiable so that the licensed certifier can keep track of a certificate revocation and third parties can verify its status, without risk of confusion among certificates.[260] Besides, the digital certificate shall include the information necessary to verify the signature, which under public key cryptography is the public key (Section 14(b)4). The period within which the digital certificate is valid shall also be mentioned in the digital certificate

---

[259] Section 14(b) of the Argentine Digital Signature Act. The application authority is in charge of determining the technological standards (Section 30(b) Argentine Digital Signature Act).

[260] Digital certificates may be revoked at the holder's request, or by decision of the licensed certifier, the application authority or a court (Section 19(e) Argentine Digital Signature Act).

indicating the exact date from which the certificate is valid as well as the expiration date (Section 14(b)1 and Section 15).

The most important requirement for a digital certificate to be valid is that the digital certificate be issued – or recognized – by a licensed certifier. Digital certificates issued by non-licensed certifiers are invalid and may not be used to create a valid digital signature (Section 2 Executive Order 2628/2002). Instead, they may only create electronic signatures (Section 2 Executive Order 2628/2002).

The Argentine Digital Signature Act establishes a mandatory license scheme requiring every entity which wishes to offer digital signature verification services to obtain a license from the licensing entity (Section 20).[261] Legal persons, public registries of contracts, government agencies (Section 17) or associations responsible for the regulation of professions (Section 18) may become licensed certifiers.

Otherwise, if a certifier is not licensed, the digital certificates it issues are not valid (Section 14) and, consequently, neither are the digital signatures created with them (Section 9(c)). The signature created with a digital certificate from a non-licensed certifier would be a digital signature in a technological sense but legally it would qualify as an electronic signature. This means that as to what technology concerns both signatures are identical. However, in one case the digital certificate has been issued by a licensed certifier while in the other it has not and this triggers the legal distinction between the former, which may create valid digital signatures, and the latter, which may only create electronic signatures.

The German Digital Signature Act in its Section 4 also required certifiers to obtain a license in order to operate. The mandatory accreditation scheme was abandoned when the German Electronic Signatures Act implementing the Electronic Signatures Directive was adopted. The Electronic Signatures Directive prohibits mandatory license schemes; only voluntary accreditation schemes are admissible.[262] However, despite this legal trend in foreign countries, Argentine legislators preferred to establish a mandatory registration scheme based on the Argentine legal tradition of having third parties certifying signatures. In Senator Del Piero's speech on the day the digital signature bill was passed, he highlighted that countries without the figure of the notary public

---

[261] The fact that the government runs the mandatory accreditation scheme and is in charge of granting and denying the licenses to prospective certifiers shall not be construed as a guarantee by any governmental agency of the services provided by the licensed certifiers (Section 25 Executive Order 2628/2002).

[262] Articles 3.1 and 3.2 Electronic Signatures Directive.

did not have mandatory accreditation schemes.[263] That is certainly not the case in countries like Spain, France or Germany, where the notary public plays a relevant role and, yet, according to the Electronic Signatures Directive, mandatory licensing schemes may not be established. Nevertheless, the remark helps to understand that the use of licensed certifiers is based on the need to grant the functioning of digital signatures a higher level of reliability.

b)   Created while the digital certificate is in force

The second requirement for a digital signature to be valid is that the signature shall be created while the digital certificate is in force (Section 9(a)). Each certificate shall indicate the period during which it is valid (Section 14(b)1 and Section 15). A signature created outside the validity period of the digital certificate (for example, after the expiration date of the digital certificate) is invalid. It should be noted that the digital certificate needs to be in force at the time of the creation of the signature but not at the time of its verification. The verification of a digital signature may take place after the expiration date of the digital certificate.

c)   Due verification

Finally, a digital signature is valid if duly verified (Section 9(b)). The verification shall be accomplished using the data contained in the certificate and following the appropriate verification procedures (Section 9(b)).[264]

IV. Electronic signatures

The Argentine Digital Signature Act governs also electronic signatures. The statute recognizes the use and validity of electronic signatures; therefore, electronic signatures are a valid type of signature.[265] However, the legal text is not clear as to when electronic signatures can be validly used. The Argentine Digital Signature Act devotes only one section, Section 5, to electronic signatures.

"An electronic signature is a set of integrated electronic data, linked or associated logically to other electronic data, used by the signing party as his means of identification, which lacks any of the necessary requirements to be

---

[263] Antecedentes Parlamentarios, 2002, 845.
[264] The proceedings for creation and verification of the signature have to be established by the application authority (Section 2 Argentine Digital Signature Act).
[265] *Altmark*, Preface, in: Luz Clara, Ley de Firma Digital Comentada, 2006, p. 16.

considered a digital signature. If an electronic signature is not recognized, it is up to the party that invokes it to prove its validity".[266]

The definition of electronic signature has two parts: first, concerning what an electronic signature is – electronic data identifying the signatory –, and second, referring to what it lacks – the requirements for being a digital signature.[267]

It is possible to identify two types of electronic signatures. On the one hand, electronic signatures that were never intended to meet the digital signature legal requirements. Examples of this type of electronic signatures are passwords, the name written at the end of an e-mail, or a scanned handwritten signature.[268] On the other hand, there are electronic signatures that were intended to be digital signatures but because of not complying with one or more of the legal requirements, the law considers them as electronic signatures. This is the case of signatures that do not comply with the requirements set forth in Section 9 – validity of digital signatures – of the Argentine Digital Signature Act; for example, a signature based on public key cryptography where the digital certificate has been issued by a non-licensed certification authority. Therefore, electronic signatures can also be based on public key cryptography.[269]

V.   Legal value of digital and electronic signatures

Under Argentine law there are important differences concerning the legal effects of digital and electronic signatures.

1.   Compliance with the legal requirement of a signature

The main difference between digital and electronic signatures results from their legal recognition as equivalents of handwritten signatures.

Section 3 of the Argentine Digital Signature Act establishes that a digital signature may be used whenever the law requires a document to be signed.[270]

---

[266] Translation obtained from the Digital Signature website of the Argentine Republic and available at <http://www.pki.gov.ar/images/stories/documents/digital%20signature%20law.pdf>.

[267] *Hocsman*, Negocios en Internet, 2005, p. 504; *Farrés*, Firma Digital, 2005, p. 95.

[268] *Fornari / Lavalle Cobo*, in: Belluscio / Zannoni (Eds.), Código Civil, Volume IX, 2007, p. 1337.

[269] Clearly shown in Section 2 of Executive Order 2628/2002 as amended by Executive order 724/2006, which establishes that digital certificates issued by non-licensed certifiers are valid to produce the effects the law establishes for electronic signatures.

[270] This section was taken almost literally from Section 3 of the bill of Congressmen Del Piero and Molinari, see Antecedentes Parlamentarios, 2002, 834.

Thus, digital signatures have the same value as handwritten signatures.[271] However, nothing is said about electronic signatures. Consequently, a first reading of the section leads to the conclusion that digital signatures comply with the legal requirement of a signature while electronic signatures do not. Therefore, the legal requirement of a signature may be fulfilled with a digital signature but not with an electronic signature.[272] The use of electronic signatures would then be excluded from legal acts.

However, as specified by its wording, Section 3 applies to situations where the law imposes the signature requirement or establishes consequences for its absence.[273] Therefore, a second reading reveals that Section 3 remains silent about the cases where the law does not require a signature or does not establish the consequences for its absence.

Under Argentine contract law the freedom of forms principle governs.[274] Therefore, there are several contracts to which the law imposes no specific form. Consequently, contracting parties may choose any form for the contract. Thus, they may execute it verbally, in writing, before witnesses, before a notary public or choose any other formal requirement that they may deem appropriate. In this scenario the question is whether an electronic signature may be used when the law does not demand a signature. If Section 3 is construed broadly, then only digital signatures may be used instead of handwritten signatures regardless of whether the signature is imposed by law or not. On the contrary, a literal interpretation of Section 3 results in narrowing its scope and limiting the use of digital signatures only to the cases where there is a legal requirement of a signature. Consequently, in those cases where the law does not impose the requirement of a signature, any type of signature – either electronic or digital – could be used.

A narrow interpretation of Section 3 is favored for several reasons. In the first place, if only digital signatures have legal value, the use of electronic signatures is completely excluded and that could not have been the intention of the lawmaker, who established the validity of electronic signatures and defined their concept (Sections 1 and 5). In the second place, the requirement of the written form being absent, the parties may choose any form. That means the parties may

---

[271] *Farrés*, Firma Digital, 2005, pp. 74-75.

[272] *Farrés*, Firma Digital, 2005, pp. 95-96.

[273] A similar provision is contained in the UNCITRAL Model Law on Electronic Commerce (Article 7.2) and the UNCITRAL Model Law on Electronic Signatures (Article 6.2).

[274] Section 974 of the Argentine Civil Code. See also *Borda*, Tratado de Derecho Civil – Parte general, Volume II, 1991, pp. 165-166; *Santos Cifuentes*, in: Belluscio / Zannoni (Eds.), Código Civil, Volume 4, 2001, Section 974, pp. 465-466; *Rivera*, Instituciones de Derecho Civil – Parte General, Volume II, 1993, pp. 625-626.

exclude the written form completely. Therefore, if they have the power not to use the written form, they should also be allowed to use a type of electronic signature other than the one imposed by the law.

However, the requirement of the written form may be imposed by the parties instead than by the law (Sections 974 and 975 Argentine Civil Code). Even if the law remains silent as to the form of a contract, the parties may agree that the contract has to be in writing. Under Argentine law every private document requires a signature (Section 1012 Argentine Civil Code); thus, the question is whether once the parties choose the written form the electronic document has to bear a digital signature. In other words, whether the need of a signature in private documents contained in Section 1012 of the Argentine Civil Code is to be construed as the law imposing the obligation of signing for the purposes of Section 3 of the Argentine Digital Signature Act.

One the one hand, it could be argued that once the written form is chosen, the rules concerning written documents apply in their entirety; therefore, that the law imposes the signature requirement and that for an electronic contract the requirement of a signature may be only fulfilled with a digital signature. On the other hand, as mentioned, contracting parties are free to exclude at all the written form. Therefore, if the parties are able to exclude the written form, they should also be able to exclude the requirement of a digital signature. Thus, it would be according to the wording of the statute to construe that the Argentine Digital Signature Act requires a digital signature only when the law imposes the signature requirement. In the cases where the parties agree on the written form electronic signatures may be used. Of course, if the parties expressly agree on the use of digital signatures, this agreement shall be respected.

This is the approach followed by the German law. Under German law when a signature is required by law, only a qualified electronic signature satisfies that requirement (Section 126a BGB). However, absent such a requirement, any type of electronic signature can be used even when the parties agree on the electronic form, except when there is an agreement of the parties to the contrary (Section 127(3) BGB).

It should be noted that the wording of Section 3 might also be misread to mean that digital signatures may only be used when the law requires a signature or establishes consequences for its absence, excluding the validity of digital signatures as equivalent to handwritten signatures in cases outside those two. However, that would not be a sound interpretation of the provision.

2. Legal presumptions

Another difference between electronic and digital signatures is that the law grants digital signatures certain protections. The Argentine Digital Signature Act contains three presumptions in favor of digital signatures: the presumption of authorship, the presumption of integrity, and the sender presumption.[275] These presumptions are rebuttable (*praesuntio iuris tantum*) and, consequently, admit evidence that may prove them wrong.[276]

a)   Authorship presumption

The authorship presumption assumes that a digital signature belongs to the holder of the digital certificate (Section 7). A signature created with a particular private key is presumed to have been created by the holder of the digital certificate containing the corresponding public key. For this reason it is so important that the private key is protected. In case of unauthorized use of a private key, it will be presumed that the signature was created by the holder of the digital certificate. On the contrary, in the case of electronic signatures the validity of the signature has to be proved by the party claiming its validity (Section 5).[277]

b)   Integrity presumption

The integrity presumption assumes that if a signature verification procedure is true, then the electronic document was not modified since the moment it was signed (Section 8). Therefore, if the verification procedure does not detect an alteration to the electronic document but the author of the document alleges the document has in fact been modified, the author will have to overcome the legal presumption that the document has not been altered since he or she signed it.

c)   Sender presumption

The sender presumption applies when an electronic document is sent automatically according to pre-programmed orders and the digital document bears a digital signature. In this case it is presumed that the signed document comes from the sender (Section 10). From the wording of the Argentine Digital Signature Act it seems that this presumption applies both to the digitally signed message and to any additional document attached to the message. For example, in the case of electronic mails, the e-mail generated automatically by a program would be covered by this presumption as well as the electronic documents, if any, attached to the message.

---

[275] *Farrés*, Firma Digital, 2005, pp. 104-120 and 126-139.
[276] *Farrés*, Firma Digital, 2005, p. 113. The three presumptions can be found in Sections 6 and 7 of the bill of Senators Del Piero and Molinari Romero, see Antecedentes Parlamentarios, 2002, 834.
[277] *Fornari / Lavalle Cobo*, in: Belluscio / Zannoni (Eds.), Código Civil, Volume IX, 2007, p. 1338.

VI. Digital or electronic document

The Argentine Digital Signature Act confers to electronic documents the same value as paper documents (Section 6).[278] The requirement of a writing and a signature go hand in hand. If the law only recognizes the validity of electronic signatures and not of electronic documents, the question of whether the written requirement can be fulfilled with the electronic form continues to be unsettled because while the signature in a form other than in writing is recognized, the recognition of the electronic document remains open. Even when the law does not specifically require a document to be in paper, it clarifies the legal scenario if a norm expressly recognizes the validity of electronic documents.

Previous legislation already recognized the value of electronic documents. The Business Companies Law 19.550 as amended allows accounting books to be carried electronically (Section 61, Business Companies Act 19.550).[279] Statute 24.264 authorizes the use and validity of electronic documents for the public administration (Section 30).[280]

Concerning terminology the Argentine Digital Signature Act is not clear. Section 6 refers to digital documents. In turn, in Section 11 the term electronic document is used. It is not certain whether the legislator meant both terms – electronic document and digital document – as equal or whether they shall be construed differently. Nevertheless, the first interpretation seems to be the most plausible.[281] In the glossary of Executive Order 2628/2002 the terms digital document and electronic document are used as synonyms. However, the term electronic document is not employed in the text of the executive order.[282]

The Argentine Digital Signature Act addresses the issue of original electronic documents. Sometimes the law imposes the requirement of an original

---

[278] Section 6 of the Argentine Digital Signature Act defines the digital document as the digital representation of acts or facts regardless of the medium to which they are affixed, or in which they are saved or stored.

[279] *Lorenzetti*, Tratado de los Contratos, Volume III, 2000, p. 841; *de Aguinis / Kleidermacher*, Nuevas formas de contratación. Contratación por ordenador, La Ley 1987-C, 892; *Hocsman*, Negocios en Internet, 2005, pp. 493-494; *Lorenzetti*, Comercio Electrónico, 2001, pp. 67-68.

[280] *Fernández Delpech*, Internet: Su Problemática Jurídica, 2004, p. 347; *Hocsman*, Negocios en Internet, 2005, pp. 494-495; *Lorenzetti*, Comercio Electrónico, 2001, p. 68.

[281] *Fernández Delpech*, Internet: Su Problemática Jurídica, 2004, p. 369.

[282] Foreign legislation uses either the term electronic document or electronic record. In German law the term electronic document is used (*elektronische Dokument*); for example Section 126a BGB. In the case of US legislation, E-Sign uses the term electronic record (Section 106.4) as well as UETA (Section 2.7). The term record is used to clarify that not only written documents in electronic form are included but also other type of media like recordings or videos.

document. For example, Section 1021 of the Argentine Civil Code requires for contracts with bilateral considerations as many originals as parties with different interests.[283] However, the nature of electronic documents makes it difficult to determine which one is the original and which one the copy.[284] The Argentine Digital Signature Act regards as originals documents created originally in digital form and digitally signed, as well as documents created originally in other forms and later digitally reproduced. In this latter case the document reproduced has to be an original itself and the digital document in which the reproduction is contained has to be digitally signed. These two types of documents are considered originals and have accordingly evidentiary value (Section 11).

Original electronic documents have to be digitally signed (Section 11). However, while a digital signature is a requirement for a digital document to be considered an original, it is not a requirement for a document to be considered an electronic document. The concept of electronic document contained in Section 6 does not require a digital signature or any other type of signature.[285]

Sometimes the law requires that documents be kept for a certain period of time. The safekeeping of digitally signed electronic documents fulfils the legal requirement of document conservation (Section 12). Furthermore, electronic documents have to remain available for consultation, and it has to be possible to accurately determine when, where and by whom the electronic document was created, sent or received.

VII. Exclusions from the Argentine Digital Signature Act

In principle, handwritten and digital signatures may be used interchangeably. However, there are certain exceptions. Section 4 of the Argentine Digital Signature Act excludes the application of the statute in some situations. Pursuant to Section 4, the Argentine Digital Signature Act does not apply to wills and testaments, legal acts governed by family law, private acts, and acts that require formalities incompatible with the use of digital signatures.[286]

---

[283] *Fornari / Lavalle Cobo,* in: Belluscio / Zannoni (Eds.), Código Civil, Volume IX, 2007, pp. 1347-1348.

[284] *Lorenzetti,* Comercio Electrónico, 2001, p. 63.

[285] Concerning the evidentiary value of digital documents, a judicial decision denied evidentiary value to an e-mail which lacked a digital signature on the ground that it did not comply with Sections 2 and 5 of the Argentine Digital Signature Act., see Henry Hirschen y Cía S.A. vs. Easy Argentina S.R.L., National Commercial Court of Appeals, February 16, 2007, DJ, 2007-II, pp. 1315.

[286] *Lorenzetti,* Comercio Electrónico, 2001, p. 65.

The direct precedent of this section is found in the bill of Senator Del Piero[287] and with some changes in the bill of Congressman Atanasof.[288] In the Senate's Session where the digital signature bill was passed Senator Del Piero explained that the reasons for the exclusions were based on the Argentine judicial tradition that certain acts be executed in the presence of the interested persons or with the intervention of a notary public. It was, therefore, considered that in these cases the implementation of the electronic form could undermine the confidence of the public in this type of acts.

1.   Dispositions in case of death

Section 4(a) states that the Argentine Digital Signature Act does not apply to provisions in case of death.[289] Consequently, wills and testaments may not be signed electronically. The Argentine Digital Signature Act neither applies to other acts that will have effect after the death of a person (Section 947 Argentine Civil Code).[290]

Under Argentine law there are three types of wills: the holographic will (*testamento ológrafo*), the notarized will (*testamento por acto público*), and the closed will (*testamento cerrado*). Notarized and closed wills require the intervention of a notary public[291] and, therefore, the exclusion is based also on Section 4(d). Concerning the holographic will the Argentine Civil Code requires that the testament be handwritten and hand signed by the testator;[292] therefore, it is not possible to use the electronic form.

It should be noted that the fact that the signatory dies does not affect the validity of a digital signature. A certificate has to be revoked once its holder dies (Section 23(f) Executive Order 2628/2002) but what is relevant is that the

---

287   See Section 4, Antecedentes Parlamentarios, 2002, 834; *Farrés*, Firma Digital, 2005, p. 90.
288   Actually, the bill of Congressman Cardesa excluded not only the acts listed in Section 4 of the Argentine Digital Signature Act but also the petition for bankruptcy or reorganization as well as cancellation of health or life insurance (Section 9 of Congressman Cardesa's bill), see Antecedentes Parlamentarios, 2002, 766.
289   The question may be raised as to whether this exception encompasses all acts governed by the law of descent and distribution. The wording of the law suggests that this interpretation is overreaching. Provision 4(a) does not refer to the acts governed by the law of descent and distribution as is the case in provision 4(b) where the legislator excluded all acts governed by family law.
290   *Fornari / Lavalle Cobo*, in: Belluscio / Zannoni (Eds.), Código Civil, Volume IX, 2007, p. 1336 (The following examples are given: donations of organs and designation of a guardian for a minor).
291   Sections 3654 and 3666 Argentine Civil Code.
292   Section 3639 Argentine Civil Code.

signature is created while the digital certificate is valid. The fact that after the signing the certificate becomes invalid does not affect the validity of the signature.

2. Acts relating to family law

Acts governed by family law are outside the scope of the Argentine Digital Signature Act (Section 4(b)). In other words, documents relating to family law may not be electronically signed. Acts of family law, such as marriage, divorce, and adoption have significant impact on the life of persons; consequently, the legislator found it wiser to exclude in these cases the application of the Argentine Digital Signature Act.

3. Acts of a personal character

The third exception, Section 4(c), refers to acts of a personal character (*actos personalísimos*), which are acts that due to their nature can only be done by the person himself.[293] Acts of a personal character are excluded from the scope of the Argentine Digital Signature Act.

4. Acts incompatible with the use of digital signatures

Finally the law is inapplicable to acts whose formal requirements are incompatible with the use of digital signatures (Section 4(d)).[294] It would have been more appropriate to refer to acts not compatible with the use of the electronic form. The use of the digital signature is not possible because the document cannot be in electronic form.

The clearest example of acts incompatible with the use of digital signatures are public deeds for they require to be done before a notary public and respecting special formal requirements such as being registered in the notary books. However, the Argentine Digital Signature Act does not expressly exclude its application to public deeds. The Argentine Digital Signature Act simply states that it does not apply to acts incompatible with the implementation of the

---

[293] *Borda*, Tratado de Derecho Civil – Parte General, Volume I, 1991, pp. 440-441. For a critical view on the drafting of this section, see *Farrés*, Firma Digital, 2005, pp. 90-91.

[294] This exception was taken from the bill of Senator Del Piero and Molinari (Section 4), see Antecedentes Parlamentarios, 2002, 834. The bill of Congressman Puiggrós also contained this exception (Section 7), see Antecedentes Parlamentarios, 2002, 759. The bill of Congressman Atanasof proposed an intermediate solution. Legal acts requiring the intervention of a notary public may be digitally signed as long as the digital certificate is issued by a notary public (Section 9), see Antecedentes Parlamentarios, 2002, 777 and 788.

electronic form. While today public deeds cannot be done in electronic form, in the future this situation might change and a notary public may be able to carry electronic books; consequently, the incompatibility may no longer exist. Thus, if the formal requirements of public deeds were compatible with the use of digital signatures, the Argentine Digital Signature Act would apply.[295]

The requirement of a public deed may be fixed by law or by the contracting parties. Once imposed, the public deed may not be replaced by another form. Nevertheless, if the parties draft a contract that requires a public deed in an electronic document digitally signed, the question is whether it could be considered as an agreement to execute a public deed. The Argentine Civil Code establishes that if a contract requiring a public deed is executed in a private instrument, that agreement does not comply with the formal requirements but it is valid as a contract to execute the public deed (Section 1185). Nothing in the Argentine Digital Signature Act indicates that an agreement to execute a public deed may not be executed electronically; therefore, the answer seems to be affirmative.

There is one judgment dealing with the exception.[296] The case deals with a settlement of claims done by e-mail. The law requires those acts to be in writing, signed and presented before the judge (Section 338 Commercial Code). The court held the e-mail as invalid based on two different sections of the Argentine Digital Signature Act. First, the e-mail lacked a digital signature under the Argentine Digital Signature Act; therefore, the instrument was not considered to be signed. Second, the settlement was, according to Section 4(d), deemed incompatible with the use of digital signatures because the law requires such an agreement to be signed and introduced in a judicial file, which is a written proceeding. It would seem overreaching to consider that the written nature of the judicial process is a ground for excluding the application of the Argentine Digital Signature Act because the scope of the electronic form would significantly reduced.

VIII. Foreign signatures and foreign certificates

The Argentine Digital Signature Act governs the recognition of foreign digital certificates. The first issue to determine is when a digital certificate is considered foreign. The answer resides in the domicile of the certifier issuing the digital certificate. Licensed certifiers must have a legal domicile in

---

[295] *Devoto,* Comercio Electrónico y Firma Digital, 2001, pp. 232-233.
[296] Coop. de Viv. Cred. y Cons. Fiduciaria Ltda. vs. Becerra Leguizamón, Hugo R., National Commercial Court of Appeals, June 27, 2006, La Ley 2006-F, 209.

Argentina (Section 21(u));[297] therefore, a certificate is foreign when issued by a certifier which is not domiciled in Argentina.

A foreign digital certificate which has been recognized has the same value as domestic digital certificates. According to Section 16(a), there are two alternative procedures to recognize a foreign certificate. One option is that the foreign certificate meets the requirements for domestic digital certificates and that a reciprocity treaty between Argentina and the country of origin of the digital certificate is in force. Another option is that a domestic licensed certifier guarantees the validity of the foreign digital certificate and that the application authority confirms the recognition (Section 16(b)).[298]

The Argentine Digital Signature Act does not contain provisions dealing with the recognition of foreign electronic signatures not based on digital certificates. Therefore, in the case of foreign electronic signatures not based on digital certificates the law does not answer the question as to their validity.

IX. Public Key Infrastructure

The Argentine Digital Signature Act devotes most of its sections to the organization of the structure needed to implement digital signatures, which is known as Public Key Infrastructure or PKI. The Argentine PKI is composed of the application authority, the licensing entity, the licensed certifiers, and the assessing commission.[299]

1. Application authority

The application authority is the highest authority within the Public Key Infrastructure. Its role is to supervise the activity of the licensed certifier and their compliance with the legal framework, to issue norms for the implementation of the Argentine Digital Signature Act and to establish the auditing system (Section 30). Moreover, the application authority is in charge of issuing the digital certificates to the licensed certifiers (Section 30(h)).[300]

---

[297] In this respect it differentiates from the Electronic Signatures Directive which allows a certification-service-provider to offer digital signature services in other countries (Article 4.2).

[298] Farrés, Firma Digital, 2005, pp. 202-204.

[299] Hocsman, Negocios en Internet, 2005, p. 511; Farrés, Firma Digital, 2005, pp. 62-71.

[300] The application authority has also duties as a holder of a digital certificate (Section 31).

The application authority of the Argentine Digital Signature Act is the Under Secretary of Public Management (*Subsecretaría de la Gestión Pública*)³⁰¹ dependant on the Chief of Ministerial Cabinet (*Jefatura de Gabinete de Ministros*) (Section 29).

2.   Licensing entity

The primary role of the licensing entity is to grant and revoke the licenses to certifiers and to control, together with the application authority, the licensed certifiers.

The licensing entity is the Under Secretary of the Public Function. That means that under the current structure the application authority and the licensing entity are centralized in the same governmental agency. This, in some respect, might avoid the problem of distributing the functions among them because the Argentine Digital Signature Act and its regulatory executive order are not accurately drafted and some functions are sometimes assigned to both the application authority and the licensing entity. For example, in different sections of the statute it is made clear that the license to operate as a certifier has to be granted by the licensing entity (Sections 14, 17 and 20). However, Section 30(h) of the Argentine Digital Signature Act assigns this function to the application authority. The same is the case with the application of sanctions. Section 40 states that the licensing entity is responsible for this while Section 30(k) designates the application authority for the same purpose.

3.   Licensed certifiers

The law lists the obligations of the licensed certifiers in Section 21 of the law. The list is not a closed one because Section 21(w) states that licensed certifiers have to comply with any other obligation arising from that condition. The licensed certifier's main role is the issuance of the digital certificates to the public.³⁰²

---

³⁰¹ Executive Order 409/2005 published in the Official Gazette on May 5, 2005. See Annex, para. 16 modifying the powers of the Under Secretary of Public Management and designing it as the application authority and licensing entity of the Argentine Digital Signature Act.

³⁰² The request of a digital certificate to the licensed certifier triggers the duty of information of the licensed certifier. The licensed certifier has to make available all the information referring to the process of obtaining a digital certificate (Section 21(h)). Prior to the issuance of a digital certificate the licensed certifier has to inform the petitioner how a digital certificate is used, its characteristics and effects, and the existence of a licensing system. Also the licensed certifier has to provide information on financial liability, the effects of the revocation of its own digital certificate and of the licence granted by the licensing entity. All of this information

Licensed certifiers may delegate some of their functions to registry authorities. The concept of registry authority is not contained in the Argentine Digital Signature Act but in the regulatory Executive Order 2628/2002. The functions that may be delegated are the reception of certificate application and certificate revocation requests, the validation of the data relating to the petitioners or holders of certificates, and the storage of information (Section 35 Executive Order 2628/2002). In case the licensed certifiers delegate these functions to registry authorities the licensed certifiers remain liable (Section 36 Executive Order 2628/2002). The issuance of certificates may never be delegated to another authority since that is an exclusive function of the licensed certifiers.

4.   Advisory Commission for Digital Signature Infrastructure

The Argentine Digital Signature Act in its Section 28 creates the Digital Signature Infrastructure Advisory Commission within the sphere of the application authority.[303] Regulatory Decree 2628/2002 deals with the Advisory Commission in Chapter III, Sections 7 to 10.

The function of the advisory commission is to assist the application authority. The advisory commission is mainly a consulting body on which the application authority can rely on issues relating to the functioning and implementation of digital signatures and their infrastructure (Section 36 Argentine Digital Signature Act). Besides, the advisory commission is to act as a link between the public and the application authority and to keep the dialogue open between those two ends (Section 35 Argentine Digital Signature Act and Section 10 Executive Order 2628/2002). The advisory commission carries out its tasks through the

---

must be drafted in an easy-to-understand manner (Section 21(a)). In addition, the licensed certifier has to notify the petitioner of his or her obligations as a holder of a certificate and of the measures needed to be taken in order to create safe digital signatures and to ensure their reliable verification (Section 21(e)). Finally, the licensed certifier has to inform in the certification policies whether the identity of the owner of the digital certificate has been verified or not (Section 21(n)). Three different verbs are used regarding the licensed certifier's obligation to inform. Section 21(a) and (n) uses the verb "inform" (*informar*), Section 21(e) uses the verb "notify" (*notificar*) and Section 21(h) uses the expression "to make available" (*poner a disposición*). "Notify" is the strongest of all the verbs, most likely meaning personally serving the person, having a secure medium to communicate something to someone and having proofs that the documents were delivered to the person. "Inform" has a softer meaning, referring to communicating something to someone but without any formal requirements in the delivery process. Finally, "to make available" is just to give someone the opportunity to have access to certain information. Therefore, to make some information available can be fulfilled by having the information online even though the information is not directly given to the person.

[303] Regulated in Section 7 to 10 of the Executive Order 2628/2002.

issuance of recommendations and the organization of public hearings (Section 35 Argentine Digital Signature Act and Section 10 Executive Order 2628/2002).

C. Conclusions

Digital signatures are predominant in Argentine legislation. The role of the rest of electronic signatures seems to be reduced. However, it is possible to construe the Argentine Digital Signature Act in a way that reconciles the goals of lawmakers of ensuring security and trust in electronic transactions while increasing the spectrum of signing technologies to be recognized. By allowing the use of electronic signatures in acts subject to no formal requirements the sphere of application of electronic signatures is significantly increased. Likewise, it is ensured that the safest technique is used for acts where the law imposes the signature requirement.

Chapter 6: The work of national and international institutions

National and international institutions such as UNCITRAL, the International Chamber of Commerce and the American Bar Association took an active role in promoting the use of electronic signatures and advancing their legal framework.

A. UNCITRAL

The United Nations Commission on International Trade Law (UNCITRAL)[304] is a subsidiary organ of the United Nations General Assembly and is responsible for furthering the harmonization and unification of international trade law.[305]

UNCITRAL issued two model laws which deal, one partially and the other entirely, with the topic of electronic signatures: The Model Law on Electronic Commerce (1996) and the Model Law on Electronic Signatures (2001).[306] In 2005, UNCITRAL adopted the Convention on the Use of Electronic Communications in International Contracts.[307]

Model laws are legislatives texts that aim at providing lawmakers with guidance when enacting national legislation in topics related to international trade. Lawmakers may adopt model laws as proposed by UNCITRAL or may freely modify them. However, the goal of model laws is not only to provide legislators with a legal text that is deemed appropriate for a certain aspect of international trade law but mainly to achieve unification of legislation in that area of law. Therefore, the larger the number of countries that enact legislation based on a model law, the fewer the chances of having divergent national legislation. In conclusion, unlike conventions model laws do not enter into force, are not enforceable and may be widely modified.[308] Nonetheless, due to their flexibility

---

[304] In Spanish the Commission's name is abbreviated CNUDMI and in French CNUDCI. The website of UNCITRAL is <http://www.uncitral.org/>.

[305] UNCITRAL was established by means of the United Nations General Assembly Resolution 2205 (XXI), in the 1497th plenary meeting on December 17, 1966. See Report of the Sixth Committee, General Assembly – Twenty-first Session, pp. 99-100 (According to para. 8 of Resolution 2205 (XXI), UNCITRAL "shall further the progressive harmonization and unification of the law of international trade".).

[306] The texts of the model laws can be found in: UNCITRAL, Model Law on Electronic Commerce with Guide to Enactment (1996), 1999, and UNCITRAL, Model Law on Electronic Signatures with Guide to Enactment (2001), 2002.

[307] In 2009 UNCITRAL published the document titled "Promoting confidence in electronic commerce: legal issues on international use of electronic authentication and signature methods" available at <http://www.uncitral.org/pdf/english/publicati ons/sales_publications/PromConfEcom_e.pdf>.

[308] UNCITRAL, Model Law on Electronic Signatures with Guide to Enactment (2001), 2002, p. 18; See UNCITRAL, FAQ, <http://www.uncitral.org/uncitral/en /uncitral_texts_faq.html>.

and lack of binding character it is normally expected that an important number of countries will use the model laws as basis for their legislation.[309]

I.   UNCITRAL Model Law on Electronic Commerce

Electronic commerce exchanges communications and data in electronic form which in certain cases need to be signed in order to comply with legal requirements. Yet, in the mid 1990s most of the national legislation was still structured around the concept of paper. The lack of certainty as to the value of electronic documents and electronic signatures was regarded as an obstacle to electronic commerce.[310] Besides, as electronic commerce occurs frequently across borders the legal uncertainty surrounding electronic commerce may hinder international trade.[311] Thus, UNCITRAL was considered the most appropriate body to work on the issue of updating and harmonizing the law regarding the legal validity of electronic documents and electronic signatures.[312]

---

[309]   UNCITRAL, Model Law on Electronic Signatures with Guide to Enactment (2001), 2002, p. 18.

[310]   UNCITRAL, Legal aspects of automatic data processing: report of the Secretary General, Yearbook of the United Nations Commission on International Trade Law, Volume XV, 1984, (A/CN.9/254), pp. 328-331 (It is pointed out that the lack of uniform rules causes legal uncertainty to transactions using electronic data. The use of electronic data in commerce grows but the absence of legal rules attempts against it. Some of the problems needing to be addressed are: the legal value of computer records, the requirement of a writing, and the authentication of signatures. Concerning this last point the question is whether an electronic authentication meets the legal requirements of a signature).

[311]   UNCITRAL, Legal Aspects of automatic trade data interchange, in: Note by the secretariat: legal aspects of automatic data processing, (A/CN.9/238), Yearbook of the United Nations Commission on International Trade Law, Volume XIV, 1983, (TRADE/WP.4/R.185/Rev.1), pp. 176-188 (This article analyzes the legal difficulties arising from the introduction of the new technologies into trade and highlights the need of international legal rules. The paper focuses mainly on international transactions for the transport of goods. The article, without saying it, contains the principle of "functional equivalence" on which the UNCITRAL Model Law on Electronic Commerce and the UNCITRAL Model Law on Electronic Signatures are based. The goal is to retain the documentary functions in a paper-less system. One of the possible techniques is public key cryptography. The authors highlight that as of the date of the article (1982) it is not commonly used and wonder whether it will be a suitable device. In brief, the authors conclude that the use of electronic documents is happening and can bring interesting benefits in reducing time and costs but the lack of legal certainty jeopardizes further developments.).

[312]   UNCITRAL, Legal Aspects of automatic trade data interchange, in: Note by the secretariat: legal aspects of automatic data processing, (A/CN.9/238), Yearbook of

The legal questions arising from the use of the electronic media in commercial transactions have been considered by UNCITRAL since the year 1982.[313] At that point in time UNCITRAL was dealing with the electronic transfer of funds and had to address the issue of the evidentiary value of computer records. It was then noted that the problem of admissibility into evidence of computer records exceeded the issue of the transfer of funds to be one common to all types of transactions using non-paper documents.[314] Soon other problems common to all transactions using electronic documents were identified, such as the legal requirement of a writing and a signature;[315] thus, the legal issues related to the use of modern technologies in international trade became a priority item in the work of UNCITRAL.[316] Indeed, according to a study done by the UNCITRAL secretariat the major obstacle to the use of new technologies in international trade was the requirement set forth in most laws of a writing and a signature.[317] Therefore, this was the reason why UNCITRAL prioritized within the topic of electronic commerce the issue of how to comply with the legal requirement of a

the United Nations Commission on International Trade Law, Volume XIV, 1983, (TRADE/WP.4/R.185/Rev.1), p. 178.

[313] UNCITRAL, Report of the United Nations Commission on International Trade Law on the work of its fifteenth Session, (A/37/17), pp. 12-13, para. 64 -73.

[314] UNCITRAL, Report of the Secretary-General: Electronic Funds Transfer, Yearbook of the United Nations Commission on International Trade Law, Volume XIII, 1982, (A/CN.9/221 ** and Corr. 1 – French only), pp. 281-283, para. 70-81.

[315] UNCITRAL; Legal Aspects of automatic trade data interchange, in: Note by the secretariat: legal aspects of automatic data processing, (A/CN.9/238), Yearbook of the United Nations Commission on International Trade Law, Volume XIV, 1983, (TRADE/WP.4/R.185/Rev.1), pp. 176-188.

[316] UNCITRAL, Report of the United Nations Commission on International Trade Law and the work of its seventeenth session, Yearbook of the United Nations Commission on International Trade Law, Volume XV, 1984, (A/39/17), pp. 19-20, para. 133-136.

[317] UNCITRAL, Report of the United Nations Commission on International Trade Law on the work of its eighteenth session, Yearbook of the United Nations Commission on International Trade Law, Volume XVI, 1985, (A/40/17), pp. 42-44; UNCITRAL, Legal value of computer records: report of the Secretary General, Yearbook of the United Nations Commission on International Trade Law, 1985, Volume XVI, (A/CN.9/265), pp. 351-365 (The paper shows the result of two surveys in which states with different legal systems took part. The results highlight that in certain circumstances electronic signatures might provide a higher degree of security than handwritten signatures. For example, when receiving a paper document with a handwritten signature the recipient cannot be sure the signature belongs to the signer. On the contrary, an electronic signature can offer a comparative advantage by allowing the recipient to verify the identity of the signatory. Concerning the writing requirement the report shows that this requirement can be met with an electronic document (called computer record). However, the major obstacle is the lack of legislation providing certainty, specially in international transactions.).

writing and a signature. Consequently, UNCITRAL sought by means of a recommendation to encourage governments to examine their legislation so as to make it compatible with the use of electronic documents and electronic signatures.[318] However, it was soon clear that a recommendation was not enough and that more guidance was needed. For this reason, the Working Group on Electronic Data Interchange prepared the Model Law on Electronic Commerce.[319]

The Model law on Electronic Commerce was adopted by UNCITRAL in its 29th session, on June 12, 1996.[320] The UNCITRAL Model Law on Electronic Commerce is divided into two parts. Part one is in turn divided into two chapters: chapter one contains the general provisions and chapter two deals with the communication of data messages. Part two covers electronic commerce in specific areas. Currently, it contains only one chapter on carriage of goods.[321]

The UNCITRAL Model Law on Electronic Commerce addresses the topic of electronic commerce as a whole. Its goal is to remove the legal obstacles to the use of the electronic media both in domestic and international electronic commerce transactions.[322] In the latter sphere, the drafters of the model law

---

[318] UNCITRAL, Report of the United Nations Commission on International Trade Law on the work of its eighteenth session, Yearbook of the United Nations Commission on International Trade Law, Volume XVI, 1985, (A/40/17), pp. 42-44.

[319] The working group was given this name starting from UNCITRAL's twenty-fifth session. Previously the group's name was Working Group on International Payments. See UNCITRAL, Report of the United Nations Commission on International Trade Law on the work of its twenty-fifth session, Yearbook of the United Nations Commission on International Trade Law, Volume XXIII, 1992, (A/47/17), p. 19, para. 147.

[320] UNCITRAL, Report of the United Nations Commission on International Trade Law on the work of its twenty-ninth session, General Assembly, Official Records, Fifty-first Session Supplement No. 17, 1996, (A/51/17), p. 47, para. 204. The Model Law on Electronic Commerce was only amended once in 1998 when article 5bis was added, see UNCITRAL, Report of the United Nations Commission on International Trade Law on the work of its thirty-first session, General Assembly, Official Records, Fifty-third Session, Supplement No. 17, 1998, (A/53/17), pp. 22-23, para. 212-221.

[321] It was designed as a flexible part with more chapters to be added if required; however, no new chapter has been added so far.

[322] For this purpose, Article 1 dealing with the sphere of application does not expressly state whether the Model Law on Electronic Commerce applies to domestic or international transactions. However, in footnote "*" to Article 1 another wording is proposed for those countries willing to limit the application of the Model Law on Electronic Commerce to international transactions.

highlighted the importance that countries have appropriate and uniform legislation on electronic commerce so as to advance international trade.[323]

The UNCITRAL Model Law on Electronic Commerce adopts the functional equivalent principle. The functional equivalent principle is based on the concept that even though paper and electronic documents are clearly different, they may however fulfill the same functions. Another principle contained in the UNCITRAL Model Law on Electronic Commerce is the non-discrimination principle against electronic documents (Article 5). This principle is also labeled media neutrality principle because it does not establish a preference of paper over electronic media.[324] The non-discrimination principle means that no document or record can be denied legal validity, enforcement or effect solely on the grounds that it is in electronic form. In other words, the form cannot be used as a single factor in determining the legal value of a record. In line with Article 5, Article 9 establishes that an electronic document cannot be denied admissibility or evidentiary value just because it is in electronic form.[325]

The core provisions of the UNCITRAL Model Law on Electronic Commerce are those which address the issues of the legal requirement of a writing, a signature and an original. The UNCITRAL Model Law on Electronic Commerce deals with each of these requirements in separate articles. Article 6 addresses the legal requirement of a writing and establishes that such a requirement is met by a data message.[326] Article 7 sets forth the signature requirement. The legal requirement of a signature is satisfied by using any method that identifies and expresses the consent of the signer. The UNCITRAL Model Law on Electronic Commerce does not designate or show a preference for any specific technology. The only requirement is that the method used is reliable and appropriate for the purpose of the message.[327] Article 7 of the UNCITRAL Model Law on Electronic Commerce later became the basis for the

---

[323] UNCITRAL, Model Law on Electronic Commerce with Guide to Enactment (1996), 1999, pp. 16-17.

[324] UNCITRAL, Model Law on Electronic Commerce with Guide to Enactment (1996), 1999, pp. 17 and 23-24.

[325] Article 9(2) of the Model Law on Electronic Commerce establishes parameters to assess the evidentiary weigh of electronic data.

[326] Data message is defined in Article 2(a) as information generated, sent, received or stored by electronic, optical or similar means including, but not limited to, electronic data interchange (EDI), electronic mail, telegram, telex or telecopy. Despite the terminology employed the concept of data message shall not be construed as referring only to documents to be sent, see UNCITRAL, Model Law on Electronic Commerce with Guide to Enactment (1996), 1999, p. 26.

[327] A list of factors that can be taken into account in determining whether a method is appropriate can be found in the Guide to Enactment of the UNCITRAL Model Law on Electronic Commerce, see UNCITRAL, Model Law on Electronic Commerce with Guide to Enactment (1996), 1999, p. 39.

UNCITRAL Model Law on Electronic Signatures. Article 8 deals with originals. In certain cases the law requires an original document. Now the question is how to provide an original document in electronic form when an electronic document can be copied and no difference can be found between the original and the copy. The UNCITRAL Model Law on Electronic Commerce bases the assessment on the integrity of the document and its capability of being reproduced.

The UNCITRAL Model Law on Electronic Commerce has been the basis for legislation in a significant number of countries, namely: the United States of America (from 1998 on depending on each state), Singapore (1998), Australia (1999), Colombia (1999), Republic of Korea (1999), Canada (from 2000 on depending on the Province), France (2000), Ireland (2000), India (2000), Mauritius (2000), Brunei Darussalam (2000), Mexico (2000), Slovenia (2000), Philippines (2000), Jordan (2001), Panama (2001),Venezuela (2001), Dominican Republic (2002), Ecuador (2002), New Zealand (2002), Pakistan (2002),Thailand (2002), South Africa (2002), Cape Verde (2003), China (2004), Viet Nam (2005), Sri Lanka (2006), United Arab Emirates (2006), Guatemala (2008).[328]

II. UNCITRAL Model Law on Electronic Signatures

1. Background

In the same session where the UNCITRAL Model Law on Electronic Commerce was passed, UNCITRAL decided to continue its work in the field of electronic commerce by focusing on digital signatures.[329] Unification on this issue was considered highly desirable in order to promote electronic contracting.[330] The national legislation under discussion or enacted in this field lacked uniformity[331] and, therefore, could hinder electronic commerce.

---

[328] UNCITRAL, Status of the 1996 Model Law on Electronic Commerce, <http://ww w.uncitral.org/uncitral/en/uncitral_texts/electronic_commerce/1996Model_status. html>.

[329] That was the terminology used by UNCITRAL, see UNCITRAL, Report of the United Nations Commission on International Trade Law on the work of its twenty-ninth session, General Assembly, Official Records, Fifty-first Session Supplement No. 17, (A/51/17), p. 52, para. 223-224. For a general review of the Model Law on Electronic Signatures, see *Sorieul*, The UNCITRAL'S Model Law on Electronic Signatures, in: Internet – International Law, International and European Studies and Comments, 2005, pp. 389-397.

[330] UNCITRAL, Report of the United Nations Commission on International Trade Law on the work of its twenty-ninth session, General Assembly, Official Records, Fifty-first Session Supplement No. 17, (A/51/17), p. 51, para. 217.

[331] UNCITRAL, Model Law on Electronic Signatures with Guide to Enactment (2001), 2002, p. 8.

The work was entrusted to the Working Group on Electronic Commerce which was the same working group which had prepared the UNCITRAL Model Law on Electronic Commerce but now bearing a different name.[332] The working group agreed that Article 7 of the UNCITRAL Model Law on Electronic Commerce would be the guideline as to the principles and vocabulary to be used in the new text.[333]

UNCITRAL authorized the working group to focus mainly on the issues of digital signatures, meaning signatures based on public key infrastructure, and certification authorities.[334] Therefore, the first documents issued between the years 1996 and 1997 addressed mainly authentication methods based on public key cryptography.[335] Also, the Secretariat proposed a first draft of articles covering only the issue of digital signatures.[336] This was also the trend in national legislation at that time. The Utah Digital Signature Act was passed in 1995 and the German Digital Signature Act, in 1997. Both statutes were based on digital signature technology and public key infrastructure. Nevertheless, UNCITRAL highlighted that the principle of technology neutrality was a key concept and that focusing on digital signatures shall not be construed as excluding or discouraging the use of electronic signatures.[337]

---

[332] UNCITRAL, Report of the United Nations Commission on International Trade Law on the work of its twenty-ninth session, General Assembly, Official Records, Fifty-first Session Supplement No. 17, (A/51/17), p. 52, para. 224.

[333] UNCITRAL, Report of the Working Group on Electronic Commerce on the work of its thirty-first session, (A/CN.9/437), p. 9, para. 26.

[334] UNCITRAL, Report of the United Nations Commission on International Trade Law on the work of its twenty-ninth session, General Assembly, Official Records, Fifty-first Session Supplement No. 17, (A/51/17), p. 52, para. 223; UNCITRAL, Report of the United Nations Commission on International Trade Law on the work of its thirtieth session, General Assembly, Official Records, Fifty-first Session Supplement No. 17, (A/52/17), p. 51, para. 250.

[335] UNCITRAL, Report of the Working Group on Electronic Commerce on the work of its thirty-first session, (A/CN.9/437), p. 8, para. 22.

[336] This first draft was considered in the 31st session of the working group and contained a very descriptive definition of digital signatures: UNCITRAL, Working Group on Electronic Commerce, Thirty-first session, Planning of future work on electronic commerce: digital signatures, certification authorities and related legal issues, Note by the Secretariat, 1996, (A/CN.9/WG.IV/WP.71), pp. 16-17.

[337] UNCITRAL, Report of the United Nations Commission on International Trade Law on the work of its thirtieth session, General Assembly, Official Records, Fifty-first Session Supplement No. 17, (A/52/17), p. 51, para. 250; UNCITRAL, Working Group on Electronic Commerce, Thirty-first session, Planning of future work on electronic commerce: digital signatures, certification authorities and related legal issues, Note by the Secretariat, 1996, (A/CN.9/WG.IV/WP.71), pp. 7-9 (However, it is worth noting that the terms media neutrality and technology neutrality are not used with precision. In the first place, because when referring to

The second draft prepared by the Secretariat, even though still focusing on digital signatures, presents significant changes concerning the role of electronic signatures.[338] First of all, the title of the document contains the words electronic signatures instead of digital signatures.[339] Likewise, along with the section on digital signatures, a new section is devoted to electronic signatures in which three categories of signatures are distinguished: signatures (based on Article 7 of the UNCITRAL Model Law on Electronic Commerce), electronic signatures and secure electronic signatures.[340] The digital signature may – if certain requirements are met – be considered a secure electronic signature.

The division between three different categories of signatures was adopted one year later by the Electronic Signatures Directive.[341] However, UNCITRAL did not follow the same criterion as the European Union. In fact, the definition of signature was soon eliminated.[342] The concept of digital signature was also abandoned even though public key infrastructure continued to be relevant in the drafting of the model law.[343] Therefore, there were electronic signatures and

---

the non-discrimination between different technologies the term media-neutrality is used when, in fact, that term is reserved for the non-discrimination principle between the written and electronic form (p. 7). Moreover, when addressing the principle of technology neutrality it is not clear whether the openness refers to all other techniques or just to new developments within signatures based on cryptography (pp. 8-9).).

[338] This draft was considered by the Working Group on Electronic Commerce on its thirty-second session (Vienna, 19-30 January, 1998), see UNCITRAL, Thirty-first session, Report of the Working Group on Electronic Commerce on the Work of its Thirty-second Session, 1998, (A/CN.9/446), pp. 4-5.

[339] UNCITRAL, Working Group on Electronic Commerce Thirty-second session, Draft Uniform Rules on Electronic Signatures, Note by the Secretariat, 1997, (A/CN.9/WG.IV/WP.73), p. 1.

[340] UNCITRAL, Working Group on Electronic Commerce Thirty-second session, Draft Uniform Rules on Electronic Signatures, Note by the Secretariat, 1997, (A/CN.9/WG.IV/WP.73), pp. 8-20.

[341] The Secretariat was aware of legislation in this direction, see UNCITRAL, Working Group on Electronic Commerce Thirty-second session, Draft Uniform Rules on Electronic Signatures, Note by the Secretariat, 1997, (A/CN.9/WG.IV/WP.73), p. 10, para. 18. An interesting document is the note by the secretariat on the draft uniform rules on electronic signatures where after each article a reference to the main electronic signature statutes or drafts existing until that moment is included, see UNCITRAL, Working Group on Electronic Commerce Thirty-fifth session, Draft Uniform Rules on Electronic Signatures, Note by the Secretariat, 1999, (A/CN.9/WG.IV/WP.82).

[342] UNCITRAL, Thirty-first session, Report of the Working Group on Electronic Commerce on the work of its thirty-second session, 1998, (A/CN.9/446), pp. 10-11, para. 27 and 29.

[343] The definition of digital signature is contained in: UNCITRAL, Working Group on Electronic Commerce Thirty-fourth session, Draft Uniform Rules on Electronic

enhanced electronic signatures.[344] Doubts were raised concerning the existence of two types of signatures. The fear was that having two types of electronic signatures would lead to construe them as two different legal concepts when actually the enhanced electronic signature just meant a signature considered reliable. Enhanced electronic signatures were the only ones that could be used whenever the law required a signature.[345] From the thirty-fifth session onwards two drafts were considered; only one of them included the concept of enhanced electronic signature.[346] The working group in its 37th session finally decided to eliminate the concept of enhanced electronic signature and to retain only the concept of electronic signature.[347] Nevertheless, digital signatures and public key cryptography have a strong influence on the model law as can be evidenced by the inclusion of the concepts of certificate and certification service providers.

The form of the document was intensively discussed and not decided until the very end. However, since the beginning the term "uniform rules" was used.[348] At its 37th session the working group finally addressed the type of instrument in

---

Signatures, Note by the Secretariat, 1998, (A/CN.9/WG.IV/WP.79). However, the working group in its 34th session did not consider that version but instead used as a basis for its debate another document (UNCITRAL, Working Group on Electronic Commerce Thirty-fourth session, Electronic Signatures, Note by the Secretariat, 1998, (A/CN.9/WG.IV/WP.80)) which does not contain the concept of digital signature, see UNCITRAL, Thirty-second session, Report of the Working Group on Electronic Commerce on the work of its thirty-fourth session, 1999, (A/CN.9/457), p. 6, para. 21. Despite the abandonment of the definition of digital signature still in the 34th session the Working Group was focusing its attention on PKI issues and technology, and considering whether it would expand it to other signature techniques, see UNCITRAL, Thirty-second session, Report of the Working Group on Electronic Commerce on the work of its thirty-fourth session, 1999, (A/CN.9/457), pp. 12-13, para. 51 and p. 16, para. 66.

[344] In its thirty-third session the Working Group abandoned the use of the term "secure electronic signature" to use the term "enhanced electronic signature", see UNCITRAL, Thirty-second session, Report of the Working Group on Electronic Commerce on the work of its thirty-third session, 1998, (A/CN.9/454), p. 9, para. 29.

[345] UNCITRAL, Thirty-third session, Report of the Working Group on Electronic Commerce on the work of its thirty-fifth session, 1999, (A/CN.9/465), p. 18, Article 6.

[346] UNCITRAL, Thirty-third session, Report of the Working Group on Electronic Commerce on the work of its thirty-fifth session, 1999, (A/CN.9/465), p. 20, para. 66.

[347] UNCITRAL, Thirty-fourth session, Report of the Working Group on Electronic Commerce on the work of its thirty-seventh session, 2000, (A/CN.9/483), p. 18, para. 64.

[348] UNCITRAL, Report of the United Nations Commission on International Trade Law on the work of its twenty-ninth session, General Assembly, Official Records, Fifty-first Session Supplement No. 17 (A/51/17), p. 52, para. 223.

which the rules concerning electronic signatures would be contained.[349] The options were between an international convention, a model law or uniform rules. An international convention was actually never seriously considered and the term uniform rules was finally discarded because it is normally reserved for instruments suggesting contractual provisions.[350] The document prepared by UNCITRAL aims at legislators or states interested in passing norms concerning electronic signatures; therefore, the name of Model Law on Electronic Signatures was adopted. Also, another debate was whether the document was going to be a separate one or to be added to the Model Law on Electronic Commerce. Preference was expressed for a separate document.[351]

In its thirty-seventh session the working group adopted the final version of the draft articles[352] and in its thirty-eighth session it revised the draft guide to enactment.[353] UNCITRAL adopted the Model Law on Electronic Signatures in its 727th meeting on July 5, 2001 and the General Assembly, in its 85th plenary meeting on December 12, 2001.[354]

2.   Goals and principles

The goal of the UNCITRAL Model Law on Electronic Signatures is to achieve unification of the legal norms governing electronic signatures. Such unification is sought mainly in commercial transaction (Article 1). Therefore, in order to broaden as much as possible the sphere of application of the UNCITRAL Model Law on Electronic Signatures the term commercial shall be construed in the

---

[349] UNCITRAL, Thirty-fourth session, Report of the Working Group on Electronic Commerce on the work of its thirty-seventh session, 2000, (A/CN.9/483), pp. 33-34, para. 134-138.

[350] Examples are the UNCITRAL Arbitration Rules (1976) and the UNCITRAL Conciliation Rules (1976).

[351] UNCITRAL, Thirty-second session, Report of the Working Group on Electronic Commerce on the work of its thirty-fourth session, 1999, (A/CN.9/457), pp. 5-6, para. 19; UNCITRAL, Working Group on Electronic Commerce Thirty-fifth session, Draft Uniform Rules on Electronic Signatures, Note by the Secretariat, 1999, (A/CN.9/WG.IV/WP.82), p. 5, para. 16; UNCITRAL, Thirty-third session, Report of the Working Group on Electronic Commerce on the work of its thirty-fifth session, 1999, (A/CN.9/465), p. 12, para. 37; UNCITRAL, Model Law on Electronic Signatures with Guide to Enactment (2001), 2002, p. 32, para. 65.

[352] UNCITRAL, Thirty-fourth session, Report of the Working Group on Electronic Commerce on the work of its thirty-seventh session, 2000, (A/CN.9/483), p. 5, para. 22.

[353] UNCITRAL, Thirty-fourth session, Report of the Working Group on Electronic Commerce in its thirty-eighth session, 2001, (A/CN.9/484), pp. 6-15, para. 21-78.

[354] UNCITRAL, Model Law on Electronic Signatures with Guide to Enactment (2001), 2002, pp. 16-17; UNCITRAL, General Assembly, Resolution 56/80, (A/R ES/56/80).

broadest sense possible.[355] Besides, the UNCITRAL Model Law on Electronic Signatures suggests other wording for states willing to expand the use of electronic signatures to non-commercial transactions.[356] Moreover, the UNCITRAL Model Law on Electronic Signatures does not differentiate between domestic and international transactions; therefore, it applies to either type of transactions.

The UNCITRAL Model Law on Electronic Signatures is based on two principles: media neutrality and technology neutrality (both contained in Article 3). Even though the wording of Article 3 seems to refer only to the principle of technology neutrality, the Guide to Enactment of the UNCITRAL Model Law on Electronic Signatures makes it clear that it embraces both principles.[357] Media neutrality means that there shall be no discrimination against the medium in which the data is contained, either on paper or electronically. It is the non-discrimination principle against the electronic form. This principle was already contained in the UNCITRAL Model Law on Electronic Commerce. In turn, the technology neutrality principle establishes the non-discrimination between different types of technologies. The importance of this principle is twofold: on the one hand, to ensure that none of the existing techniques is discriminated, and on the other hand, to ensure that the model law applies and encompasses future techniques, unknown at the time of its enactment.

The UNCITRAL Model Law on Electronic Signatures has twelve articles. Basically it defines and governs the use and consequences of electronic signatures, as well as establishes the responsibilities for the parties involved. It should be noted that the UNCITRAL Model Law on Electronic Signatures does not deal with all the topics related to electronic signatures[358] but aims mainly at resolving the issues referring to the private law aspects of electronic transactions.[359]

3.   Electronic signatures

An electronic signature is "data in electronic form in, affixed to or logically associated with, a data message, which may be used to identify the signatory in

---

[355] UNCITRAL Model Law on Electronic Signatures, footnote to Article 1.
[356] UNCITRAL Model Law on Electronic Signatures, footnote to Article 1.
[357] UNCITRAL, Model Law on Electronic Signatures with Guide to Enactment (2001), 2002, p. 9.
[358] The UNCITRAL Model Law on Electronic Signatures does not address issues of national security, public policy, criminal and administrative law, see UNCITRAL, Report of the Working Group on Electronic Commerce on the work of its thirty-first session, (A/CN.9/437), p. 8, para. 23.
[359] UNCITRAL, Working Group on Electronic Commerce Thirty-sixth session, Draft Uniform Rules on Electronic Signatures, Note by the Secretariat, 1999, (A/CN.9/WP.84), p. 4, para. 15.

relation to the data message and to indicate the signatory's approval of the information contained in the data message" (Section 2(a)).

The definition leads to four remarks. First, an electronic signature is itself a data message; that is, it exists in electronic form. Second, an electronic signature is invariably linked to a data message. Whereas a handwritten signature can only be used to sign paper documents, electronic signatures can only be used to sign electronic documents, which the UNCITRAL Model Law on Electronic Signatures names data messages. A data message is information generated, sent, received or stored by electronic or other similar means (Section 2(c)). The UNCITRAL Model Law on Electronic Signatures followed the concept of data message used in the UNCITRAL Model Law on Electronic Commerce and, therefore, the term data message shall not be construed as referring only to data to be sent. The Guide to Enactment of the UNCITRAL Model Law on Electronic Signatures makes it clear that the term shall be construed broadly including also electronic records.[360] Third, the signature is in, attached ("affixed") or linked ("logically associated") to the data message. This means that either the electronic signature is contained in the document or is separate from the document but intrinsically linked to it. Fourth, an electronic signature *may* serve to establish the identity of the signatory and the consent of the signatory.[361] Therefore, these two functions do not have to be always present. Not every signature may be aimed at establishing the consent of the signer. Electronic signatures may be also used for security reasons and thus, just to identify a person. Consequently, the UNCITRAL Model Law on Electronic Signatures does not want to limit the definition of electronic signatures to the legal concept.[362] However, the wording of the definition is confusing because according to it a signature *may* be used for the purpose of establishing identity. *A contrario sensu*, it is possible that an electronic signature is not employed for the purpose of establishing the identity of the signatory. It is difficult to conceive the use of an electronic signature that is neither for authentication purposes nor for establishing consent. An electronic signature may have only the first purpose and, therefore, not aim to be a signature in the legal sense but only serve to identify a person. However, it is difficult to find signatures that do not seek to accomplish the identity function.

Electronic signatures may satisfy the legal requirement of a signature (Article 6.1) and, therefore, may be used either when the law establishes the obligation to sign or establishes the consequences for not signing (Article 6.2). The electronic

---

[360] UNCITRAL, Model Law on Electronic Signatures with Guide to Enactment (2001), 2002, p. 45.

[361] The signatory is the person who holds the signature-creation data, Article 2(d) of the UNCITRAL Model Law on Electronic Signatures.

[362] UNCITRAL, Model Law on Electronic Signatures with Guide to Enactment (2001), 2002, pp. 43-44.

signature in order to be used on an equal basis with the handwritten signature shall be "as reliable as was appropriate for the purpose for which the data message was generated or communicated, in the light of all the circumstances, including any relevant agreement" (Article 6.1). This wording is the same as the one contained in Article 7.1(b) of the UNCITRAL Model Law on Electronic Commerce.

The UNCITRAL Model Law on Electronic Signatures does not require a special type of electronic signature or a special technique. According to the principle of technology neutrality embedded in Article 3 every electronic signature technique is able to comply with the legal requirements of a signature. Whether an electronic signature may be used instead of a handwritten signature will depend on a balancing test between reliability and appropriateness for the purpose of the message. Reliability is not an absolute concept. Contrarily, reliability of an electronic signature is measured taking into account the purpose of the message. That is a factual appreciation and in its determination all the circumstances shall be considered including any relevant agreements between the parties (Article 6.1).

During the preparation of the UNCITRAL Model Law on Electronic Signatures the choice of the reliability test was questioned. The main drawback is the lack of certainty and predictability. Assessment of the reliability of a signature is done after the document has been signed and does not serve the needs of legal security contracting parties are looking for.[363] Despite the criticism the reliability test was kept but in order to increase the level of legal security the UNCITRAL Model Law on Electronic Signatures contains two provisions aiming at establishing *ex-ante* when electronic signatures are deemed valid for legal purposes.

The first of those provisions, Article 6, establishes that an electronic signature is considered reliable if the following three requirements are met: first, the elements used to create the signature (private key, PIN, etc.) link to the signatory; second, the elements used to create the signature are under the sole control of the signatory; and third, any alteration to the electronic signature is detectable. In case the goal of the legal provision is to guarantee the integrity of the document, a fourth requirement needs to be present: any alteration to the data message introduced after signed has to be detectable (Article 6.3). These requirements are similar to the advance electronic signature requirements of the Electronic Signatures Directive (Article 2.2).

---

[363] The Working Group in its 35th session discussed the issue. It was made clear that this is one of the ways in which certainty and predictability could be achieved and not the only way. See UNCITRAL, Thirty-third session, Report of the Working Group on Electronic Commerce on the Work of its Thirty-fifth session, 1999, (A/CN.9/465), pp. 19, 27-28 and 29, para. 64, 91, 93 and 98.

The second provision is Article 7 which determines who is able to make an *ex-ante* determination of whether a signature is reliable in the terms of Article 6.[364] States may vest any authority, organ or person with that power. UNCITRAL was, however, very careful when drafting this article to prevent states from imposing a particular technique or certain particular techniques. Therefore, the determination of the types of electronic signatures considered reliable for the purposes of Article 6.1 has to be made in accordance with international standards and cannot affect the operation of the rules of private international law (Article 7.2 and 7.3).[365] This last requirement means that foreign signatures shall be governed by the law resulting from the application of the rules of private international law so as to prevent states from requiring foreign signatures to comply with their own criteria of reliable signatures.[366]

4.   Recognition of foreign electronic signatures and foreign certificates

In its last article the UNCITRAL Model Law on Electronic Signatures deals with foreign electronic signatures and foreign certificates.[367] One of the peculiarities of electronic commerce is that Internet has reduced considerably the distances and persons living in different cities, countries and continents can easily interact with each other. Therefore, transactions may fall within different legal systems and be subject to different and sometimes conflicting rules. If electronic signatures want to be a useful tool for electronic commerce, it is necessary that electronic signatures and certificates are not only recognized

---

[364] UNCITRAL, Model Law on Electronic Signatures with Guide to Enactment (2001), 2002, p. 58.

[365] UNCITRAL, Model Law on Electronic Signatures with Guide to Enactment (2001), 2002, pp. 58-59. In the 36th session it was decided to include the reference to the private international rules to ensure non-discrimination of foreign electronic signatures on the basis of non- compliance with the rules set out by the governmental body or person designated by the state, see UNCITRAL, Thirty-third session, Report of the Working Group on Electronic Commerce on the work of its thirty-sixth session, 2000, (A/CN.9/467), p. 19, para. 94. Also, the Note of the Secretariat clearly states that this provision does not limit the power of variation by agreement of Article 5, see UNCITRAL, Working Group on Electronic Commerce Thirty-sixth session, Draft Uniform Rules on Electronic Signatures, Note by the Secretariat, 1999, (A/CN.9/WP.84), p. 18, para. 49.

[366] UNCITRAL, Model Law on Electronic Signatures with Guide to Enactment (2001), 2002, p. 59.

[367] During the preparation of the Model Law it was noted that while a certificate is foreign when invoked outside the jurisdiction of the issuing certification authority, a signature can be qualified as foreign based on the place of signing, the nationality of the signers or the place of operations of the certification authorities and, therefore, the concept of foreign signature was ambiguous, see UNCITRAL, Thirty-fourth session, Report of the Working Group on Electronic Commerce on the work of its thirty-seventh session, 2000, (A/CN.9/483), p. 7, para. 26.

where issued but also in other countries. A mechanism designed to be implemented in electronic transactions whose validity is limited to the territory of a state will not be successful or as successful as could otherwise be.

The UNCITRAL Model Law on Electronic Signatures distinguishes between foreign electronic signatures and foreign certificates. The rules concerning foreign certificates apply to electronic signatures based on certificates. In turn, electronic signatures not based on certificates shall be governed by the rules for foreign electronic signatures.

The UNCITRAL Model Law on Electronic Signatures does not define when a certificate or a signature is foreign nor discusses this point in its Guide to Enactment. However, the wording of paragraphs 2 and 3 of Article 12 shed some light. Concerning certificates, a certificate is deemed foreign if issued by a certification service provider outside the state where recognition is sought.[368] Therefore, the domestic or foreign nature of a certificate is linked to its place of issuance. Concerning electronic signatures, an electronic signature is foreign if created or used outside the state where recognition is sought. Thus, the place of creation or use is the relevant factor to establish the domestic or foreign nature of electronic signatures. The Model Law on Electronic Signatures does not, however, define where a signature is deemed created or used. The place of creation of the signature might refer to the place where the signatory is physically present at the time of signing even if there just for a short period of time. Most likely it does not refer to the habitual residence or domicile of the signatory. Concerning the concept of use, a signature may be considered used when sent to another person.

For the recognition of foreign electronic signatures and foreign certificates the UNCITRAL Model Law on Electronic Signatures chooses a flexible criterion: reliability. This is the same standard Article 6 uses to determine whether an electronic signature complies with the legal requirement of a signature.

The parameter to assess the recognition of foreign signatures and certificates is whether their level of reliability is substantially equivalent to signatures or certificates in the country where recognition is sought. Concerning certificates the certificate issued in a foreign country is going to be compared with certificates issued where recognition takes place (Article 12.2). The reliability is not based on the practices of the certification authority but instead on the reliability of the certificate itself.[369] For foreign electronic signatures the

---

[368] UNCITRAL, Thirty-fourth session, Report of the Working Group on Electronic Commerce on the work of its thirty-seventh session, 2000, (A/CN.9/483), p. 7, para. 26.

[369] In earlier drafts the reliability test was based on the practices of the certification authority, see UNCITRAL, Thirty-fourth session, Report of the Working Group on

comparison is going to be made between a foreign signature and a signature created or used where recognition is sought (Article 12.3). In both cases the level of reliability does not have to be exactly the same but substantially equivalent (Article 12.2 and 12.3). The assessment of reliability has to be done on the basis of recognized international standards and other relevant factors (Article 12.4). In a draft version the provision contained an open-ended list of factors to be taken into account to carry out this determination but it was later eliminated.[370] When the level of reliability of certificates or signatures is substantially equivalent the foreign electronic signature cannot be discriminated against and has to be recognized and be granted the same legal effects as domestic signatures or certificates. The UNCITRAL Model Law on Electronic Signatures uses the verb shall and, therefore, once the reliability test has been met the foreign signature or certificate has to be recognized (Article 12.2 and 12.3).

In order to reinforce the idea that only reliability is to be taken into account in assessing recognition of a foreign electronic signature the UNCITRAL Model Law on Electronic Signatures expressly excludes as a factor in that determination the place of creation of the electronic signature and the place of business of the signatory (Article 12.1). The same principle applies for the recognition of foreign certificates; the place of creation of the certificate and the place of business of the issuer of the certificate are not relevant factors in the recognition of the certificate (Article 12.1).

Contracting parties may agree on the use of certain types of electronic signatures. When this type of agreement exists it is not necessary to assess the reliability of electronic signatures. Thus, the parties' agreement on electronic signatures replaces the reliability test. However, those agreements are subject to their recognition under applicable law (Article 12.5).

Article 12 used to contain another paragraph which was left out of the final version. The provision established that parties to a commercial transaction could establish the particular supplier or the class of supplier or the class of certificate to be used. The scenario in mind for this provision was that of companies or governmental institutions receiving a large volume of communications per day

---

Electronic Commerce on the work of its thirty-seventh session, 2000, (A/CN.9/483), p. 10, para. 35.

[370] UNCITRAL, Model Law on Electronic Signatures with Guide to Enactment (2001), 2002, p. 71; UNCITRAL, Thirty-third session, Report of the Working Group on Electronic Commerce on the Work of its Thirty-fifth session, 1999, (A/CN.9/465), p. 8; UNCITRAL, Working Group on Electronic Commerce Thirty-fifth session, Draft Uniform Rules on Electronic Signatures, Note by the Secretariat, 1999, (A/CN.9/WG.IV/WP.82), pp. 36-37; UNCITRAL, Thirty-fourth session, Report of the Working Group on Electronic Commerce on the work of its thirty-seventh session, 2000, (A/CN.9/483), pp. 12-14, para. 483.

and, therefore, wanting to limit the scope of authorities and certificates to be used. However, the prevailing view was that the provision was unnecessary since nothing in the UNCITRAL Model Law on Electronic signatures prohibits agreements between parties as to the use of a certain technology. Moreover, the main concern was the fear that a misinterpretation of the provision would restrict electronic signature techniques.[371]

5.   Effect on national legislation

So far only Thailand (2001), Cape Verde (2003), Mexico (2003), China (2004), Viet Nam (2005), United Arab Emirates (2006) and Guatemala (2008) have enacted legislation based on the UNCITRAL Model Law on Electronic Signature.[372] The success of the model law is not as wide as expected and the field of electronic signature remains governed by different domestic norms. One of the reasons for this situation is that the UNCITRAL Model Law on Electronic Signatures came late in time. The Electronic Signatures Directive was enacted two years before the final version of the UNCITRAL Model Law on Electronic Signatures was approved. In the United States of America, both UETA and E-Sign predate the UNCITRAL Model Law on Electronic Signatures. Another reason was the fact that the UNCITRAL Model Law on Electronic Signatures, despite promoting the principle of technology neutrality, was largely based on digital signature technology at a time where some countries – especially the United States of America – were abandoning that approach. However, it should be noted that the main principles contained in the UNCITRAL Model Law on Electronic Signatures can be found in other legislation.[373] In US legislation the principle of media neutrality is predominant. The Electronic Signatures Directive also recognizes all type of signatures but with different degrees and effects.

III.   United Nations Convention on the Use of Electronic Communications in International Contracts

UNCITRAL continued its work towards the harmonization of international trade law in the field of electronic commerce by working on international

---

[371] UNCITRAL, Thirty-fourth session, Report of the Working Group on Electronic Commerce on the work of its thirty-seventh session, 2000, (A/CN.9/483), pp. 14-15, para. 50-53.

[372] Costa Rica has in turn legislation influenced by the Uncitral Model Law on Electronic Signatures, see UNCITRAL, Status of the 2001 Model Law on Electronic Signatures, <http://www.uncitral.org/uncitral/en/uncitral_texts/electroni c_commerce/2001Model_status.html>.

[373] *Hultmark,* Interpretation of legal text in an electronic and international environment, in: Hohloch (Ed.), Recht und Internet, 2001, p. 48; *Heydn,* Germany, in: Campbell (Ed.), E-Commerce and the Law of Digital Signatures, 2005, p. 224.

conventions. Once the Model Law on Electronic Signatures was finished, the Working Group on Electronic Commerce debated the next steps. The topic the working group found more compelling and needing uniformity was that arising from international electronic contracting.[374] To this end the Convention on the Use of Electronic Communications in International Contracts was adopted on November 23, 2005.[375] The convention deals with several topics in the field of international contracts entered into through electronic means. The convention is opened for signatures from January 16, 2006[376] and has not yet entered into force.[377]

The Convention on the Use of Electronic Communications in International Contracts did not come up with new rules. In general the provisions contained therein were taken from the UNCITRAL Model Law on Electronic Commerce and UNCITRAL Model Law on Electronic Signatures as well as from other national statutes. The fact that the convention was adopted in 2005, when a large number of countries had already enacted legislation on electronic commerce issues and the approaches that have worked the best could be assessed, may be regarded as an advantage. Besides, it is normal that some principles and ideas were repeated as some of them were never included in a convention.

The convention contains the principle of media neutrality – present also in other texts such as the UNCITRAL Model Law on Electronic Signatures (Article 3), UETA (Section 7) and E-Sign (Section 101(a)) – whereby a contract shall not be denied validity or enforceability just because it is in electronic form (Article 8.1). Thus, the use of paper or of electronic means shall not be the decisive factor in determining whether a contract is legally valid. The convention does not address the principle of technology neutrality. However, this may be due to the fact that the convention does not deal directly with the regulation of electronic signatures but only with the legal requirement of a signature.

An agreement of the parties is required in order to use the electronic form; however, this agreement does not need to be express but it can be inferred from

---

[374] UNCITRAL, Thirty-fourth session, Report of the Working Group on Electronic Commerce in its thirty-eighth session, 2001, (A/CN.9/484), p. 19, para. 95.

[375] United Nations General Assembly, Resolution 60/21, <http://daccessdds.un.org/do c/UNDOC/GEN/N05/488/80/PDF/N0548880.pdf?OpenElement>.

[376] So far eighteen countries have signed the convention, namely: Central African Republic, China, Colombia, Honduras, Iran, Lebanon, Madagascar, Montenegro, Panamá, Paraguay, Philippines, Republic of Korea, Russian Federation, Saudi Arabia, Senegal, Sierra Leone, Singapore and Sri Lanka, see UNCITRAL, Status of the 2005 United Nations Convention on the Use of Electronic Communications in International Contracts, <http://www.uncitral.org/uncitral/en/uncitral_texts/elect ronic_commerce/2005Convention_status.html>.

[377] To enter into force the convention needs to be ratified by at least three States or regional economic integration organizations (Article 23 and 17).

the parties' conduct (Article 8.2). E-Sign and UETA also require the parties to previously agree to the use of the electronic form (Section 101(b)(2) E-Sign; Section 5(b) and 5(c) UETA); however, this requirement is broadly construed.[378] In Germany, the majority opinion also holds that the previous consent of the parties is required in order to use the electronic form.[379]

The Convention on the Use of Electronic Communications in International Contracts is also applicable to other conventions so that communications relating to the formation or performance of contracts may be conducted via electronic means. Article 20 lists six conventions to which the Convention on the Use of Electronic Communications in International Contracts is applicable but this list is open-ended (Article 20.2).[380] It should be noted that the Convention on the Use of Electronic Communications in International Contracts

---

[378] Uniform Electronic Transactions Act with preparatory note and comments, 1999, p. 21.

[379] According to Section 126(3) BGB the written form *can* be replaced by the electronic form. As a result, the majority opinion argues that the electronic form cannot be imposed by one of the parties unilaterally; therefore, if an agreement between the parties is missing, it is not possible to use the electronic form. See Gegenäußerung der Bundesregierung, BT-Drucks. 14/4987, p. 41; *Marly*, in: Soergel, Bürgerliches Gesetzbuch, 13th Edition, 2002, Section 126a, marginal number 26; *Heinrichs / Ellenberger*, in: Palandt, Bürgerliches Gesetzbuch, 68th Edition, 2009, Section 126a, marginal number 6; *Prütting / Wegen / Weinreich*, BGB Kommentar, 4th Edition, 2009, Section 126a, marginal number 7; *Hertel*, in: Staudinger, Kommentar zum Bürgerlichen Gesetzbuch, New Edition, 2004, Section 126, marginal number 167; *Palm*, in: Erman, Bürgerliches Gesetzbuch, 12th Edition, 2008, Section 126a, marginal number 6; *Roßnagel*, Die europäische Richtlinie für elektronische Signaturen und ihre Umsetzung im neuen Signaturgesetz, in: Lehman (Ed.), Electronic Business in Europa – Internationales, europäisches und deutsches Online-Recht, 2002, marginal number 61; *Bettendorf*, Elektronische Dokumente und Formqualität, RNotZ 2005, 277, 284; *Steinbeck*, Die neuen Formvorschriften im BGB, DStR, 2004, 644-645. The minority opinion, on the contrary, believes that the only requirement for the use of the electronic form is that the law does not, explicitly or implicitly, exclude the electronic form; therefore, no previous agreement between the parties would be required in order to use the electronic form. See *Einsele*, in: Münchener Kommentar zum Bürgerlichen Gesetzbuch, 5th Edition, 2006, Section 126, marginal numbers 27 and 29.

[380] The six conventions are: Convention on the Recognition and Enforcement of Foreign Arbitral Awards (New York, 10 June 1958); Convention on the Limitation Period in the International Sale of Goods (New York, 14 June 1974) and Protocol thereto (Vienna, 11 April 1980); United Nations Convention on Contracts for the International Sale of Goods (Vienna, 11 April 1980); United Nations Convention on the Liability of Operators of Transport Terminals in International Trade (Vienna, 19 April 1991); United Nations Convention on Independent Guarantees and Stand-by Letters of Credit (New York, 11 December 1995); United Nations Convention on the Assignment of Receivables in International Trade (New York, 12 December 2001).

does not have a higher hierarchy than these six conventions and that they have not been amended.[381] This was a solution that UNCITRAL found to try to reduce the obstacles posed to the use of electronic communications in international conventions.

The convention will be analyzed in further detail in chapter 8.

IV. Signature requirement in United Nations conventions

Formal requirements are also present in international treaties. Several United Nations conventions (most of them within UNCITRAL's domain) make reference to writings, documents and signatures. Some of them were drafted in a broad way and the use of the electronic form does not conflict with the form provisions. In others, the question was not so clear and UNCITRAL took action in this respect.

1. Convention on the Recognition and Enforcement of Foreign Arbitral Awards

The Convention on the Recognition and Enforcement of Foreign Arbitral Awards (1958) is commonly known as the New York Convention. An agreement to submit to arbitration shall be contained either in a signed contract or arbitration agreement, or in exchanged letters or telegrams (Article II). In order to make sure that arbitral agreements or provisions in electronic form are recognized UNCITRAL issued a recommendation to construe Article II.2, defining the term agreement in writing, broadly.[382]

2. United Nations Convention on the Carriage of Goods by Sea

The United Nations Convention on the Carriage of Goods by Sea was adopted in 1978 and is also known as the Hamburg Rules. When addressing the signature requirement of a bill of lading the convention states that a signature can be in

---

[381] UNCITRAL, Explanatory note by the UNCITRAL secretariat on the United Nations Convention on the Use of Electronic Communications in International Contracts, in: United Nations Convention on the Use of Electronic Communications in International Contracts, 2007, p. 91, para. 289.

[382] UNCITRAL, Recommendation regarding the interpretation of article II, paragraph 2, and article VII, paragraph 1, of the Convention on the Recognition and Enforcement of Foreign Arbitral Awards, issued in New York, 10 June 1958, adopted by the United Nations Commission on International Trade Law on 7 July 2006 at its thirty-ninth session (A/6/17). In the same session where this recommendation was adopted UNCITRAL approved the modification of the UNCITRAL Model Law on Commercial Arbitration so as to admit the use of the electronic form. See Article 7 of the UNCITRAL Model Law on International Commercial Arbitration (amended 2006).

electronic form as long as it is not inconsistent with the law of the country where the bill of lading is issued (Article 14.3). Therefore, the convention does not govern the issue of electronic signatures; instead, the convention refers to the national law of the place where the bill of lading is issued to determine whether electronic means could be validly used to sign.

3. United Nations Convention on International Bills of Exchange and International Promissory Notes

The United Nations Convention on International Bills of Exchange and International Promissory Notes was adopted in 1988 but has still not entered into force. However, it is worth mentioning that in the definition of signature not only handwritten signatures are included but also an "equivalent authentication effected by any other means" (Article 5(k)).

4. United Nations Convention on the Assignment of Receivables in International Trade

The Convention on the Assignment of Receivables in International Trade (2001) was approved on the same date as the UNCITRAL Model Law on Electronic Signatures; therefore, the language of the convention follows that of the UNCITRAL Model Law on Electronic Signatures. According to Article 5(c) the writing requirement is fulfilled by any form of information that is accessible and usable for subsequent reference. In turn, the requirement of a signature is met by using a procedure that serves to identify the signatory and to indicate the signatory's approval to the content of the writing (Article 5(c)). This convention is not yet in force.

B.   Other organizations

I.   International Chamber of Commerce

The International Chamber of Commerce (ICC) within its goal to further international commerce got actively involved in the field of electronic commerce. In 1997, the ICC issued the General Usage for International Digitally Ensured Commerce (GUIDEC) and a second version of it, GUIDEC II, was presented in 2001.[383] The GUIDEC was prepared in the framework of the Electronic Commerce Project (ECP) that aims at furthering electronic commerce. The goal of the GUIDEC is to provide a general framework for the authentication of electronic communications. In this respect the GUIDEC is primarily based on digital signatures and certification authorities.

---

[383] International Chamber of Commerce, General Usage for International Digitally Ensured Commerce (GUIDEC II), 2001.

Together with the other international institutions forming the Alliance for Global Business, the International Chamber of Commerce issued "A Global Action Plan for Electronic Business"[384] in 2002. The document focuses primarily on the role of governments in electronic commerce.

Governments have the power to further electronic transactions. On the one hand, governments can use the new technologies to communicate, offer services to the citizens and to contract. On the other hand, governments are able to structure a legal framework so as to advance legal security in electronic commerce. Although governmental action is needed, it should find its limits, which has sometimes been a major problem in electronic commerce. Governments shall refrain from invading areas reserved to the private sphere. In this respect it is stressed that governments shall present technical neutral legal frameworks where no special technology is imposed. Moreover, so as not to impinge on international electronic transactions governments shall take actions having in mind that electronic commerce is mainly transnational.

The International Chamber of Commerce also issued the ICC eTerms 2004 and the ICC Guide to eContracting.[385] The ICC eTerms 2004 are contractual provisions to help contracting parties in establishing the validity of electronic contracting. Parties to a contract may incorporate these provisions in their agreements expressly or by reference. The ICC eTerms 2004 propose two provisions: one establishes the validity, enforceability and admissibility into evidence of electronic messages; the other sets forth the rules for dispatch and receipt of electronic messages.[386]

II.   Internet Law & Policy Forum

The Internet Law & Policy Forum (ILPF) furthers the use of the Internet by providing a forum for the discussion and finding of solutions to the new legal challenges.[387] The organization was founded in 1995 and is non-governmental. Its members are companies mainly in the Internet and communications business. ILPF is divided in different working groups among which there is one devoted

---

[384] The text may be found in: International Chamber of Commerce, <http://www.iccw bo.org/uploadedfiles/3EdGAP.pdf?terms=GUIDEC+II>.

[385] The documents are available in: International Chamber of Commerce, <http://ww w.iccwbo.org/policy/law/id279/index.html>.

[386] According to Article 2 of the ICC Terms 2004, the relevant factor to determine when a message is considered sent or received is the moment the message exits or enters the information system, respectively. Consequently, a message is deemed sent when it exits the information system of the sender. In turn, a message is deemed received when it inters the information system of the recipient. Only in the case a message is sent to another information system than the one designated is the time of reception based on awareness.

[387] Internet Law & Policy Forum, <http://www.ilpf.org/>.

to the issue of electronic authentication. One of the studies prepared by this working group is "An Analysis of International Electronic and Digital Signature Implementation Initiatives". The study was published in the year 2000 when the electronic legislation was booming and presents a synthesis of the legislative situation per country until then. The conclusions of the study were not promising. It is argued that the approaches taken by national legislation are sometimes so divergent that they might put at stake the application of electronic signatures in international cases.[388] Also, public key infrastructure is the predominant technology even in statutes which claim to be technology neutral.[389]

III. American Bar Association

The American Bar Association (ABA) issued two documents relating to digital signatures: The Digital Signature Guidelines in the year 1996 and the PKI Assessment Guideline in the year 2003. The Digital Signature Guidelines focus on the functioning of digital signatures and explain their concept, functions and general principles.[390] The PKI Assessment Guideline deals with public key infrastructure in a more extended way as well as covers other topics of an electronic transaction such as governing law and consumer protection. Both texts are based on digital signatures and public key infrastructure.

C. Conclusions

Organizations of different nature have sought to further the discussion of topics related to the legal aspects of electronic signatures as well as to promote the legal regulation of electronic signatures. The main concern addressed by international institutions is the uniformity in electronic signature legislation. Therefore, they strive to achieve harmonization of the principles governing electronic signature recognition and the validity of electronic signatures as equivalents to handwriting signatures.

---

[388] ILPF, An Analysis of International Electronic and Digital Signature Implementation Initiatives, in International Chamber of Commerce, GUIDEC II – General Usage for International Digitally Ensured Commerce (version II), 2001, p. 52.

[389] ILPF, An Analysis of International Electronic and Digital Signature Implementation Initiatives, see International Chamber of Commerce, GUIDEC II – General Usage for International Digitally Ensured Commerce (version II), 2001, p. 60.

[390] For a comment on the ABA Digital Signature Guidelines see *Kania,* The ABA's Digital Signature Guidelines: An Imperfect Solution to Digital Signatures on the Internet, CommLaw Conspectus: Journal of Communications Law and Policy, Volume 7, 1999, 297-313.

UNCITRAL has sought to achieve uniformity of electronic signature legislation by issuing two model laws and an international convention. While the Model Law on Electronic Commerce seems to have had a significant impact on national legislation, fewer states have followed the UNCITRAL Model Law on Electronic Signatures. A new attempt to agree on some basic, uniform principles concerning electronic commerce, including electronic signatures, has been made with the Convention on the Use of Electronic Communications in International Contracts. Other organizations such as the ICC and ILPF and the American Bar Association have conducted studies relating to the state of electronic signature regulation or provided rules for the implementation of electronic signatures.

Part III: Electronic signatures and international contracts

The regulation of electronic signatures differs throughout different countries – or sometimes even within one same country; therefore, contracting parties must know in advance the law that will establish the electronic signature requirements. The application of one electronic signature legislation or another may determine whether a contract complies with the legal requirement of a signature or not. For instance, if a law requires that an electronic signature be based on public key cryptography to be considered equivalent to handwritten signatures, a signature based on any other technique, even if it is valid under a foreign law, may not be considered to comply with the signature legal requirements of the law governing the formal validity of the contract.

The question of which law establishes the formal requirements arises in international contracts. A contract which is linked to one country only will be governed by the law of that country. Contrarily, in the case of international contracts their contacts to more than one country result in the situation that more than one law may potentially determine their formal requirements. Therefore, a contract with links to two or more countries triggers the question of which national law will determine the form requirements of the contract. Among those formal requirements is encompassed the signature requirement.

Thus, it first has to be established when a contract is international. Second, it is necessary to determine which law, of the multiple possible laws, will govern the form requirements of the contract. Depending on the law that a legal system determines applicable to the formal requirements, a contract may end up being formally valid or not. For example, a legal system may consider the formal validity of a contract subject to the law of the place of location of the parties. If the contracting parties followed the formal requirements of another law with different requirements as to form, the formal validity of the contract may be at stake. Therefore, contracting parties need to know how the legal systems linked to the contract determine the law governing the formalities of international contracts.[391] One of the laws which has been accepted as the law governing the form is the law applicable to the contract. As the contracting parties can choose the law applicable to the contract it is important to determine the scope and extent of the contracting parties' power because their choice has an impact on the formal validity of the contract.

---

[391] The parties can include in the contract a choice of forum clause determining the jurisdiction that will have the power to hear the contractual claims. In this manner, the contracting parties reduce the jurisdictions and legal systems to take into account in their analysis of the laws connected with the contract because a court applies its own conflict of laws rules.

These three questions as to the nature of an international contract, the formal validity and the law applicable to the contract are within the scope of private international law. Each legal system has and applies its own rules of private international law and, therefore, the answer may vary from one legal system to another.[392] International conventions also address these issues with the goal to achieve unification in the field of private international law.

Chapter 7: General aspects of international contracts

This chapter introduces the concepts of international contract, law applicable and formal validity.

A.　The international contract

I.　Concept

It is not difficult to recognize when a contract is international;[393] however, to provide a definition of international contract is not that simple.[394] International contracts have elements that link them to more than one country and, consequently, to more than one legal system. Therefore, what differentiates a domestic contract from an international one is that in an international contract at least one of its elements has contacts with a foreign country and with a foreign legal system.[395] That is the case, for example, of a contract entered into in one country to be performed in another one. It may also be possible that all of the elements are related to different countries: a contract entered into in one country

---

[392] *Bachman,* Internet und IPR, in: Lehman (Ed.), Internet- und Multimediarecht (Cyberlaw), 1997, p. 171; *Huet,* The law applicable to digital networks, in: Internet – International Law, International and European Studies and Comments, 2005, p. 65; *Audit,* Droit International Privé, 2006, p. 19.

[393] *Holleaux / Foyer / La Pradelle,* Droit International Privé, 1987, p. 592 ("Tout d'abord, dans la pratique, la qualification de contrat international fait rarement difficulté: la plupart des contrats internationaux apparaissent objectivement comme tels.").

[394] *Jacquet,* Le contrat international, 1999, p. 5 ("... la notion de contrat international est d'une simplicité trompeuse."); *Delaume,* What is an International Contract? An American and Gallic Dilemma, The International and Comparative Law Quarterly, Volume 28, 1979, 258-259; *Pommier,* Principe d'Autonomie et Loi du Contrat en Droit International Privé Conventionnel, 1992, pp. 141-142 ("Et, en effet, la définition du contrat international a toujours donné lieu à des discussions très controversées."); *Feldstein de Cárdenas,* Derecho Internacional Privado – Parte Especial, 2000, p. 342.

[395] *Audit,* Droit International Privé, 2006, p. 656 footnote 4; *Holleaux / Foyer / La Pradelle,* Droit International Privé, 1987, pp. 590-592; *Jacquet,* Le contrat international, 1999, p. 5.

between contracting parties domiciled in two other different countries and to be performed in a fourth country.

II.   Elements determining the internationality of a contract

A contract may be deemed international based on several factors, such as, the domicile of the parties, the nationality of the parties, the place of contracting, the place of performance, or the links of the contract with international trade.[396] However, each legal system establishes the elements that will be taken into account to characterize a contract as international.[397] Not every element triggering a connection with a foreign law might be considered legally relevant to render a contract international.[398] Consequently, depending on the criterion followed a same contract may be considered international under one law or convention and domestic under another one.[399]

One important issue is whether the elements connecting a contract to a foreign legal system need to be objective elements or whether it is sufficient that they are subjective elements. Objective elements mean the real existence of a connection between a contract and a foreign country. Examples of objective elements are the place of performance, the place of execution or the domicile of the parties. On the contrary, subjective elements are those which depend on the sole will of the parties. The paradigmatic example of a subjective element is the choice of law provision. By means of the choice of a foreign law the parties link a contract to a foreign legal system; in other words, a domestic contract exclusively connected with one country and one legal system comes into contact with another legal system by the sole existence of a choice of law clause. Nonetheless, it can be argued that the international nature of a contract is, to a certain extent, always within the control of the contracting parties. Contracting parties are free to decide where to enter into a contract and in some cases, the place where it will be performed. Also a party may have several domiciles and

---

[396] *Estrella Faria*, Harmonizing the Law of International Electronic Contracting: Adjust the Rules but don´t Rewrite Them, in: Schulz (Ed.), Legal Aspects of an E-Commerce Transaction, 2006, p. 76.

[397] *Feldstein de Cárdenas*, Derecho Internacional Privado – Parte Especial, 2000, p. 343; *Boggiano*, Derecho Internacional Privado, Volume I, 2006, p. 13; *Delaume*, What is an International Contract? An American and Gallic Dilemma, The International and Comparative Law Quarterly, Volume 28, 1979, 261-262.

[398] For example *Jacquet* wonders whether a local merchant of foreign nationality enters into international contracts with his or her regular customers because of his or her foreign nationality, see *Jacquet*, Le contrat international, 1999, p. 6.

[399] *Lorenzo Idiarte*, ¿Cuándo un contrato es internacional? Análisis desde una perspectiva regional, in: Kleinheitsterkamp / Lorenzo Idiarte (Eds.), Avances del Derecho Internacional Privado en América Latina, 2002, pp. 109-110 (The author stresses that the determination of the elements that render a situation international must be conducted reasonably.).

may choose which one of those domiciles will be relevant for the contractual purposes. However, in these cases, even though these connecting factors may depend to a certain degree on the will of the parties, there is a real international contract because the way the contract is structured triggers two or more laws.[400]

The connecting points linking a contract with a foreign country may be characterized as strict or flexible. Strict points of connection are, for example, the domicile of the parties, the place of contracting or the place of performance. In these cases it needs to be determined in which country the connecting factor is located to decide whether the contract is international or not. However, the trend is to abandon the strict connecting points for more flexible ones in order to give more leeway when determining the domestic or international nature of a contract.[401] Examples of flexible connecting factors are, for instance, the objective ties with a foreign country or the connection of a contract with international commerce. Under these criteria, a court may consider different elements to determine whether the contract is international including the place of performance, of contracting or of the domicile of the parties.

The most common connecting points are:

1.   Domicile of the parties

Contracting parties may have their domiciles or places of business in different countries. Several international conventions use this connecting factor for the determination of the internationality of a contract.[402] Whether the persons have

---

[400] *Lorenzo Idiarte*, ¿Cuándo un contrato es internacional?, Análisis desde una perspectiva regional, in: Kleinheitsterkamp / Lorenzo Idiarte (Eds.), Avances del Derecho Internacional Privado en América Latina, 2002, p. 132.

[401] According to *Lorenzo Idiarte* the adoption of objective connecting points means the abandonment of strict points of connections while still ensuring internationality. In this manner, it is not possible that the parties have the power to determine whether a contract is international, see *Lorenzo Idiarte*, ¿Cuándo un contrato es internacional? Análisis desde una perspectiva regional, in: Kleinheitsterkamp / Lorenzo Idiarte (Eds.), Avances del Derecho Internacional Privado en América Latina, 2002, p. 119.

[402] That is the case of the United Nations Convention on Contracts for the International Sale of Goods (1980), the Convention on the Law Applicable to Contracts for the International Sale of Goods (1986), the Inter-American Convention on the Law Applicable to International Contracts (1994), the Protocol of Buenos Aires on International Jurisdiction in Contractual Matters (1994), the United Nations Convention on Independent Guarantees and Stand-by Letters of Credit (1955) (see also its explanatory note, UNCITRAL, <http://www.uncitral.org/pdf/english/texts/payments/guarantees/guarantees.pdf>, p. 20), and the UNCITRAL Convention on the Use of Electronic Communications in International Contracts (2005) (see also UNCITRAL, Explanatory note by the UNCITRAL secretariat on the United Nations Convention on the Use of Electronic

the same nationality or not is not relevant; the relevant factor is the parties' domicile. Therefore, a contract between two persons of the same nationality but domiciled in different countries could be deemed international.

2.   Place of contracting or execution

The place of contracting is the place where a contract is executed. A contract may be executed in a country other than where the contracting parties are domiciled or where the contract is going to be performed.

The place of contracting is easily determined when all the parties gather and sign the contract in the presence of each other. However, that is not the case in many contracts. When a contract is entered into between persons located in different countries, it might be difficult to establish the place of contracting. The difficulty in determining the place of execution may be more patent in electronic contracts because of the very essence of the Internet and electronic means of communications without real physical location.

3.   Place of performance

The place of performance of a contract is another element that may be taken into account when determining whether a contract is international or not. A contract may be executed in one country between contracting parties domiciled in that same country but the contract is to be performed in a foreign country – or even in several foreign countries.

4.   The economic criterion

Sometimes a contract is considered international if the business generated by the contract affects the interests of international trade; that is, the contract has an economic impact on more than one country. This category is much more abstract than the other ones and must be assessed on a case by case basis. The economic criterion was developed in France in the beginning of the XX century. Case law evolved from the concept of "flow of values"[403] to "interests of international trade" until the most recent concept of a transaction going "beyond

---

Communications in International Contracts, in: United Nations Convention on the Use of Electronic Communications in International Contracts, 2007, p. 14, para. 6 and p. 29, para. 60).

[403] The concept of "*movement de flux et de reflux*" was used in the conclusion of the General Attorney (*procureur général*) Matter in the case Pélissier du Besset (Civ. 17 May 1927), see *Audit*, Droit International Privé, 2006, p. 656 footnote 4; *Holleaux / Foyer / La Pradelle*, Droit International Privé, 1987, pp. 590-591; *Jacquet*, Le contrat international, 1999, p. 10.

the barriers of the domestic economy".[404] A contract may go beyond the barriers of international trade and still have all of its elements connected with one country. Therefore, the use of the economic approach may render international a contract that would otherwise be considered entirely domestic because of the lack of a foreign element.[405] Contrarily, a contract with links to several countries may lack connections with foreign trade.[406] Therefore, the economic criterion differs from the legal criterion, which requires the presence of factual elements linking the contract to another country. However, more often than not the economic criterion goes hand in hand with the legal one.[407]

5.   Nationality of the parties

The nationality of the parties is generally not relevant for the determination of a contract as international. Actually, some conventions expressly clarify that the nationality of the parties is to be disregarded.[408] Also some legal systems exclude the consideration of this connecting factor.[409] However, in the United States of America the nationality of the parties is one of the factors that courts may consider relevant to establish the internationality of a contract.[410]

---

[404] *Holleaux / Foyer / La Pradelle*, Droit International Privé, 1987, pp. 590-591; *Delaume*, What is an International Contract? An American and Gallic Dilemma, The International and Comparative Law Quarterly, Volume 28, 1979, 258, 269; *Lando*, The Conflict of Laws on Contracts – General Principles, 1985, pp. 286-287; *Pommier,* Principe d'Autonomie et Loi du Contrat en Droit International Privé Conventionnel, 1992, pp. 149-150. The new procedural code of France adopts this test to determine whether an arbitration is international. Section 1492 of the New Code of Civil Procedure establishes that an arbitration is international if it affects the interests of international trade.

[405] *Jacquet*, Le contrat international, 1999, pp. 11-12; *Audit*, Droit International Privé, 2006, p. 656 footnote 4.

[406] *Pommier,* Principe d'Autonomie et Loi du Contrat en Droit International Privé Conventionnel, 1992, pp. 150-151.

[407] *Batiffol / Lagarde*, Droit International Privé, Volume II, 1983, p. 276 ("... l'un allant d'ailleurs rarement sans l'autre."); *Jacquet*, Le contrat international, 1999, p. 10 ("... de l'une à l'autre, il n'y a pas contradiction, mais bien au contraire, le plus souvent convergence."); *Holleaux / Foyer / La Pradelle*, 1987, p. 591 ("En réalité, la qualification du contrat international exige une double approche économique et juridique.").

[408] United Nations Convention on Contracts for the International Sale of Goods (1980), Article 1.3, and United Nations Convention on the Use of Electronic Communications in International Contracts (2005), Article 1.3; UNCITRAL, Digest of case law on the United Nations Convention on the International Sale of Goods, Article 1, p. 5, para. 14.

[409] That is the case of Argentine law, see Section 1210 Argentine Civil Code.

[410] *Delaume*, What is an international contract? An American and a Gallic Dilemma, The International and Comparative Law Quarterly, Volume 28, 1979, 262-266.

6. Choice of law provision

Some legal systems consider international a contract whose only contact with a foreign country originates in the existence of a choice of law provision. Therefore, the contract becomes international when the parties subject the contract to a foreign law (that is the case of the Convention on the Law Applicable to Contractual Obligations (1980) – Rome Convention – Article 3.3).[411] Before that moment the contract is only connected with one legal system and, thus, is domestic. However, other legal systems (Argentina, for example) and international conventions (such as the Convention on the Law Applicable to International Sales of Goods and the Convention on the Law Applicable to Contracts for the International Sale of Goods) do not accept that a domestic contract is internationalized by the sole inclusion of a choice of law clause.[412]

B. The laws governing substance and form

A contract is composed of substance and form. Substance is the content of a contract, the parties' agreement. Form is how an agreement is externalized, the medium through which the agreement is formalized (on paper, in an electronic document, verbally). Substance and form may be governed by different laws. Therefore, in an international contract there are two laws to be determined: the applicable law to the contract and the law establishing the formal requirements of the contract.[413] However, the fact that it is necessary to locate the applicable law to the contract and the law that will govern its formal validity does not mean that substance and form will necessarily be subject to different legal systems. The same legal system may govern the form and substance of a contract. This has actually been the usual case when the principle of *locus regit actum* applied both to substance and form.[414] The substitution of that rule for the principle of party autonomy in the determination of the law applicable to the contract resulted in the possible disassociation between the law governing substance and

---

[411] *Pommier*, Principe d'Autonomie et Loi du Contrat en Droit International Privé Conventionnel, 1992, pp. 130-131. The Rome Convention is to be replaced by the Regulation 593/2008 of the European Parliament and the Council of 17 June 2008 on the law applicable to contractual obligations (Rome I), (Rome I Regulation), which shall enter into force on December 17, 2009.

[412] *Pommier*, Principe d'Autonomie et Loi du Contrat en Droit International Privé Conventionnel, 1992, p. 134; *Lorenzo Idiarte*, ¿Cuándo un contrato es internacional?, Análisis desde una perspectiva regional, in: Kleinheitsterkamp / Lorenzo Idiarte (Eds.), Avances del Derecho Internacional Privado en América Latina, 2002, p. 119.

[413] *Gutmann*, Droit International Privé, 2000, p. 170.

[414] *Audit*, Droit International Privé, 2006, p. 151; *Gutmann*, Droit International Privé, 2000, p. 170; *Loussouarn / Bourel / de Vareilles-Sommières*, Droit International Privé, 2004, p. 484; *Mayer / Heuzé*, Droit International Privé, 2004, p. 509.

form.[415] However, the principle of *locus regit actum* has also been relaxed in the issue of form and, therefore, the formal requirements of a contract may be subject to the law chosen by the parties to govern the substance of the contract.[416]

I. Formal validity

A contract may need to comply with certain formal requirements regarding form. A legal system may require a contract to be in writing or evidenced in a writing, made before a notary public or registered before a relevant authority. Parties to an international contract must be aware which law is going to set forth the formal requirements of the contract because lack of compliance with them may affect the validity or enforceability of the contract.[417] For instance, if the legal system governing the formal requirements of a contract requires that a contract be signed and the contract bears electronic signatures which do not comply with the electronic signature statute of that legal system, the contract lacks a valid signature.[418]

An international contract has contacts with several laws; thus, it has to be determined which one of those laws will establish the formal validity of the contract.

Traditionally, the law governing the form has been the law of the place where the contract is entered into.[419] This principle is known as *locus regit actum* and means that the forms are governed by the law of the place of execution of the act.[420] The principle of *locus regit actum* has been for long time the main rule to determine the law applicable to the formal validity of a contract.[421] However, nowadays the facultative nature of this principle is recognized and, consequently, other laws may also govern the formal validity of an act.[422]

---

[415] *Audit*, Droit International Privé, 2006, pp. 141-142 and 151.

[416] *Audit*, Droit International Privé, 2006, p. 679; *Mayer / Heuzé*, Droit International Privé, 2004, p. 510.

[417] *von Savigny*, System des heutigen Römischen Rechts, Volume 8, 1974, p. 349.

[418] A very simple example illustrating this situation is included in *Atreya / Hammond / Paine / Starrett / Wu*, Digital Signatures, 2002, pp. 235-236 (A painter accepts an offer to paint a house but because the painter does not comply with the legal signature requirements – in this case that the digital signature bear a timestamp – the homeowner may disregard the painter's acceptance.).

[419] *Audit*, Droit International Privé, 2006, pp. 151 and 679.

[420] *Foelix*, Traité du Droit International Privé, 1866, pp. 164-177.

[421] *Audit*, Droit International Privé, 2006, pp. 679-680; *Holleaux / Foyer / La Pradelle*, Droit International Privé, 1987, p. 602.

[422] *Holleaux / Foyer / La Pradelle*, Droit International Privé, 1987, p. 602; *Audit*, Droit International Privé, 2006, p. 153; *Mayer / Heuzé*, Droit International Privé,

Savigny explains that the law governing the formal requirements of an act shall be determined based on the same rules used to determine the applicable law. Accordingly, he sustains that the form of a contract should be governed by the law of the place of performance.[423] However, the application of this rule presents difficulties when the contract is entered into in a place that is not the place of performance for the forms imposed by the law of the place of performance may be unknown or not available in the place where the contract is entered into. *Savigny* gives the example of a Prussian who becomes sick while in France and wants to draft a will there.[424] According to the rule that the form be governed by the same law applicable to the act, a will has to comply with the law of the domicile of the testator. Prussian law requires the intervention of a court while in France wills require the intervention of a notary public and not of a court. Therefore, the requirement that a Prussian has to comply with the law of his or her domicile may hinder the execution of the will in a valid form.

That is when the rule *locus regit actum* comes into play. According to it, a legal act is governed, as far as form requirements are concerned, by the law of the place where the act is executed.[425] Therefore, it is considered that the *locus regit actum* principle originated in the fact that parties may find it difficult to comply with the forms imposed by the law governing the transaction; in other words, that the rule is based on the convenience of the parties.[426] This feature has led to the conclusion that the principle of *locus regit actum* is not mandatory; thus, a contract may be formally valid under other laws as well.

A law commonly recognized for the determination of the formal requirements is the law governing the substance of the contract, that is, the *lex causae*.[427] Also, the national law common to the parties[428] or the laws of the place where the

---

2004, p. 551; *Foelix,* Traité du Droit International Privé, 1866, pp. 180-184; *Gutmann,* Droit International Privé, 2000, pp. 179-181; *Loussouarn / Bourel / de Vareilles-Sommières,* Droit International Privé, 2004, pp. 485-486; *Feldstein de Cárdenas,* Derecho Internacional Privado – Parte Especial, 2000, pp. 269-270.

[423] *von Savigny,* System des heutigen Römischen Recht, 1974, Volume VIII, pp. 205-214.

[424] *von Savigny,* System des heutigen Römischen Recht, 1974, Volume VIII, pp. 350-351.

[425] *von Savigny,* System des heutigen Römischen Recht, 1974, Volume VIII, pp. 350-351.

[426] *Audit,* Droit International Privé, 2006, p. 152; *Loussouarn / Bourel / de Vareilles-Sommières,* Droit International Privé, 2004, p. 485.

[427] *Loussouarn / Bourel / de Vareilles-Sommières,* Droit International Privé, 2004, p. 486; *Audit,* Droit International Privé, 2006, pp. 153 and 679; *Gutmann,* Droit International Privé, 2000, p. 181.

[428] In France three options have been recognized: the law of the place of execution, the law of the contract or the national law common to the parties. However, the latter has not been contemplated in the Convention on the Law Applicable to

parties are[429] have been accepted to govern the form of a contract. Moreover, some authors reckon that the parties have ample freedom to choose the law governing the form and, therefore, could subject the contract to the formal requirements of any law.[430] Nevertheless, when determining the law governing the form the contracting parties do not have the same freedom as when choosing the law applicable to the contract. With respect to the formal validity of a contract, the parties have to choose between a limited number of laws, most commonly being the law of the place of contracting or the law governing the contract. Therefore, the principle *locus regit actum* has more strength in the determination of the law governing the form than in the determination of the law applicable to the contract.[431] However, the *lex causae* may be chosen by the parties; thus, the parties can to this extent choose the law governing the form.

II.   The law applicable to the contract

Due to the fact that an international contract has connections with more than one country, two or more legal systems are potentially applicable to the contract. This means that the law applicable to the contract has to be determined among two or more laws. Thus, the question is which one of the different laws triggered shall be the law applicable to the contract. In common law, this is referred to as the proper law of the contract, and in the French literature, as the *localisation du contrat*.[432]

The determination of the applicable law is made in the first place by the contracting parties, and lacking a choice of law, by the forum judge. Currently, it is deeply rooted, both in national law and in international conventions that the parties to an international contract have the power to choose the law the contract

---

Contractual Obligations (1980), see *Holleaux / Foyer / La Pradelle*, Droit International Privé, 1987, p. 602; *Audit*, Droit International Privé, 2006, pp. 679-680; *Loussouarn / Bourel / de Vareilles-Sommières*, Droit International Privé, 2004, pp. 486-487; *Gutmann*, Droit International Privé, 2000, pp. 181-182.

[429] This is the approach followed by the Convention on the law Applicable to Contractual Obligations (1980) (Article 9.2) and by the Convention on the Law Applicable to Contracts for the International Sale of Goods (1986) (Article 11.2), for contracts entered into between parties in different countries.

[430] *Boggiano*, Derecho Internacional Privado, Volume II, 2006, p. 214. With a different view, see *Audit*, Droit International Privé, 2006, p. 679; *Loussouarn / Bourel / de Vareilles-Sommières*, Droit International Privé, 2004, pp. 486-487.

[431] *Mayer / Heuzé*, Droit International Privé, 2004, pp. 509-510 and 551; *Audit*, Droit International Privé, 2006, p. 151; *Gutmann*, Droit International Privé, 2000, p. 170.

[432] *Marzorati*, Jurisdicción competente y la ley aplicable en las relaciones jurídicas formalizadas en el ciberespacio, La Ley 2004-D, 1373; *Batiffol / Lagarde*, Droit International Privé, 1983, pp. 265-272; *Audit*, Droit International Privé, 2006, pp. 655 and 663.

is to be subject to.[433] Party autonomy[434] was recognized in England in the year 1865 and in France in the year 1910, but it is claimed to go back to the XVI century.[435] In the United States of America, the power of the parties to choose the applicable law has also been recognized since the XIX century.[436]

The consecration of the principle of party autonomy meant the abandonment of the *locus regit actum* principle according to which a contract is governed by the law of the place of contracting (*lex loci contractus*).[437] The principle of *locus regit actum* was used to determine the law applicable to the contract as well as the formal validity of the contract.[438] Therefore, the whole contract used to be subject to the law of the place of execution. However, as far as the applicable law is concerned the principle of *locus regit actum* plays currently only a secondary role and party autonomy has become the main rule.[439] In turn, in the issue of formal validity of the contract the principle has retained a preponderant role even though other criteria to determine the formal validity of a contract are also admitted.[440]

The power of contracting parties to choose the law applicable to the contract is based on several reasons. First, in contracts freedom shall be the rule and,

---

[433] *Holleaux / Foyer / La Pradelle*, Droit international privé, 1987, p. 589; *Lando*, Conflict of Laws of Contracts – General Principles, 1985, pp. 237-238 (*Lando* also includes a historical review for the determination of the applicable law (pp. 240-244) and the evolution of party autonomy (pp. 256-284)); *Audit*, Droit International Privé, 2006, pp. 141-142 and 655.

[434] In French *autonomie de la volonté*; in Spanish *autonomía de la voluntad*; in German *Parteiautonomie*.

[435] *Holleaux / Foyer / La Pradelle*, Droit international privé, 1987, p. 593; *Lando*, Conflict of Laws of Contracts – General Principles, 1985, pp. 257-265; *Batiffol / Lagarde*, Droit International Privé, 1983, pp. 260-262; *Mayer / Heuzé*, Droit international privé, 2004, p. 511; *Audit*, Droit international privé, 2006, p. 142; *Fresnedo de Aguirre*, La autonomía de la voluntad en la contratación internacional, 1991, pp. 12-14; *Gutmann*, Droit International Privé, 2000, p. 171; *Marzorati*, Reflexiones sobre jurisdicción y ley aplicable en internet, in: Kleinheisterkamp / Lorenzo Idiarte (Eds.), Avances del Derecho Internacional Privado en América Latina, 2002, p. 317; *Morris / McClean*, The Conflict of Laws, 2000, p. 320.

[436] *Scoles / Hay / Borchers / Symeonides*, Conflict of Laws, 2000, pp. 860-861.

[437] *Audit*, Droit International privé, 2006, p. 141.

[438] *Audit*, Droit International Privé, 2006, p. 151; *Gutmann*, Droit International Privé, 2000, p. 170; *Loussouarn / Bourel / de Vareilles-Sommières*, Droit International Privé, 2004, p. 484; *Mayer / Heuzé*, Droit International Privé, 2004, p. 509.

[439] *Audit*, Droit International Privé, 2006, pp. 141-142; *Gutmann*, Droit International Privé, 2000, pp. 170-171; *Mayer / Heuzé*, Droit international privé, 2004, p. 509.

[440] *Audit*, Droit International Privé, 2006, p. 151; *Gutmann*, Droit International Privé, 2000, pp. 179-180; *Mayer / Heuzé*, Droit international privé, 2004, p. 510.

therefore, parties shall have the power to choose the law for their contract.[441] Second, party autonomy increases legal certainty because contracting parties know in advance the law that is going to govern the contract.[442] Third, parties to an international contract may require a greater degree of flexibility in choosing the law applicable to the contract.[443] This may occur when a certain type of contract is unknown under a certain law but well-regulated under another one,[444] a legal system is more advanced than another one in certain legal topics,[445] or the parties are more familiar with a foreign law. Finally, another argument in favor of party autonomy is that the parties are considered to be in a better position than a court to decide the law that best suits the contract.[446]

Normally, the power to choose the applicable law is limited to international contracts[447] and subject to certain constraints.[448] However, certain legal systems allow contracting parties to subject a domestic contract to a foreign law. This approach was adopted by the Rome Convention (Article 3.3). Actually, the contract is internationalized by the inclusion of a choice of law provision; until that point the contract is domestic. This means that the international nature of the contract does not pre-exist the choice of the foreign law. Nevertheless, in these cases the freedom of the parties is subject to restrictions which are inoperative when party autonomy is exercised in international contracts.

The forum judge will determine whether party autonomy has been exercised within its limits. If in fact the parties made a valid choice of law, the contract is governed by that law. Absent a choice of law by the parties, the judge will

---

[441] *Audit*, Droit International Privé, 2006, p. 147; Restatement (Second) of Conflict of Laws, Section 187, comment (e).

[442] *Pommier*, Principe d'Autonomie et Loi du Contrat en Droit International Privé Conventionnel, 1992, pp. 17-18; *Scoles / Hay / Borchers / Symeonides*, Conflict of Laws, 2000, p. 857; Restatement (Second) of Conflict of Laws, Section 187, comment (e).

[443] *Lando* refers to this aspect as the "need for freedom" of the contracting parties, see *Lando*, The Conflict of Laws of Contracts – General Principles, 1985, p. 285.

[444] *Holleaux / Foyer / La Pradelle*, Droit international privé, 1987, p. 593.

[445] Restatement (Second) of Conflict of Laws, Section 187, comment (f).

[446] *Boggiano*, Contratos internacionales – International Contracts, 1995, p. 39.

[447] *Pommier*, Principe d'Autonomie et Loi du Contrat en Droit International Privé Conventionnel, 1992, pp. 129-141; *van der Hof*, Party autonomy and International Online Business-to-Business Contracts in Europe and the United States, in: Schulz (Ed.), Legal Aspects of an E-Commerce Transaction, 2006, p. 130; *Boggiano*, Derecho Internacional Privado, Volume II, 2006, p. 175; *Lorenzo Idiarte*, ¿Cuándo un contrato es internacional? Análisis desde una perspectiva regional, in: Kleinheitsterkamp / Lorenzo Idiarte (Eds.), Avances del Derecho Internacional Privado en América Latina, 2002, p. 106.

[448] *Fresnedo de Aguirre*, La autonomía de la voluntad en la contratación internacional, 1991, pp. 83-88 (The author analyzes the limits normally imposed to the freedom of choice.).

determine the applicable law according to the forum's rules of private international law.

Like the determination of the international nature of a contract, the determination of the applicable law is carried out following connecting factors.[449] Connecting factors used to be rigid, such as the place of contracting, the place of performance, the domicile of the parties, and the nationality of the parties, and this is still the case in some legal systems.[450] However, the trend is to evolve towards more flexible points of connection,[451] such as the law most closely connected to the contract.[452] Thus, the different elements of the contract will be taken into account to determine to which country and, consequently, to which law a contract has its closest connections.

The reason for the change is that rigid connecting factors may be cumbersome in practice. The place where the contract was entered into may be difficult to determine or accidental.[453] The difficulty to determine the place of contracting arises when the parties are located in different places and, therefore, it is burdensome to determine where a contract was executed. Additionally, the place of contracting may bear no relation to the contract (for example, a contract executed in an airport or train station or in any other place where the parties were only temporarily and bearing no other connection to the contract); therefore, it would sometimes not be reasonable to subject a contract to the law of that place. The place of performance also presents difficulties since performance may take place in different countries, or it may be difficult to decide which of the parties' performance to take into account.[454] The same problem is present with the domicile of the parties when the parties are domiciled in different countries. Moreover, these concepts may be especially

---

[449] For an analysis of the different connecting factors, see *Lando*, The Conflict of Laws in Contracts – General Principles, 1985, pp. 379-394.

[450] This is the approach of the rules of private international law contained in the Argentine Civil Code, Sections 1205, 1209 and 1210.

[451] *Lando*, The Conflict of Laws in Contracts – General Principles, 1985, pp. 238-239 and 321-358 (The author also analyzes the connecting factors in different legal systems.); *Scoles / Hay / Borchers / Symeonides*, Conflict of Laws, 2000, pp. 123-124.

[452] This is the solution adopted by the Convention on the Law Applicable to Contractual Obligations (1980), Article 4.1. However, some authors reckon that flexible points of connections are inappropriate for determining the law in Internet cases, see *Burnstein,* A Global Network in a Compartmentalised Legal Environment, in: Boele-Woelki / Kessedjian (Eds.), Internet – Which Court Decides? Which Law Applies?, Law and Electronic Commerce, Volume 5, 1998, pp. 27-28.

[453] *von Savigny*, System des heutigen Römischen Recht, 1974, Volume VIII, p. 207.

[454] *Audit*, Droit international privé, 2006, p. 150; *Morris / McClean,* The Conflict of Laws, 2000, pp. 320-321.

difficult to apply in electronic contracts.[455] The nationality has in general not been in itself a relevant factor for determining the applicable law.[456]

C. Conclusions

Legal systems seek to ensure the formal validity of international contracts, in the first place, by allowing that the formal validity of a contract be subject to the *lex causae*. This means that the contracting parties may freely choose the law applicable to the contract knowing that that law can also determine the formal validity of the contract. Party autonomy means a radical change in the power of the parties over the contractual relationship. In the second place, several laws are recognized to govern the formal requirements of a contract so that the parties have different legal systems to choose from when it comes to executing a contract.

---

[455] *Calvo Caravaca / Carrascosa González*, Conflictos de leyes y conflictos de jurisdicción en Internet, 2001, pp. 24-31.
[456] *Holleaux / Foyer / La Pradelle*, Droit international privé, 1987, pp. 598-599; *Batiffol / Lagarde*, Droit International Privé, 1987, pp. 296-297.

Chapter 8: The international contract in international legal instruments

The determination of the international character of a contract, of the law applicable to it and of its formal requirements is made by each national law. The private international law of a given legal system includes also the rules set forth in the international conventions a country has ratified. This part will cover international conventions and international instruments dealing with contracts. For completeness purposes, conventions which have not entered into force as well as conventions not ratified by the jurisdictions analyzed in this work – Argentina, Germany and the United States of America – will also be covered.

The issue of the law establishing the formal requirements will be addressed together with other two topics to which it is directly linked. First, the international nature of the contract. A contract connected only with one country does not raise questions as to which law is to govern its formal requirements. Therefore, it will be analyzed when a convention dealing with contractual matters considers a contract to be international. Most of the international norms to be covered, notwithstanding the fact that they deal with issues of international contracts, do not define this concept. Nevertheless, conventions normally determine their sphere of application; that is, they describe the situations that fall within their domain. In doing so, the conventions establish the boundaries within which they will be applicable. However, the concept of international contract does not equal the sphere of application.[457] The concept of international contract is normally wider than the scope of application; nevertheless, when determining the scope of application a convention selects within the large amount of international contracts those it will apply to.

The second topic related to the law governing the formal validity of contracts is the law applicable to the contract. With regard to the law governing the substance and formal validity of a contract two types of international conventions are to be differentiated. On the one hand, there are conventions whose purpose is to establish uniformity in the field of private international law by means of harmonizing the criteria for the determination of those laws. This type of conventions does not contain material rules; that is, it does not provide the answers to the parties' legal questions but determines the law of the country that will. For example, they determine that the law applicable to the contract will be the law with which a contract has its closest connections or that the formal requirements are governed by the law of the place of execution. On the other hand, there are conventions containing material provisions aimed at governing a certain type of international contract or at least an aspect of it. In this case the

---

[457] *Lorenzo Idiarte*, ¿Cuándo un contrato es internacional? Análisis desde una perspectiva regional, in: Kleinheitsterkamp / Lorenzo Idiarte (Eds.), Avances del Derecho Internacional Privado en América Latina, 2002, pp. 110-112.

convention provides the material rules to which the contract is subject.[458] Nevertheless, in these cases the determination of the applicable law is still needed because conventions normally do not cover all contractual aspects.[459]

A.   Convention on the Law Applicable to International Sales of Goods

I.   Background

The Convention on the Law Applicable to International Sales of Goods was approved on June 15, 1955 and entered into force on September 1, 1964.[460] The convention is the result of the work of the Hague Conference on Private International Law, an intergovernmental organization which works towards the "progressive unification of the rules of private international law".[461] The Hague Conference on Private international law has its seat in The Hague, The Netherlands, it was first established in 1893 and has currently more than sixty member states. The work of the Hague Conference on Private International Law focuses mainly on issues of family and commercial law.

The Convention on the Law Applicable to International Sales of Goods is in force in Denmark, Finland, France, Italy, Norway, Sweden, Switzerland and Niger.[462]

II.   International contracts

The convention does not include a definition of international contract. It simply states that it applies to sales of international nature (Article 1). Therefore, it is up to the forum judge to determine when a sale is international. However, the inclusion of choice of law or choice of forum clauses does not render a contract international (Article 1). This means that the contracting parties may not internationalize a domestic contract by choosing a foreign law to a contract which otherwise lacks links to a foreign country. In other words, the contract

---

[458] *Pommier*, Principe d'Autonomie et Loi du Contrat en Droit International Privé Conventionnel, 1992, pp. 2-5.

[459] *Audit*, Droit International Privé, 2006, p. 7. For example, the Convention on the Law Applicable to Contractual Obligations (1980) excludes several topics from its scope (Article 1.2). The Convention on the International Sales of Goods applies only to the issues of formation and rights and obligations of the contracting parties (Article 4); moreover, it does not cover certain sales (Articles 2 and 3).

[460] Hague Conference on Private International Law, Status Table of the Convention of 15 June 1955 on the Law Applicable to International Sales of Goods, <http://www .hcch.net/index_en.php?act=conventions.status&cid=31>.

[461] Statute of the Hague Conference of Private International Law, Article 1.

[462] Hague Conference on Private International Law, Status table of the Convention of 15 June 1955 on the Law Applicable to International Sales of Goods, <http://www .hcch.net/index_en.php?act=conventions.status&cid=31>.

requires objective links to a foreign country in order to be considered international.

III. Formal validity

The formal validity of contracts is expressly excluded from the scope of the convention (Article 5.2). Therefore, the law applicable to the form will be established according to the rules of private international law of the forum judge. However, those rule may determine that a contract is governed by the law applicable to the contract. In this case, if the convention is applicable, the law applicable is determined in accordance with the convention.

IV. Applicable law

The contracting parties may choose the law applicable to an international contract for the sale of movable goods (Article 2).[463] The choice shall result from an express clause or from the provisions of the contract (Article 2). If the parties fail to choose the law governing the contract, the convention considers the domicile as the connecting factor to determine the applicable law. The rule is that the law applicable will be the one of the country where the seller has his or her domicile or place of business at the time of receiving the purchase order.

However, there is an exception to this principle. If the seller receives the purchase order in the country where the buyer is domiciled or has his or her place of business, then the law of the buyer's country is applicable (Article 3). In this manner, the convention contemplates the situation where the seller targets the buyer in the buyer's country but lacks a domicile or place of business in that country. The convention wants to avoid the situation where a buyer places a purchase order in his or her country and the seller receives it in that country but the transaction is subject to a law foreign to the buyer because the seller does not have a domicile or place of business in the buyer's country, when until that point in time all of the transaction steps have taken place in the buyer's country.

---

[463] *Pommier,* Principe d'Autonomie et Loi du Contrat en Droit International Privé Conventionnel, 1992, p. 9 ("La Convention de la Haye de 1955 sur la loi applicable aux ventes à caractère international d'objets mobiliers corporels est la première pierre constitutive d'un droit international privé conventionnel positif qui réserve une fonction dans la désignation de la loi applicable au contrat à la volonté des parties.").

B.   United Nations Convention on Contracts for the International Sale of Goods

I.   Background

The Convention on Contracts for the International Sale of Goods (commonly known as CISG) was approved on April 10, 1980 in the United Nations Conference on Contracts for the International Sale of Goods and has been opened for signature and accession as from April 11, 1980.[464] Since then around 70 countries have become members of CISG, including Argentina, Germany and the United States of America.[465] The goal of CISG is the unification of the rules for sale of goods contracts of international nature so as to promote international trade and remove legal barriers.[466] CISG applies both to electronic and non-electronic contracts.[467]

CISG is the result of the work of the United Nations Commission on International Trade Law. On the very first UNCITRAL session the topic of the international sale of goods was included in the commission's work program.[468] In order to carry out the task of harmonizing the law of the international sale of goods, UNCITRAL instituted the Working Group on International Sale of Goods, which held its first session in January 1970[469] and continued its work

---

[464]   UNCITRAL, Final Act of the United Nations Conference on Contracts for the International Sale of Goods, Ycarbook of the United Nations Commission on International Trade Law, Volume XI, 1980, (A/CONF.97/18), p. 150, para. 13.

[465]   UNCITRAL, Status of the United Nations Convention on the Contracts for the International Sale of Goods, <www.uncitral.org/uncitral/en/uncitral_texts/sale_goo ds/1980CISG_status.html>. Some countries have recently acceded to the convention, like Paraguay, El Salvador, Japan, Lebanon, Albania and Armenia.

[466]   Preamble of CISG. However, there are opinions that CISG has not helped in the advancement of international trade, see *Cuniberti*, Is the CISG Benefiting Anybody?, Vanderbilt Journal of Transnational Law, Volume 39, 2006, 1511-1550 (According to the author, CISG has neither increased legal certainty nor helped reduce transaction costs).

[467]   *Fallon / Meeusen*, Le commerce électronique, la directive 2000/31/CE et le droit international privé, Revue Critique de droit international privé, July-September 2002, 435, 441.

[468]   The first session of UNCITRAL took place from January 29 to February 28, 1968 at the United Nations Headquarters. In this session the international sale of goods was the topic most supported by the delegations to be addressed by UNCITRAL, see UNCITRAL, The First Session, Yearbook of the United Nations Commission on International Trade Law, Volume I, 1970, (A/7216), p. 75, para. 34.

[469]   UNCITRAL, Report of the Working Group on the international sale of goods, First session, Yearbook of the United Nations Commission on International Trade Law, Volume I, 1970, (A/CN.9/35), pp. 176.

until its ninth session in 1977.[470] The working group was assigned the task of taking steps towards the harmonization of the law of the international sale of goods either by means of amending the existing texts or drafting a brand new one.[471] The latter was decided.

The texts considered by the working group when drafting CISG were three. On the one hand, the two so-called Hague Conventions of 1964 prepared by the International Institute for the Unification of Private Law (UNIDROIT): the Convention relating to a Uniform Law on the International Sale of Goods, approved in The Hague on July 1, 1964 and containing as an Annex the Uniform Law on the International Sale of Goods,[472] and the Convention relating to a Uniform Law on the Formation of Contracts for the International Sale of Goods approved in The Hague in 1964, and containing as an Annex the Uniform Law on the Formation of Contracts for the International Sale of Goods[473].[474] The third text was the Convention on the Law applicable to the International Sale of Goods concluded in 1955 and commented above.

UNCITRAL approved the draft of the Convention on Contracts for the International Sale of Goods at its 209th meeting on June 16, 1978.[475] Thereafter

---

[470] UNCITRAL, Report of the Working Group on the International Sale of Goods on the work of its ninth session, Yearbook of the United Nations Commission on International Trade Law, 1978, Volume IX, (A/CN.9/142), pp. 61-85; UNCITRAL, Report of the United Nations Commission on International Trade Law on the work of its eleventh session, Yearbook of the United Nations Commission on International Trade Law, Volume IX, 1978, (A/33/17), pp. 12-13.

[471] UNCITRAL, Report of the United Nations Commission on International Trade Law on the work of its second session, Yearbook of the United Nations Commission on International Trade Law, Volume I, 1970, (A/7618), pp. 99-100, para. 38.

[472] Sometimes referred to as ULIS.

[473] Sometimes referred to as ULFIS.

[474] The Hague Conventions were not ratified by a large number of countries. The Hague Conventions entered into force on August 1, 1972 and are in effect in only four countries: Gambia, Israel, San Marino and the United Kingdom. In turn, Belgium, Germany, Italy, Luxemburg, the Netherlands denounced both conventions. See UNIDROIT, Status of UNIDROIT Conventions, <http://www.uni droit.org/english/implement/i-64ulis.pdf> and <http://www.unidroit.org/english/im plement/i-64ulf.pdf>. According to *Gillette / Walt* the failure of the conventions can be attributed to the fact that they only embraced the legal principles of western European countries, see *Gillette / Walt*, Sales Law – Domestic and International, 1999, p. 4. See also *Marzorati*, Derecho de los negocios internacionales, Volume 1, 2003, pp. 106-107.

[475] UNCITRAL, Report of the United Nations Commission on International Trade Law on the work of its eleventh session, Yearbook of the United Nations Commission on International Trade Law, Volume IX, 1978, (A/33/17), p. 14, para. 27.

the General Assembly convened an international conference to submit the draft convention to the consideration of all states and organizations.[476]

II. International contracts

CISG is applicable to sales of goods of international nature but does not define that concept.[477] Nevertheless, for the purposes of determining the sphere of application CISG takes into account the location of the places of business of the contracting parties. Article 1(1) establishes the application of CISG when the contracting parties have their places of business in different states. The location of the parties´ places of business in different states is the first and unavoidable threshold for the application of CISG. Based on this requirement as to the application of the convention it can be inferred that the international nature of a contract is based on where the places of business of the parties are.[478] However, there are further requirements to be taken into consideration when determining the applicability of CISG; therefore, the sales contract may be international but not subject to CISG.

III. Formal validity

CISG does not establish which law will govern the formal requirements of contracts for the sale of international goods; instead it contains its own rules concerning the formal validity of the contracts falling within its sphere of application. CISG adopted the freedom of forms rule. Contracts for the international sale of goods are not subject to any formal requirement (Article 11).[479] Thus, the formal requirements, if any, imposed by national law are overridden.[480]

---

[476] United Nations General Assembly, General Resolution 33/93, Resolutions adopted on the reports of the Sixth Committee, pp. 217-218.

[477] UNCITRAL, Comments by Governments and international organizations on the draft convention on the international sale of goods, Yearbook of the United Nations Commission on International Trade Law, 1977, Volume VIII, (A/CN.9/125 and A/CN.9/125/Add. 1 to 3), p. 138.

[478] UNCITRAL, Digest of case law on the United Nations Convention on the International Sale of Goods, Article 1, p. 5, para. 11; *Garro*, La Convención de las Naciones Unidas sobre los contratos de compraventa internacional de mercaderías: su incorporación al orden jurídico argentino (Segunda parte), La Ley 1985-A, 930. The nationality of the parties is not relevant to the determination of a sale of goods contract as international under CISG (Article 1(3)), see UNCITRAL, Digest of case law on the United Nations Convention on the International Sale of Goods, Article 1, pp. 5-6, para. 14.

[479] UNCITRAL Digest of case law on the United Nations Convention on the International Sale of Goods, Article 11, p. 2 (It mentions a case ruled by a Swiss court which decided that a signature is not required according to the principle of

However, contracting states whose legislation require a writing can opt out of this provision by declaring that written form requirements imposed by national law cannot be fulfilled by using another type of form (Article 96). According to Article 12 the freedom of forms principle does not apply when a contracting state has made a declaration under Article 96.[481] In these cases, the form of the contract is not covered by CISG; thus, the law that will govern the form has to be determined. However, CISG does not address how the determination of the applicable law is made. On the one hand, it is sustained that the law governing the form is the law of the state that made the reservation.[482] On the other hand, it is considered that the rules of private international law of the forum judge shall determine the law governing the form.[483]

If the law of the contracting state making an Article 96 reservation is determined as the one governing the form – either based on the first position or on the forum judge's private international law – the law of that country governs the formal requirements of the contract. Nevertheless, it does not mean that the contract necessarily has to comply with a form requirement. Several legal systems follow the rules of the principle of freedom of forms and it may be that under the national law governing the form, the sale contract at stake does not need to comply with any formal requirements. On the contrary, if the law indicated as applicable is the one of the state not making the reservation, the question is whether Article 11 imposing the principle of freedom of forms applies.[484] This may mean an important difference because the principle of freedom of forms might be an exception in the legal system of the non-reservation state or, even if recognized, certain contracts may be required to be in or evidenced by a writing.

IV. Applicable law

CISG does not contain choice of law provisions because in the matters falling within its scope CISG itself is the applicable law to the contract. However,

---

freedom of form established by CISG.). It should be noted that cases ruling on CISG may be relevant in other jurisdictions because according to Article 7 of CISG, when construing the convention regard is to have to its international nature.

[480] UNCITRAL, Digest of case law on the United Nations Convention on the International Sale of Goods, Article 11, p. 3, para. 4.

[481] The states having made an Article 96 declaration are: Argentina, Armenia, Belarus, Chile, Hungary, Latvia, Lithuania, Paraguay, Russian Federation and Ukraine, see UNCITRAL, Status of the United Nations Convention on the Contracts for the International Sale of Goods, <www.uncitral.org/uncitral/en/uncitra l_texts/sale_goods/1980CISG_status.html>.

[482] UNCITRAL, Digest of case law on the United Nations Convention on the International Sale of Goods, Article 11, pp. 3-4, para. 7.

[483] *Menicocci*, Prueba del contrato y ley aplicable al pago del precio de la compraventa internacional de mercaderías, La Ley 2006-C, 776.

[484] *Gillette / Walt*, Sales Law – Domestic and International, 1999, pp. 137-138.

CISG does not govern every aspect of an international sale but only its formation and the rights and obligations of the parties (Articles 4 and 5).

The first requirement for CISG to apply is that the contracting parties have their domicile in two different states (Article 1(1)). Moreover, the parties must be aware of this situation (Article 1(2)); that is, the fact that the parties shall have their domiciles in different countries has to appear from the contract, its negotiations or from the information disclosed by the parties on or before the execution of the contract (Article 1(2)). Therefore, the location of the places of business in different states is an objective as well as a subjective element.

The election of the places of business of the parties in different states was also the approach taken by the Uniform Law on the International Sale of Goods (Article 1) and the Uniform Law on the Formation of Contract for the International Sale of Goods (Article 1). However, these two uniform laws contain also three other requirements for their application. In addition to the parties having their places of business in different states one of the following situations has to be present: (a) at the time of the execution of the contract the goods have to be in the course of carriage or to be carried from the territory of one state to the territory of another; (b) the offer and the acceptance has to be effected in different States, or (c) the delivery of the goods is to be made in the territory of a State that is not where the offer and acceptance have been effected. The working group on the international sale of goods decided to eliminate these additional requirements.[485]

Instead, CISG requires that the places of business be located in different contracting states (Article 1(1)(a)).[486] When one party does not have its place of business in a contracting state the convention is nonetheless applicable if the rules of private international law determine the application of the law of a contracting state (Article 1(1)(b)) and the contracting state has not declared the

---

[485] UNCITRAL, Working Group on the International Sale of Goods, Report on the work of the Second Session, Yearbook of the United Nations Commission on International Trade Law, 1971, Volume II, (A/CN.9/52), pp. 52-54, para. 13-31; UNCTRAL, Report of the Secretary-General: pending questions with respect to the revised text of a uniform law on the international sale of goods, Yearbook of the United Nations Commission on International Trade Law, 1975, Volume VI, (A/CN.9/100, annex III), pp. 88-89, para. 4-8; UNCITRAL, Comments by Governments and international organizations on the draft convention on the international sale of goods, Yearbook of the United Nations Commission on International Trade Law, 1977, Volume VIII, (A/CN.9/125 and A/CN.9/125/Add. 1 to 3), p. 138.

[486] UNCITRAL, Digest of case law on the United Nations Convention on the International Sale of Goods, Article 1, pp. 7-11, *Gillette / Walt*, Sales Law – Domestic and International, 1999, pp. 28-29.

inapplicability of this section pursuant to Section 95.[487] A contracting state may make an Article 95 reservation limiting the application of CISG to the cases where both parties have their places of business in different contracting states and excluding the possibility that CISG applies based on the fact that the law of a contracting state has been determined as the law applicable.[488]

Additionally, CISG applies as long as the sales are not excluded under Articles 2 and 3, and the parties have not opted out of the convention as authorized by Article 6.[489]

The contracting parties have the power to designate CISG as the applicable law despite the lack in CISG of an express provision allowing the choice.[490] A draft version of CISG contained a provision allowing the parties to choose CISG as the law governing the contract.[491] This provision was considered useful for

---

[487] UNCITRAL, Digest of case law on the United Nations Convention on the International Sale of Goods, Article 1, pp. 11-14; *Gillette / Walt*, Sales Law – Domestic and International, 1999, pp. 29-32. The Czech Republic, Saint Vincent and the Grenadines, Singapore, Slovakia, and the United States of America have declared, according to Article 95, that Article 1(1)(b) is not applicable. In turn, Germany declared that it will not apply Article 1(1)(b) with regard to a state that has made an Article 95 declaration, see UNCITRAL, Status of the 1980 Convention on the International Sale of Goods <http://www.uncitral.org/uncitral/e n/uncitral_texts/sale_goods/1980CISG_status.html>.

[488] *Gillette / Walt*, Sales Law – Domestic and International, 1999, pp. 30-32.

[489] CISG does not apply to all contracts for the sale of goods. Article 2 excludes certain contracts for the sale of goods based on the purpose of the purchase (subparagraph a), the way of acquiring the goods (subparagraphs b and c) or the types of goods (subparagraphs d, e and f). Article 3 excludes contracts where the predominant purpose of the contract is not the sale of goods, see *Marzorati*, Derecho de los negocios internacionales, Volume 1, 2003, pp. 118-121; *Gillette / Walt*, Sales Law – Domestic and International, 1999, pp. 36-41. Even when all the elements triggering the application of CISG are present, the contracting parties are free to modify its provisions and to derogate any of its norms (except for Article 12 which may not be derogated or varied by the parties). Moreover, the parties are also free to opt out of CISG and, therefore, exclude its application completely (Article 6), see *Gillette / Walt*, Sales Law – Domestic and International, 1999, pp. 32-33.

[490] UNCITRAL, Digest of case law on the United Nations Convention on the International Sale of Goods, Article 1, p. 14. The choice of CISG by the parties has been recognized by courts (UNILEX, CISG, U.S. District Court, Northern District of Illinois, East. Div, Raw Materials Inc. v. Manfred Forberich GmbH & Co., KG, 6/7/2004, <http://www.unilex.info/case.cfm?pid=1&id=987&do=case>) and in arbitrations (UNILEX, CISG, Arbitral Institute of the Stockholm Chamber of Commerce, 5/4/2007, <http://www.unilex.info/case.cfm?pid=1&id=1194&do=cas e>).

[491] UNCITRAL, Working Group on the International Sale of Goods, Report on the work of the Second Session, Yearbook of the United Nations Commission on

businesses contracting with companies located in contracting states and non-contracting states of CISG because it would make it possible to apply the same rules regardless of whether the requirements of Article 1 were met.[492] However, that provision was eliminated from the final draft. The arguments raised by Germany and Norway addressed the fear that contracting parties may designate CISG as the applicable law to a pure domestic contract derogating mandatory provisions.[493] It should be noted that under the Rome Convention the choice of a foreign law in a domestic contract is currently possible in EU member states but the mandatory rules of the country which the domestic contract is related to are safeguarded (Article 3.3).

C.   Convention on the Law Applicable to Contractual Obligations

I.   Background

The Convention on the Law Applicable to Contractual Obligations,[494] also known as the Rome Convention, was approved on June 19, 1980 and entered into force almost eleven years later, on April 1, 1991.[495] The Rome Convention sets forth the rules of private international law on contractual matters for the EU member states.[496] Its rules apply both to paper as well as to electronic

---

    International Trade Law, 1971, Volume II, (A/CN.9/52), pp. 52 para. 13 and pp. 54-55, para. 36-42.

[492] UNCITRAL, Commentary on the draft convention on the International Sale of Goods, Yearbook of the United Nations Commission on International Trade Law, Volume VII, 1976, (A/CN.9/116, annex II), p. 99.

[493] UNCITRAL, Comments by Governments and international organizations on the draft convention on the international sale of goods, Yearbook of the United Nations Commission on International Trade Law, 1977, Volume VIII, (A/CN.9/125 and A/CN.9/125/Add. 1 to 3), pp. 116 and 120-121; UNCITRAL, Report of the Secretary-General: Analysis of comments by Governments and international organizations on the draft Convention on the international sale of goods as adopted by the Working Group on the international sale of goods, 1977, Yearbook of the United Nations Commission on International Trade Law, Volume VIII, (A/CN.9/126), p. 146.

[494] On December 17, 2009 the Regulation 593/2008 of the European Parliament and the Council of 17 June 2008 on the law applicable to contractual obligations (Rome I), (Rome I Regulation), shall enter into force, which establishes the rules concerning the applicable law to contractual obligations.

[495] See <http://europa.eu/legislation_summaries/justice_freedom_security/judicial_co operation_in_civil_matters/l33109_en.htm>.

[496] *Giuliano / Lagarde*, Report on the Convention on the law applicable to contractual obligations, Introduction, para. 7. However, certain contractual matters are excluded from the scope of the convention like capacity and agency as well as certain contractual obligations such as those relating to wills and family law, and negotiable instruments (Article 1 Rome Convention). See *Giuliano / Lagarde*,

contracts.[497] The Rome Convention overrides the national choice of law rules on the issues governed by it.[498]

II. International contracts

The Rome Convention does not contain a definition of international contract. Actually, the convention does not even refer to international contracts.[499] According to Article 1, the convention is applicable to "any situation involving a choice between the laws of different states".[500] Therefore, the Rome Convention does not only apply to international contracts but to any type of contract where a conflict of laws is present. For example, in the case of a country with different legal systems the determination of the applicable law to the contract will be answered by the Rome Convention.[501]

Nevertheless, the convention contains two indications to determine when a contract may be considered international: (i) the existence of a choice between laws of different countries (Article 1) and (ii) the presence of relevant elements connecting the contract with more than one country (*a contrario sensu* Article 3.3). Therefore, what is important is the existence of a foreign element in the

---

Report on the Convention on the law applicable to contractual obligations, Article 1, para. 2-11. *Boggiano* proposes that the Rome Convention be taken as a model for the unification of choice of law provisions in America due to the fact that the Rome Convention brings together the rules of common law and civil law legal systems. The author also regards as a guiding model the 1986 Hague Convention on the applicable law to contracts for the international sales of goods, see *Boggiano*, Contratos Internacionales – International Contracts, 1995, pp. 151-153.

[497] *Calvo Caravaca / Carrascosa González*, Conflictos de leyes y conflictos de jurisdicción en Internet, 2001, p. 58; *Fallon / Meeusen*, Le commerce électronique, la directive 2000/31/CE et le droit international privé, Revue Critique de droit international privé, July-September 2002, 435, 439.

[498] *Giuliano / Lagarde,* Report on the Convention on the law applicable to contractual obligations, Article 2. Nevertheless, the rules existing prior to the entrance into force of the Rome Convention are still applicable to contracts executed before April 1, 1990 as well as to the issues not covered by the Rome Convention, see *Clarkson / Hill,* Jaffey on the Conflict of Laws, 2002, p. 200; *Audit,* Droit International Privé, 2006, p. 655; *Mayss*, Principles of Conflict of Laws, 1996, p. 109.

[499] *Lando*, The Conflict of Laws of Contracts – General Principles, 1985, p. 287; *Jacquet*, Le contrat international, 1999, pp. 7-8.

[500] The Rome I Regulation establishes that the regulation applies "in situations involving a conflict of laws".

[501] However, when the conflict of laws arises only between the territorial units of a state it is not mandatory that the rules of the Rome Convention apply (Article 19.2). See 19 of the Rome Convention and *Giuliano / Lagarde,* Report on the Convention on the law applicable to contractual obligations, Article 1, para. 1 and Article 19. The Rome I Regulation contains the same rules on Article 22.

contract that connects it with a foreign country triggering a choice of law. Whenever a contract gives rise to a choice of law between two or more countries the contract may be deemed international. In other words, any element triggering a choice of law is enough.[502] Therefore, a simple choice of law clause renders a contract international even if this is the only connecting factor with a foreign legal system; that is, even if all the other elements of the contract are linked only to one country.[503]

III. Formal validity

According to the Rome Convention the formal validity of a contract may be governed by the law of the place of execution, the law governing the contract or the law of the place where the parties are.[504] The convention applies the *lex causae*, the *lex loci actus*, or the law of the country of the parties alternatively without establishing any priority between them.[505] However, these three connecting factors do not apply to all contracts; depending on where the parties are at the time of entering into the contract, the connecting factors that are eligible to govern the formal requirements of the contract vary.

If the parties are in the same country, there are two laws that may establish the formal validity of a contract: the law of the country where the contract has been executed (*lex loci contractus*) or the law governing the contract (*lex causae*) (Article 9.1).[506] If, on the other hand, the parties are in different countries, then

---

[502] Contratos Internacionales – International Contracts, 1995, p. 439.

[503] This approach has been defended by M. Curti-Gialdino, see *Pommier, Principe d'Autonomie et Loi du Contrat en Droit International Privé Conventionnel*, 1992, pp. 131-133. For authors with a contrary view, see *Jacquet, Le contrat international*, 1999, p. 8; *Pommier, Principe d'Autonomie et Loi du Contrat en Droit International Privé Conventionnel*, 1992, p. 133.

[504] The same rule is contained in Article 11 of the Rome I Regulation. The Rome Convention does not define the concept of form but the *Giuliano / Lagarde* Report states that form may be construed "as including every external manifestation required on the part of a person expressing the will to be legally bound", see *Giuliano / Lagarde*, Report on the Convention on the law applicable to contractual obligations, Article 9, para. 2. See also: *Clarkson / Hill*, Jaffey on the Conflict of Laws, 2002, p. 242.

[505] *Giuliano / Lagarde*, Report on the Convention on the law applicable to contractual obligations, Article 9, para. B1; *Audit*, Droit International Privé, 2006, p. 680. However, in France the *Cour de Cassation* used to give priority to the law of the place of execution over the law governing the contract or the national law common to the contracting parties, see *Holleaux /Foyer / La Pradelle*, Droit International Privé, 1987, p. 602; *Mayer / Heuzé*, Droit International Privé, 2004, p. 552.

[506] The Rome Convention did not include the law of the common nationality or habitual residence of the parties. See *Giuliano / Lagarde*, Report on the Convention on the law applicable to contractual obligations, Article 9, para. B.1;

three laws come into play: the laws of the countries where the parties are or the law governing the contract (*lex causae*) (Article 9.2).[507] Consequently, in the case the parties are in different countries, the place of contracting (*lex loci contractus*) is abandoned. Instead, the contract may be formally valid according to the laws of one of the countries where the parties are. This solution is adopted in view of the difficulty to determine the place where the contract is entered into when the parties are in different countries.[508]

A contract is always formally valid if it complies with the formal requirements of the law governing the contract regardless of the location of the parties.[509] In the event the parties change the law applicable to the contract, this change must not affect the formal validity of the contract (Article 3.2).[510]

In the case the contract is entered into by an agent, the country where that agent acts is the one relevant for the determination of the applicable law (Article 9.3).[511] The location of a contracting party acting through an agent is not relevant for the determination of the law applicable to the form; the location of the agent is. Acts accessory to the contract are governed by the law of the contract or by the law of the country where the act is done (Article 9.4).

The convention contains two exceptions to the general rule determining the law governing the formal requirements. Consumer contracts falling within Article 5.2 are governed by the law of the country where the consumer has his or her habitual place of residence (Article 9.5). Also, a contract concerning rights in or rights to use immovable property has to comply with the formal mandatory requirements imposed by the law where the property is situated (Article 9.6).[512]

IV. Applicable law

The Rome Convention recognizes party autonomy as well as establishes the rules to determine the proper law of the contract absent a choice by the parties.

Holleaux /Foyer / La Pradelle, Droit International Privé, 1987, p. 602; *Mayer / Heuzé*, Droit International Privé, 2004, p. 551 and 554.

[507] The Rome I Regulation adds also the law of the habitual residence of the parties at the time the contract was concluded (Article 11.2).

[508] *Giuliano / Lagarde*, Report on the Convention on the law applicable to contractual obligations, Article 9, para. B.3.

[509] *Morris / McClean,* The Conflict of Laws, 2000, p. 341.

[510] Article 3.2 of the Rome I Regulation contains the same rule.

[511] The same principle is reflected in Articles 9.1 and 9.2 of the Rome I Regulation.

[512] An example of this type of norm is Section 1211 of the Argentine Civil Code which requires a public instrument for contracts relating to real property located in Argentina. This norm is contained in Article 9.5 of the Rome I Regulation, which, unlike the Rome Convention, expressly states that this rule applies when the mandatory requirements of form cannot be derogated by agreement.

The choice of the applicable law is connected with the formal validity of the contract. Under the Rome Convention a contract is formally valid if it complies with the *lex causae*. Therefore, the freedom of the parties to choose the applicable law entails also the possibility to subject the formal requirements of the contract to that law.

1. Party autonomy

The Rome Convention establishes the freedom of the parties to choose the law they deem most appropriate to govern the contract (Article 3).[513] The choice of a foreign law is authorized even in contracts which have, except for the choice of law clause, their entire links to one country.[514] In general, in order for the parties to subject a contract to a foreign law the contract has to be objectively international;[515] this means that the contract has to be international before the parties exercise the power to choose the applicable law.[516] However, under the Rome Convention a contract simultaneously becomes international and subject to a foreign law by means of introducing a choice of law provision. This is an exception to the usual practice[517] and, consequently, it is the reason why Article 3.3 restricts the scope of application of the foreign law when the choice of law provision is the only foreign element in the contract. It does so by establishing the prevalence of the mandatory rules of the law of the country with which the contract is entirely connected, over any provisions to the contrary of the chosen foreign law.[518] In objective international contracts the foreign law chosen by the parties overrides, with certain exceptions, the mandatory provisions of the forum judge.[519]

---

[513] *Gutmann*, Droit International Privé, 2000, pp. 174-175. The same principle is found in Article 3.1 of the Rome I Regulation.

[514] *Scoles / Hay / Borchers / Symeonides*, Conflict of Laws, 2000, p. 872; *Jacquet*, Le contrat international, 1999, p. 8.

[515] *Lando*, The Conflict of Laws on Contracts – General Principles, 1985, pp. 286-287.

[516] *Pommier*, Principe d'Autonomie et Loi du Contrat en Droit International Privé Conventionnel, 1992, pp. 129-141; *Lorenzo Idiarte*, ¿Cuándo un contrato es internacional? Análisis desde una perspectiva regional, in: Kleinheitsterkamp / Lorenzo Idiarte (Eds.), Avances del Derecho Internacional Privado en América Latina, 2002, p. 119 footnote 65.

[517] *Pommier*, Principe d'Autonomie et Loi du Contrat en Droit International Privé Conventionnel, 1992, p. 133.

[518] *Chissick*, Electronic Commerce: Law and Practice, 1999, p. 118; *Jacquet*, Le contrat international, 1999, p. 8. Article 3.3 of the Rome I Regulations refers to provisions which cannot be derogated from by agreement.

[519] *van der Hof*, Party autonomy and International Online Business-to-Business Contracts in Europe and the United States, in: Schulz (Ed.), Legal Aspects of an E-Commerce Transaction, 2006, p. 130.

This solution was adopted in order to reconcile the opinions of those rejecting the choice of law in contracts whose only foreign element is the choice of law clause, and of those in favor of it.[520] The main concern when choosing a foreign law for an otherwise domestic contract is that the choice may seek solely to avoid mandatory provisions of the domestic law otherwise applicable. Therefore, the Rome Convention recognizes party autonomy in contracts without any other relevant foreign element but the choice of a foreign law subject to the application of the mandatory provisions of the law which would have otherwise governed the contract.

The choice of law may be made at the time the contract is executed or at a later stage (Article 3.2).[521] The law applicable to the contract is the law in force in the designated country; however, the private international law rules of the applicable law are excluded (Article 15).[522] The law chosen does not need to have a connection with the contract or the parties,[523] nor be that of an EU member state (Article 2).[524] The choice of the applicable law may be made for the whole contract or just for a part of it (Article 3.1).[525] Then, it is possible to choose different laws for different parts of the contract, what in French is known as *dépeçage* (severability) of the law applicable to the contract. It was debated whether to allow the *dépeçage* or not. The dominant view held that the *dépeçage* is a consequence of the freedom of choice and could therefore not be prohibited.[526]

In conclusion, the freedom given to the parties is wide admitting the choice of law at any time, of any foreign law, and even of multiple laws.[527]

---

[520] *Giuliano / Lagarde,* Report on the Convention on the law applicable to contractual obligations, Article 3, para. 8.

[521] *Audit,* Droit International Privé, 2006, pp. 662-663; *Mayss,* The Principles of Conflict of Laws, 1996, p. 115. Article 3.2 of the Rome I Regulation.

[522] In the Rome I Regulation this rule is to be found in Article 20.

[523] *Holleaux / Foyer / La Pradelle,* Droit International Privé, 1987, p. 596; *Audit,* Droit International Privé, 2006, p. 657; *Mayer / Heuzé,* Droit International Privé, 2004, p. 522.

[524] Also contained in Article 2 of the Rome I Regulation.

[525] See Article 3.1 of the Rome I Regulation.

[526] *Giuliano / Lagarde,* Report on the Convention on the law applicable to contractual obligations, Article 3, para. 4; *Audit,* Droit International Privé, 2006, pp. 660-662; *Lando,* The Conflict of Laws of Contracts – General Principles, 1985, pp. 250-254 (The author disfavors the approach of the Rome Convention as well as clarifies that applying different laws to a complex contract with several separable parts is not actually *dépeçage.*).

[527] The choice has even been characterized as unlimited, see *Loussouarn / Bourel / de Vareilles-Sommières,* Droit International Privé, 2004, p. 497.

Together with the freedom to choose the law applicable to the contract, the parties also have the freedom to amend that choice and to choose another law. However, there are two limitations to said power. First, the change of the applicable law shall not affect the formal validity of the contract (Article 3.2); therefore, the contract remains formally valid despite the change of the applicable law. The second limitation to the freedom of the parties to amend the applicable law is that the rights of third parties are not adversely affected (Article 3.2).[528]

For the provisions of Article 3 to apply, there needs to be a choice of law. The choice of law "must be expressed or demonstrated with reasonable certainty by the terms of the contract or the circumstances of the case" (Article 3.1).[529] An express choice is normally made in a contractual provision establishing the law of a certain country or territorial unit as applicable. The choice may also be demonstrated by the terms of the contract or the circumstances of the case.[530] This means that the contract or the circumstances of the case have to reveal a real choice of law made by the parties.[531] The situation has to be distinguished from the absence of choice, where a court deduces what the parties may have chosen had they made a choice of law.[532] The Rome Convention does not allow the courts to elucidate a choice of law if the parties did not, in fact, agree on one.[533] In the absence of a choice of law, either explicit or implicit, Article 4

---

[528] The parties have the power to decide the retroactive effect, or not, of the new law – or of the law chosen at a later point, see *Audit*, Droit International Privé, 2006, pp. 662-663. The same rules are contained in Article 3.2 of the Rome I Regulation.

[529] The wording in the Rome I Regulation is slightly different. According to the Rome I Regulation, the choice "shall be made expressly or clearly demonstrated by the terms of the contract or the circumstances of the case"; that is, the choice has to be "clearly demonstrated" instead of "demonstrated with reasonable certainty".

[530] *Giuliano / Lagarde*, Report on the Convention on the law applicable to contractual obligations, Article 3, para. 3; *Morris / McClean*, The Conflict of Laws, 2000, pp. 328-329.

[531] *Pommier*, Principe d'Autonomie et Loi du Contrat en Droit International Privé Conventionnel, 1992, pp. 105-109; *Holleaux / Foyer / La Pradelle*, Droit International Privé, 1987, p. 595.

[532] *Chissick*, Electronic Commerce: Law and Practice, 1999, p. 115; *Giuliano / Lagarde*, Report on the Convention on the law applicable to contractual obligations, Article 3, para. 3.

[533] *Chissick*, Electronic Commerce: Law and Practice, 1999, pp. 115-116. The *Giuliano / Lagarde* Report gives examples of cases where a court may consider that there was an express choice by the parties: a contract entered into in a standard form which is always governed by a certain law, previous contracts between the parties with express choice of law provisions (course of dealing), inclusion in the contract of references to a certain law, etc. See *Giuliano / Lagarde*, Report on the Convention on the law applicable to contractual obligations, Article 3, para. 3. In the case Egon Oldendorff v Liberia Corp (1996) an English court found that the parties had made a choice of law based on the fact that the parties' contract

governs because there is no choice made by the parties.[534] However, if a choice of law is not made expressly in a contract, there is actually no certainty as to whether the parties reached an agreement on the applicable law.[535]

2.   Choice of law rules

In the absence of a choice of law, the contract is governed by the law of the country with which it has the closest connection (Article 4.1).[536] The Rome Convention contains some guidelines, in the form of presumptions, to determine the country with which a contract is most closely connected.[537] The presumptions are rebuttable.[538]

a)   General presumption

It is presumed that a contract is most closely connected with the country where the party with the characteristic performance has, at the time of execution of the contract, his or her habitual residence or central administration (Article 4.2).[539] Therefore, in order to find the applicable law it is necessary to elucidate in the first place, the characteristic performance, in the second place, the residence or central administration of the characteristic performer, and, in the third place, the time when the contract was executed.

The presumption contained in Section 4.2 may be disregarded if there is evidence that the contract is most closely connected with a country other than

---

contained an arbitration clause in London as well as clear references to English law – quoted in *Mayss*, Principles of Conflict of Laws, 1996, pp. 113-114 and in *Morris / McClean,* The Conflict of Laws, 2000, p. 329.

[534] *Morris / McClean,* The Conflict of Laws, 2000, pp. 328-330.

[535] *Clarkson / Hill*, Jaffey on the Conflict of Laws, 2002, p. 212.

[536] By this means the Rome Convention abandons the use of rigid points of connection, see *Audit*: Droit International Privé, 2006, pp. 663-664 (Also, the author states that Article 4.1 is not technically a conflict of law rule because it does not designate the applicable law but only states a general rule on how to determine the applicable law, pp. 664-665). The Rome I Regulation in its Article 4.1 establishes the law that will govern each type of contract therein enumerated. Contracts for the sale of goods and provision of services are governed by the law of the habitual residence of the seller or service provider, respectively (Article 4.1(a) and 4.1(b)). Only in case the contract is not listed in Article 4.1 the contract is subject to the law of the country where the party with the characteristic performance has his or her habitual residence (Article 4.2).

[537] *Gutmann*, Droit International Privé, 2000, pp. 176-178.

[538] *Giuliano / Lagarde*, Report on the Convention on the law applicable to contractual obligations, Article 4, para. 4; *Gutmann*, Droit International Privé, 2000, p. 178.

[539] *Lord Mance*, The Future of Private International Law, Journal of Private International Law, Volume 1, No. 2, 1995, 185, 188 (The author also addresses the different interpretations of the presumption by national courts.).

the country where the party with the most characteristic performance has the habitual residence or central administration at the time the contract is executed (Article 4.5).[540]

Besides, a court may apply a different law to a separable part of the contract as long as it is more closely connected to a country other than the country designated by the application of the presumption (Article 4.1). However, courts cannot designate different laws with the same freedom as contracting parties can. A court may determine a different law to a part of a contract as long as the part is separable from the rest of the contract and more closely connected with the country whose law will govern the separable part.[541]

i)   The characteristic performance

It is necessary to determine who the contractual party with the characteristic performance is. The characteristic performance is linked to the place where the contract has its social and economic impact; where the contract has its center of gravity.[542] It is the performance that is particular to a contract and, therefore, allows the differentiation of contracts.[543] For example, what differentiates a contract for the sale of goods from a service contract is the performance of the seller in the former and the rendering of the service in the latter and not the performance of the person paying for the goods or the services. The payment of the monies is not considered to be the characteristic performance because it is present in almost every contract and does not allow us to differentiate one from another.[544] However, there are cases where the characteristic performance cannot be determined and, therefore, the presumption does not apply (Article 4.5).[545] Examples of these situations are contracts where both parties exchange

---

[540]   The Rome I Regulation establishes that if the applicable law to the contract cannot be determined according to Articles 4.1 and 4.2 then the law of the country with which the contract is most closely connected is to be applied (Article 4.4).

[541]   *Giuliano / Lagarde*, Report on the Convention on the law applicable to contractual obligations, Article 4, para. 8.

[542]   *Giuliano / Lagarde*, Report on the Convention on the law applicable to contractual obligations, Article 4, para. 3.

[543]   *Menicocci*, Compraventa internacional de mercaderías y derecho aplicable al pago del precio, La Ley Impuestos 2006-11, 1143.

[544]   In contracts where both parties′ performances are the payment of money, then the party with the greater risks is considered to be the one with the characteristic performance, see *Clarkson / Hill*, Jaffey on Conflict of Laws, 2002, p. 216 (The example given is a re-insurance contract where both parties have to pay money. Because the reinsurer carries the greater risks then this party is considered to be the one with the characteristic performance.).

[545]   According to Article 4.3 of the Rome I Regulation, the law determined as applicable by Articles 4.1. and 4.2 shall be disregarded when the contract is manifestly more closely connected with another country.

goods, and complex contracts with multiple parties, such as joint ventures, where all the parties' performances are characteristic.[546] In these cases, a court will need to find another way to elucidate which one is the law most closely connected to the contract.

ii)   The habitual residence or central administration

Once the party with the characteristic performance has been determined it is required to find out where his or her habitual residence (in case of a physical person) or its central administration (for legal persons) is.[547] However, for contracts executed in the course of a party's trade or profession the convention takes into account the principle place of business instead of the habitual residence or central administration (Article 4.2).[548] Physical persons may be engaged in business activities and conduct them from a location different than their habitual residence. Likewise, legal persons may have their central administration and principal place of business in different locations. Nevertheless, the connecting factor of the principal place of business is also abandoned in favor of a non-principal place of business if it is the one in charge of performing the contract (Article 4.2).

iii)   The time of execution of the contract

The Rome Convention wants to determine a connecting factor which does not change in time. Therefore, the habitual residence or central administration of the person with the characteristic performance at the time of execution of the contract is the relevant one for determining the law applicable to the contract. This means that the exact point in time when the contract was entered into needs to be determined.[549] At that point in time the residence or central administration of the party with the characteristic performance is fixed. Subsequent changes to the habitual residence or central administration of the party with the characteristic performance do not affect the attributive factor. The applicable law will continue to be that of the habitual residence or central administration

---

[546]   *Clarkson / Hill*, Jaffey on Conflict of Laws, 2002, pp. 216-217; *Kronke, Applicable law in Torts and Contracts in Cyberspace*, in: Boele-Woelki / Kessedjian (Eds.), Internet – Which Court Decides? Which Law Applies?, Law and Electronic Commerce, Volume 5, 1998, pp. 74-75.

[547]   The Rome Convention does not define the concepts of habitual residence and central administration. According to *Mayss* the forum judge will define the terms according to the forum's law, see *Mayss*, The Principles of Conflict of Laws, 1996, p. 117.

[548]   *Chissick*, Electronic Commerce: Law and Practice, 1999, p. 117 ("Article 4(2) changes the presumption slightly for commercial contracts.").

[549]   The place where the contract is executed has no relevance in determining the applicable law, see *Giuliano / Lagarde*, Report on the Convention on the law applicable to contractual obligations, Article 4, para. 3.

that the party with the characteristic performance had at the time of entering into the contract.

b)   Other presumptions

In the search to elucidate which law is most closely connected to the contract the Rome Convention abandons for certain contracts the characteristic performance presumption. For special types of contracts other presumptions apply. Thus, contracts relating to real property are governed by the law of the country where the real property is located (Article 4.3).[550] Contracts for the carriage of goods are governed by the law of the country where the carrier has his principal place of business at the time the contract is entered into as long as that country is also the place of loading, discharge, or the consignor's principal place of business (Article 4.4).[551] Also, consumer contracts – analyzed below – and employment contracts are subject to special rules (Articles 5 and 6 respectively).[552]

3.   Consumer contracts

a)   Concept of consumer contract

Whether a contract is a consumer contract is determined based on the purpose for which a person acquires the goods or services. If goods or services are acquired for purposes falling outside the trade or profession of the buyer, then the contract is a consumer contract (Article 5.1). Furthermore, a credit contract for financing the acquisition of those goods or services is also considered a consumer contract (Article 5.1). In case of contracts partially for consumer purposes and partially for commercial purposes, the prevailing purpose will determine the nature of the contract.[553]

b)   Article 5.2 consumer contracts

Consumer contracts are subject to special rules if the seller has an active attitude towards the consumer; in other words, if the seller targets and directs the offer of products and services to that consumer.[554] The Rome Convention lists three

---

[550] The Rome I Regulation determines in Article 4.1(c) the law which is applicable to contracts dealing with rights in immovable property.

[551] The Rome I Regulation devotes Article 5 to contracts of carriage.

[552] Consumer contracts are regulated in Article 6 and employment contracts in Article 8 of the Rome I Regulation.

[553] *Giuliano / Lagarde*, Report on the Convention on the law applicable to contractual obligations, Article 5, para. 2.

[554] *Audit*, Droit International Privé, 2006, pp. 670-671. Nevertheless, certain consumer contracts are excluded. The rules of Article 5 do not apply to contracts of carriage, or certain services that are provided exclusively in a country that is not where the consumer resides, for example, hotel accommodation or language courses (Rome Convention Article 5.4.(a)) unless it is an "inclusive price" contract or a package

situations in which it is considered that consumers are passive and that the seller is the one taking the initiatives towards them (Article 5.2).[555] First, if the seller makes the offer in the country where the consumer resides and the consumer takes all relevant actions to execute the contract in that same place. Second, if the place of residence of the consumer is also the place where the order is received.[556] Third, if the consumer gives his or her purchase order in a foreign country because of arrangements made by the seller. Unlike the other two situations, in this case the contract is not entered into in the country where the consumer resides.[557]

c)   Freedom of choice

In a consumer contract the parties are free to choose the applicable law; therefore, the rules of Article 3 apply. Consequently, the power to choose the law for the whole contract or just for a part as well as to amend the governing law is fully applicable to consumer contracts. However, the mandatory consumer protection rules afforded by the country where the consumer has his or her habitual residence are applicable to consumer contracts falling within Article 5.2, irrespective of the law chosen by the parties (Article 5.2).[558] Therefore, the provisions more favorable to the consumer contained in the law of his or her place of residence remain applicable despite the valid choice of a foreign law.[559] On the contrary, if none of the Article 5.2 situations are present, then Article 3 apply without modifications and the contract is governed entirely by the law chosen by the parties.

---

tour (Rome Convention Article 5.5). See *Giuliano / Lagarde*, Report on the Convention on the law applicable to contractual obligations, Article 5, para. 5-6. The Rome I Regulation also excludes the consumer contracts listed in its Article 6.4.

[555] For the concept of passive and active consumers in online contracts and the application of the Rome Convention to those types of contracts see *Fallon / Meeusen*, Le commerce électronique, la directive 2000/31/CE et le droit international privé, Revue Critique de droit international privé, July-September 2002, 435, 445-449. The Rome I Regulation applies the consumer provision in two cases: when the seller pursues in or directs his activities to the country where the seller has his or her habitual residence (Article 6.1 (a) and (b)).

[556] For example, in a fair taking place in the country where the consumer resides or the consumer going to a branch of a company located in his or her country, see *Giuliano / Lagarde*, Report on the Convention on the law Applicable to contractual obligations, Article 5, para. 3.

[557] This is known as "border-crossing excursion-selling" and applies only to the sale of goods, see *Giuliano / Lagarde*, Report on the Convention on the law applicable to contractual obligations, Article 5, para. 3.

[558] The Rome I Regulation contains the same principle but uses the terminology „provisions that cannot be derogated from by agreement" (Article 6.2).

[559] *Audit*, Droit International Privé, 2006, p. 671.

d) Absence of choice

In case that the parties to a consumer contract did not make a choice of law, there is also a different regime depending on whether the contract falls under Article 5.2 or not. When the contract falls within any of the three cases listed in Article 5.2 the contract is governed by the law of the country where the consumer has his or her habitual residence. The residence of the consumer is the connecting point and the law of that country applies entirely – and not only its mandatory consumer protection rules as is the case when the parties make a choice of law. That means Article 4, determining the applicable law in absence of a choice, is excluded in its totality. If the contract does not fall within the cases listed in Article 5.2, the normal provisions of Article 4 apply to determine the applicable law.

D. Convention on the Law Applicable to Contracts for the International Sale of Goods

I.   Background

On December 22, 1986, the Hague Conference on Private International Law issued a new convention: the Convention on the Law Applicable to Contracts for the International Sale of Goods.[560] This convention took into account the developments made by CISG and was to replace the 1995 Convention on the Law Applicable to International Sales of Goods for states ratifying both conventions (Article 28). However, the 1986 Convention on the Law Applicable to Contracts for the International Sale of Goods has not yet entered into force.

II. International contracts

A contract for the international sale of goods has to trigger "a choice between the laws of different states" (Article 1b).[561] The domicile of the parties in different states is one of the triggering factors (Article 1a). The choice of law needs to arise from objective ties with different states; therefore, the convention regards as irrelevant for the determination of a contract as international the choice of a foreign law, even if accompanied by a choice of forum, for an otherwise domestic contract (Article 1b).

---

[560] For a brief analysis of this convention, see *Balestra*, Ley aplicable a los contratos de compraventa internacional de mercaderías, La Ley 1987-E, 752; *Marzorati*, Derecho de los negocios internacionales, Volume 1, 2003, pp. 190-198.

[561] According to *Lando* this Convention does not require a contract to be international, see *Lando*, The Conflict of Laws of Contracts – General Principles, 1985, pp. 287-288.

III. Formal validity

In the issue of the formal validity of a contract, the Convention on the Law Applicable to Contracts for the International Sale of Goods follows the approach of the Rome Convention and distinguishes whether the contracting parties – or their agents – are in the same country or not at the time of entering into the contract (Article 11). If the parties – or their agents – are in the same country, the formal validity of the contract is governed by the law of the country where the contract is executed (*lex loci contractus*) or by the law governing the contract (*lex causae*). If the parties – or their agents – are in different countries, the contract is formally valid if it complies with the law governing the contract (*lex causae*) or with one of the laws of the countries where the parties are.

The convention allows that contracting states make a reservation so as to exclude the application of the convention to the issue of the formal validity of the contract. The exclusion of the convention operates when the legislation of a state requires a contract to be executed or evidenced in writing and one of the contracting parties has his or her domicile in that state at the time of the execution of the contract (Article 11(5) and Article 21(1)(c)). Argentina is one of the countries that has signed and ratified the convention – however, as mentioned, the convention has not yet entered into force. In accordance with Article 21(1)(c) Argentina made a reservation stating that the convention does not apply to the formal validity of the contract when a party has the place of business or central administration in its territory at the time of the execution of the contract.

IV. Applicable law

Contracting parties have the freedom to choose the law applicable to their contract.[562] The choice may be made expressly or result unambiguously from the contract or conduct of the parties. The law chosen can govern the whole contract or just a part of it (Article 7(1)). The choice of law may be changed by the parties as long as neither the validity of the contract nor the right of third parties is affected (Article 7(2)). The contracting parties may limit the choice of law to a part of the contract.

Absent a choice of law by the parties, the connecting factor which determines the applicable law is the domicile of the seller at the time of execution of the contract, except in certain circumstances where the domicile of the buyer is the relevant one (Article 8.1 and 8.2). The domicile of the buyer is the one to take into account when most parts of the contract are linked to the country where the

---

[562] *Kronke*, Applicable law in Torts and Contracts in Cyberspace, in: Boele-Woelki / Kessedjian (Eds.), Internet – Which Court Decides? Which Law Applies?, Law and Electronic Commerce, Volume 5, 1998, pp. 75-77.

buyer is domiciled. Moreover, when elucidating the applicable law, conventions always try to find the country and, therefore, the legal system to which the contract is most closely connected. In this line, whenever the contract is "manifestly more closely connected with a law" other than the one that results from using the domicile connecting factor, the former law is to be applied (Article 8 (3)).

The law that results applicable either by the choice of the parties or by application of the rules of the convention may be the law of a non-contracting state (Article 6). The choice of law provisions of the applicable law are to be excluded (Article 15). In addition, the mandatory provisions of the law of the forum are applicable and prevail over the applicable law to the contract (Article 17). The designated law may be excluded only if manifestly incompatible with the public policy of the forum (Article 18).

E.   Inter-American Convention on the Law Applicable to International Contracts

I.   Background

The Inter-American Convention on the Law Applicable to International Contracts was adopted in Mexico in 1994 with the aim of harmonizing the rules of private international law of the country members of the Organization of American States.[563] However, as of this date only two states, Mexico and Venezuela, have ratified the convention. The convention has been in force in these two countries since December 15, 1996.[564]

II.   International contracts

The Inter-American Convention on the Law Applicable to International Contracts defines when a contract is international. According to Article 1, a contract is international if the contracting parties have their habitual residence or establishments in different contracting states, or if the contract has objective ties with more than one contracting state. Therefore, the convention requires the presence of an objective foreign element to consider a contract international.

---

[563] According to the information provided in: Organization of American States, Member states and permanent missions, <http://www.oas.org/documents/eng/mem berstates.asp>, "all 35 independent countries of the Americas have ratified the OAS Charter and belong to the Organization. Cuba remains a member, but its government has been excluded from participation in the OAS since 1962."

[564] Organization of American States, <http://www.oas.org/juridico/English/sigs/b-56.html>.

III. Formal validity

The Inter-American Convention on the Law Applicable to International Contracts distinguishes whether the parties are located in the same country at the time of execution of the contract or not (Article 13). However, unlike the criterion of the Rome Convention that subjects the formal validity of the contract to different laws depending on the location of the parties, the Inter-American Convention subjects the formal validity of the contract to the same laws in both cases. A contract is formally valid if it complies with the requirements of the law governing the contract, the law of the place of execution,[565] or the law of the place of performance.

IV. Applicable law

The Inter-American Convention allows the parties to choose the law applicable to the contract. The choice must result from an express provision in the agreement or it must be evident from the behavior of the parties and the provisions of the contract (Article 7). Therefore, the convention requires a real choice of law by the parties and does not allow courts to infer the intention of the parties in that respect. Therefore, when the choice of law is not express, it has to be evident for the judge which law the parties have chosen. In the same line, a choice of forum provision shall not be construed as an express agreement of the parties to designate the law of the forum as the applicable law (Article 7). However, a choice of forum provision may be taken into account to assess whether there is a tacit agreement on the applicable law.

The law chosen may later be changed as long as the change does not impinge on the formal validity of the contract nor on the rights of third parties (Article 8). The choice of law may embrace the whole contract or just a part of it (Section 7). The parts not covered by the choice of law are to be governed by the law resulting from the application of the choice of law provisions contained in the convention.

---

[565] The English and Spanish versions of Article 13 first paragraph are not equally drafted. The English version reads that the contract entered into between parties in the same country is formally valid if among others it meets the requirements "of the law of the State in which the contract is valid". On the other hand, the Spanish version states that the contract is formally valid if it meets the requirements *"fijados en el derecho del Estado en que se celebre"*, which means the law of the place of execution of the contract. Even though the English and Spanish versions have the same value (Article 30), the Spanish text seems to be more appropriate and also in line with the second paragraph of Article 13, which refers to the place of execution for determining the law for contracts entered into by parties in different states.

In the case there is no choice of law, the contract is governed by the law of the country with the closest ties to the contract (Article 9). The judge shall make that determination taking into account all objective and subjective elements of the contract. There is one exception to the rule of the closest ties and it is for determining whether a party has duly consented to the contract or not. In that case, the law of the habitual residence or principal place of business is to govern that particular matter (Article 12 second paragraph). Exceptionally, a part of the contract may be subject to a law to which it has closer connections (Article 9). However, that part must be separable from the rest and have a closer connection to another state (Article 9).

The law chosen by the parties or the one designated by the judge shall yield to the mandatory rules of the forum. Also, the mandatory rules of a law closely connected to the contract may result applicable (Article 11).

F.   UNIDROIT Principles of International Commercial Contracts

I.   Background

The International Institute for the Unification of Private Law (UNIDROIT) is an international body whose main function is to work towards the harmonization and coordination of private law between states (UNIDROIT Statute, Articles 1 and 2.1). UNIDROIT dates from 1926 and used to be a body of the League of Nations.[566] It later became an independent organization through the adoption of its Statute on March 15, 1940.[567] Currently sixty-one states are members of UNIDROIT.[568]

One of its most successful works in harmonizing private law is the UNIDROIT Principles of International Commercial Contracts (UNIDROIT Principles).[569] UNIDROIT issued a first version in 1994 and a second edition ten years later, in 2004. The UNIDROIT Principles contain substantive rules on contract law.

---

[566] UNIDROIT, <http://www.unidroit.org/english/presentation/main.htm>.
[567] UNIDROIT, <http://www.unidroit.org/english/presentation/main.htm>.
[568] UNIDROIT, <http://www.unidroit.org/english/presentation/main.htm>.
[569] *Bonell*, UNIDROIT Principles 2004 – The New Edition of the Principles of International Commercial Contracts adopted by the International Institute for the Unification of Private Law, Uniform Law Review, 2004, p. 6; *Hartkamp*, Principles of contract law, in: Grosheide / Hondius (Eds.), International Contract Law, 2004, pp. 172-174.

II. International contracts

As its name indicates, the UNIDROIT Principles apply to and set forth the rules for international commercial contracts.[570] The UNIDROIT Principles do not define international contract and the omission is intentional.[571] There are multiple criteria to determine the international character of a contract and the UNIDROIT Principles prefer to remain neutral in this respect so as to avoid restricting the concept of international contract. However, according to the official comment a contract shall be considered international when an international element is present.[572] Contrarily, a contract is not deemed international when there are no international elements involved; in other words, "where all the relevant elements of the contract in question are connected with one country only".[573]

III. Formal validity

The UNIDROIT Principles contain material rules concerning the formal requirements of a contract. A contract governed by the UNIDROIT Principles does not need to comply with any particular form (Article 1.2). Freedom of forms is the rule and the contracting parties are able to choose the form that they consider more appropriate for the transaction. Nevertheless, mandatory requirements as to form established by norms of national, international or supranational origin remain applicable (Article 1.4). For example, if the contract is governed by Argentine law and under Argentine law a contract is to be in writing, this form requirement is still valid. Likewise, forms may be mandatory if so established by the parties (Articles 2.1.13 and 2.1.18).

IV. Applicable law

The UNIDROIT Principles apply when the parties to a contract have so agreed (Preamble).[574] The parties can also exclude or modify its application (Article 1.5). Nevertheless, the UNIDROIT Principles may apply even if the parties have not expressly stated so. It is enough that the parties agree that the contract is to

---

[570] UNIDROIT Principles, Preamble.
[571] UNIDROIT Principles, Official Comment, Preamble, para. 1.
[572] UNIDROIT Principle, Official Comment, Preamble, para. 1.
[573] UNIDROIT Principle, Official Comment, Preamble, para. 1.
[574] *Drobnig,* The use of the UNIDROIT Principles by National and Supranational Courts, in: Institute of International Business Law and Practice – International Chamber of Commerce, UNIDROIT Principles for International Commercial Contracts: A new lex mercatoria?, 1995, pp. 225.

be governed by the general principles of the law or by the *lex mercatoria* (Preamble).[575]

The application of the UNIDROIT Principles does not preclude the application of mandatory law (Article 1.4). The UNIDROIT Principles are not enforceable law; that is why it is debatable whether parties may choose them as the applicable law to the contract.[576] For that reason, for contracting parties wishing to have their contracts governed by the UNIDROIT Principles it is safer to subject their contract to arbitration.[577]

---

[575] *Bonell*, UNIDROIT Principles 2004 – The New Edition of the Principles of International Commercial Contracts adopted by the International Institute for the Unification of Private Law, Uniform Law Review, 2004, p. 13. The UNIDROIT Principles may also serve as guidance for construing or filling the gaps of national and international law (UNIDROIT Principles, Preamble), see *Drobnig*, The use of the UNIDROIT Principles by National and Supranational Courts, in: Institute of International Business Law and Practice – International Chamber of Commerce, UNIDROIT Principles for International Commercial Contracts: A new lex mercatoria?, 1995, pp. 227-228; *Bonell*, UNIDROIT Principles 2004 – The New Edition of the Principles of International Commercial Contracts adopted by the International Institute for the Unification of Private Law, Uniform Law Review, 2004, pp. 13-16.

[576] The majority opinion finds that the UNIDROIT Principles may not be chosen as the applicable law to the contract, see *Martiny*, in: Münchener Kommentar zum Bürgerlichen Gesetzbuch, 4th Edition, 2006, Section 27 EGBGB, marginal number 33; *Heldrich*, in: Palandt, Bürgerliches Gesetzbuch, 68th Edition, 2009, Section 27 EGBGB, marginal numbers 1 and 3 (However, the author states that it would be possible to choose the UNIDROIT Principles if permitted by the relevant legal system but it is not the case under German law); *Calvo Caravaca / Carrascosa González*, Conflictos de leyes y conflictos de jurisdicción en Internet, 2001, pp. 59-60 (Non-national law is applicable only if allowed by the law of the contract.); *Drobnig*, The use of the UNIDROIT Principles by National and Supranational Courts, in: Institute of International Business Law and Practice – International Chamber of Commerce, UNIDROIT Principles for International Commercial Contracts: A new lex mercatoria?, 1995, pp. 226-227. With a different view: *Hartkamp*, The use of the UNIDROIT Principles of International Commercial Contracts by National and Supranational Courts, in: Institute of International Business Law and Practice – International Chamber of Commerce, UNIDROIT Principles for International Commercial Contracts: A new lex mercatoria?, 1995, p. 256. The possibility to modify Article 3 of the Rome Convention in order to allow parties to choose non-national law was under consideration, see *Marella*, Choice of Law in the Third-Millennium Arbitrations: The Relevance of the UNIDROIT Principles of International Commercial Contracts, Vanderbilt Journal of Transnational Law, Volume 36, May 2003, 1137, 1142.

[577] UNIDROIT Principles, Official Comments, comment on the Preamble, para. 4a; *Bonell*, UNIDROIT Principles 2004 – The New Edition of the Principles of International Commercial Contracts adopted by the International Institute for the

G.   United Nations Convention on the Use of Electronic Communications in International Contracts

I.   Background

Aware of the increasing use of electronic communications in international trade and within its powers to further the harmonization of international trade law, UNCITRAL prepared the Convention on the Use of Electronic Communications in International Contracts. This convention has not yet entered into force.

II.   International contracts

The Convention on the Use of Electronic Communications in International Contracts determines the international character of a contract based on the location of the places of business of the contracting parties (Article 1.1). A contract is deemed international when the parties have their places of business in different states.

UNCITRAL decided to follow the same criterion adopted in CISG. Other criteria were considered such as the place of formation or center of gravity of the contract; however, the decision to adopt the criterion of the location of the places of business of the parties was based on the fact that it had been the traditional criterion used by UNCITRAL as well as on the difficulty of applying the other two criteria mentioned. The criterion of the place of formation of the contract may be especially cumbersome to apply to an electronic contract where it might be difficult to determine the place from where a message was sent or received.[578]

The Convention on the Use of Electronic Communications in International Contracts contains, unlike CISG, a definition of place of business. Place of business means "any place where a party maintains a non-transitory establishment to pursue an economic activity other than the temporary provision of goods or services out of a specific location" (Article 4(h)). The place of business of the parties is linked to a physical place and it is presumed to be the place indicated by the contracting party (Article 6.1). Consequently, the location of the equipment, the place where the information can be accessed or the

---

Unification of Private Law, Uniform Law Review, 2004, pp. 10-12; *Hartkamp*, Principles of contract law, in: Grosheide / Hondius (Eds.), International Contract Law, 2004, pp. 176-177. For the application of the UNIDROIT Principle in arbitrations, see *Marzorati*, Derecho de los negocios internacionales o Derecho Internacional de los negocios, La Ley 2005-E, 1418 (The author summarizes some arbitration decisions based on the UNIDROIT Principles.).

[578] UNCITRAL, Working Group IV (Electronic Commerce), Thirty-ninth session, Legal aspects of electronic commerce – Electronic contracting: provisions for a draft convention, Note by the Secretariat, 2001, (A/CN.9/WG.IV/WP.95), pp. 8-9.

country identified in the domain name or electronic e-mail address are, on their own, not conclusive of the place of business of a party (Articles 6.4 and 6.5). The underlying reason for this approach is to avoid having different places of business depending on whether the contract was executed electronically or not.

III. Formal validity

The convention adopts the principle of freedom of forms and, therefore, it does not require any particular formal requirement for the execution of contracts (Article 9).[579] However, the Convention on the Use of Electronic Communication in International Contracts does not derogate the form requirements established by national law; therefore, if a law requires a contract to be in writing, that requirement remains unmodified. In other words, the convention does not interfere with national law; simply aims at allowing the compliance of domestic formal requirements by electronic means. This is an important difference with CISG. Under CISG a contract does not have to comply with any requirement with respect to form (unless a reservation according to Articles 12 and 96 is made). CISG prevails over the formal requirements imposed by national law. In contrast, the freedom of forms established in the Convention on the Use of Electronic Communications in International Contracts does not prevail over formal requirements of national law; that means, if the law governing the contract imposes a formal requirement, it has to be fulfilled. In this manner, the requirement of a writing and a signature imposed by national law are still applicable but they can be met by means of an electronic communication or an electronic signature – only to this extent is domestic law modified.[580]

The same is the case with the requirement of a signature. The convention defers to national law the determination of whether a signature is required. However, if a signature is required, it is possible that the parties sign with electronic signatures. It should be noted that the term electronic signature is not used in the text of the convention but in the Explanatory Notes by the UNCITRAL Secretariat.

Nevertheless, the convention provides a uniform standard for the assessment of whether an electronic signature complies with the legal requirements. The

---

[579] UNCITRAL, Explanatory note by the UNCITRAL secretariat on the United Nations Convention on the Use of Electronic Communications in International Contracts, in: United Nations Convention on the Use of Electronic Communications in International Contracts, 2007, p. 49, para. 136.

[580] UNCITRAL, Explanatory note by the UNCITRAL secretariat on the United Nations Convention on the Use of Electronic Communications in International Contracts, in: United Nations Convention on the Use of Electronic Communications in International Contracts, 2007, p. 49, para. 137.

electronic signature has to be reliable in order to fulfill the requirements of a signature (Article 9.3). The analysis of whether a signature is reliable will be influenced by the legal approach adopted in each country concerning the recognition of electronic signatures. It is quite likely that Argentina and Germany demand high standards for establishing the reliability of an electronic signature on account of the fact that their national legislation requires the use of signatures based on public key cryptography when the law establishes the signature requirement. Contrarily, the concept of reliability is much more flexible and open to different techniques in US law. However, when construing the convention, courts are to bear in mind the international origin of the convention (Article 5.1). Therefore, a more flexible approach adopted by foreign courts may have an impact on those countries with stricter standards for electronic signatures. Consequently, it is still to be seen whether any progress is achieved in the harmonization of electronic signature rules through this new convention.

IV. Applicable law

The Convention on the Use of Electronic Communications in International Contracts is a convention providing material rules for the issues of formation and performance of contracts using electronic communications.

The convention applies if the parties are domiciled in different states and aware of this situation (Article 1). However, there is no requirement that the states be contracting states nor is included a provision similar to Article 1(1)(b) of CISG whereby the convention applies if it is in force in the country whose law governs the contract. Therefore, it is enough that the contracting parties have their domiciles in different states and that the law chosen is that of a contracting state.[581]

Nevertheless, the convention allows states to declare the convention applicable only when the domiciles are in contracting states (Article 19.1(a)). Also, it is possible to limit the scope of application of the convention to contracts where parties have agreed to its application. For this option to be applicable a state has to make a declaration allowing that option (Article 19.1(b)). The nationality of the parties does not play a role in determining the application of the convention (Article 1 (3)).

---

[581] UNCITRAL, Explanatory note by the UNCITRAL secretariat on the United Nations Convention on the Use of Electronic Communications in International Contracts, in: United Nations Convention on the Use of Electronic Communications in International Contracts, 2007, p. 14, para 6. and pp. 29-30, para. 60-63.

Certain transactions are excluded from the scope of application of the convention (Article 2) and the parties may exclude the convention as a whole or modify its provisions (Article 3).

H. Conclusions

The analysis of international conventions on topics of international contracts allows tackling the issue of the formal validity of contracts from an international perspective. The conventions recognize the formal validity of a contract if it complies with the formal requirements of at least the law governing the substance or of the law of the place of execution. That is the case of the Rome Convention, the Convention on the Law Applicable to Contracts for the International Sale of Goods and the Inter-American Convention on the Law Applicable to International Contracts. The Rome Convention even simplifies the rules for contracts with parties in different countries disregarding the place where they are executed. On the other hand, conventions and international instruments containing material norms adopt the principle of freedom of forms (CISG, Convention on the Use of Electronic Communications in International Contracts, and the UNIDROIT Principles). The goal is to seek to free contracts from formal requirements or to subject the formal validity of the contract to several laws so as to facilitate the execution of formally valid contracts. Moreover, the conventions dealing with applicable law recognize the freedom of the parties to choose the law applicable to the contract. Therefore, the parties can choose the law that will govern the formal validity of the contract by designating that law as the law of the contract.

However, the conventions have not been ratified by several states with the exception of CISG and the Rome Convention (which, however, entered into force more than a decade after its enactment). This shows how difficult it is to achieve uniformity within the international sphere. Even when conventions are ratified it is possible that states make valid use of the exceptions and subject the formal validity to national law. That is the case of Argentina with regard to CISG and the Inter-American Convention on the Law Applicable to International Contracts.

The issue of the law governing the formal validity of a contract arises when the contract is international. The conventions follow in general an objective approach to the concept of internationality in contracts (Convention on the Law Applicable to International Sales of Goods, United Nations Convention on Contracts for the International Sale of Goods, Convention on the Law Applicable to Contracts for the International Sale of Goods, Inter-American Convention on the Law Applicable to International Contracts, UNIDROIT Principles of International Commercial Contracts, United Nations Convention on the Use of Electronic Communications in International Contracts). However, the Rome Convention considers international a contract that except for the inclusion of the choice of law provision would be regarded as domestic.

Chapter 9: The international contract under domestic law

The concept of international contract, its formal validity and the law applicable to it will be analyzed in three national legal systems: Argentina, Germany and the United States of America.

A. Argentine law

I. International contracts

The domestic rules of private international law contained in the Argentine Civil Code do not define when a contract is international. However, from its provisions it follows that the Argentine Civil Code takes into account the place of execution and the place of performance of a contract to determine whether it is international or not. The disassociation between the place of execution and the place of performance is what renders a contract international.[582] Consequently, if a contract is executed in one country and performed in another, it is considered international. In turn, if the places of execution and performance are in the same country, the contract is domestic. This reasoning can be inferred from Sections 1209 and 1210 of the Argentine Civil Code which determine the law applicable to a contract when its place of execution and its place of performance are not in the same country. The Argentine Civil Code excludes the nationality of the parties as an element for characterizing a contract as domestic or international (Section 1210).

Argentine law also encompasses international treaties and conventions. Thus, the concept of international contract has broaden through the international treaties and conventions Argentina has ratified, such as CISG, which considers international a contract based on the domicile of the parties in different states. This is the same criterion of the Protocol of Buenos Aires on International Jurisdiction in Contractual Matters (Buenos Aires Protocol).[583] The Buenos Aires Protocol was signed in Buenos Aires, Argentina, on August 5, 1994, and establishes the rules to elucidate the proper forum in issues arising out of international contracts within the Mercosur (*Mercado Común del Sur* - Southern Common Market).[584] The Buenos Aires Protocol does not define the concept of

---

[582] *Lorenzo Idiarte*, ¿Cuándo un contrato es internacional?, Análisis desde una perspectiva regional, in: Kleinheitsterkamp / Lorenzo Idiarte (Eds.), Avances del Derecho Internacional Privado en América Latina, 2002, p. 124; *Marzorati*, Derecho de los negocios internacionales o Derecho Internacional de los negocios, La Ley 2005-E, 1418.

[583] *Protocolo de Buenos Aires sobre Jurisdicción Internacional en Materia Contractual*. Contained in the Decision 01/94 of the Council of Common Market.

[584] The Protocol entered into force on June 6, 1996 for Paraguay and Brazil, on November 30, 1996 for Argentina and on August 28, 2004 for Uruguay, see

international contract. However, the sphere of application provision considers the domicile of the parties for its application. Therefore, contracts entered into between parties domiciled in different contracting states may be considered international.[585]

In turn, the Inter-American Convention on General Rules of Private International Law (1979) follows a more abstract and wider approach.[586] The convention sets forth the rules to determine the applicable law to "facts connected with foreign law" (Article 1). Therefore, the key idea is that internationality is present when there are facts connected with a foreign law. The convention does not specify when a fact[587] is connected to a foreign law but it is sustained that the term fact makes reference to objective standards.[588]

<www.mre.gov.py/paginas/boletines/tratados/anteriores/Boletin2972004.asp>. The Mercosur is composed of four full members: Argentina, Brazil, Paraguay and Uruguay. In turn, Chile, Bolivia, Peru, Ecuador, Colombia are associate members. Venezuela, currently an associate member, is in the process of becoming a full member by means of the Adhesion Protocol of July 4, 2006, see <http://www.merc osur.int/msweb/portal%20intermediario/es/index.htm>. The Adhesion Protocol has been ratified by Argentina and Uruguay. As of September 2009, the ratifications of Brazil and Paraguay are still pending. Nevertheless, Venezuela has been authorized to participate in the meetings dealing with economic and commercial matters which are reserved for the full members (Decision 29/05 of the Council of Common Market available at <http://www.mercosur.int/msweb/portal%20interme diario/es/index.htm>).

[585] The Buenos Aires Protocol applies if both parties have their domiciles in different Mercosur member states (Article 1(a)). If this is not the case, the Buenos Aires Protocol may nonetheless be applicable if the three following requirements are met: one of the parties has his or her domicile in a Mercosur member state, a choice of forum provision exists in favor of a court of a member state, and the connection is reasonable (Section 1(b)).

[586] The Inter-American Convention on General Rules of Private International Law was adopted, alongside with six other conventions and a protocol, in the Second Inter-American Specialized Conference on Private International (CIDIP-II) law held in Montevideo, Uruguay in 1979. See Organization of American States, CIDIP-II, <http://www.oas.org/dil/CIDIPII_home.htm>. The Inter-American Convention on General Rules of Private International Law entered into force on October 6, 1981 and is in force in Argentina, Brazil, Colombia, Ecuador, Guatemala, Mexico, Paraguay, Peru, Uruguay and Venezuela. See Organization of American States, <http://www.oas.org/juridico/english/sigs/b-45.html>.

[587] In the Spanish version the word *situaciones* is used.

[588] *Lorenzo Idiarte*, ¿Cuándo un contrato es internacional?, Análisis desde una perspectiva regional, in: Kleinheitsterkamp / Lorenzo Idiarte (Eds.), Avances del Derecho Internacional Privado en América Latina, 2002, pp. 117-118.

Argentine legal scholars have taken different approaches with regard to the concept of international contract.[589] *Goldschmidt* considers a contract international when the place of execution of the contract, the domicile of one of the parties at the time of the execution of the contract, or the place of performance of the contract is in a foreign country.[590] According to *Boggiano* the relevant factor is that the contract is international from an objective perspective.[591] Thus, a contract is international either because the parties have their domiciles in different countries at the moment the contract is entered into, the performance takes place abroad, or the obligations of the parties link the contract to other countries (economic criterion).[592]

Feldstein de Cárdenas provides a very accurate concept of international contract establishing that it is the one that presents relevant objective foreign elements during its formation, performance or termination from the point of view of a determined legal system.[593] According to this definition, the concept of international contract is not limited to fixed connecting points but allows considering different elements that may render a contract international. Moreover, it reinforces the idea that the concept of international contract depends on the elements considered relevant by a particular legal system, it being therefore possible that different jurisdictions take dissimilar approaches. Also, it is required that the connections are objective excluding the internationalization of the contract by the sole will of the parties.[594] This is the main trend in Argentina, to require that a contract has objective contacts with a foreign law. However, there are views following a much wider approach. *Kaller de Orchansky* distinguishes between contracts that are objectively international because the domicile of the parties or the places of execution and performance are in different countries and contracts that are domestic but that the parties render international because of the choice of a foreign tribunal or law.[595]

---

[589] *Lorenzo Idiarte*, ¿Cuándo un contrato es internacional?, Análisis desde una perspectiva regional, in: Kleinheitsterkamp / Lorenzo Idiarte (Eds.), Avances del Derecho Internacional Privado en América Latina, 2002, pp. 125-126.
[590] *Goldschmidt*, Derecho Internacional Privado, 2002, p. 393. With the same view: *Weinberg*, Contratos internacionales, La Ley 1984-C, 915.
[591] *Boggiano*, Contratos Internacionales – International Contracts, 1995, p. 39 (The author refers to an "objectively international" contract.).
[592] *Boggiano*, Derecho Internacional Privado, Volume II, 2006, p. 175.
[593] *Feldstein de Cárdenas*, Derecho Internacional Privado – Parte Especial, 2000, p. 343.
[594] *Feldstein de Cárdenas*, Derecho Internacional Privado – Parte Especial, 2000, p. 350.
[595] *Kaller de Orchansky*, in: Bueres / Highton (Eds.), Código Civil, 2005, Volume 3C, Sections 1205 to 1210, p. 72.

II. Formal validity

According to private international law of domestic origin, the formal validity of a contract is always governed by the law of the place of execution (*lex loci celebrationis*) (Sections 12 and 950 Argentine Civil Code). Thus, the Argentine Civil Code follows the principle *locus regit actum.* Form is defined as the solemnities required at the time of execution of the act (Section 973 Argentine Civil Code).[596]

Therefore, contracting parties do not have several laws to choose from when it comes to the law determining the formal requirements of a contract. However, the predominant view is that the principle *locus regit actum* is not mandatory; therefore, the form of the contract may be subject to other laws.[597] The laws that might determine the formal validity of an international contract are the law applicable to the contract (*lex causae),* the law which a contract has a reasonable contact with, or even any law that the parties especially choose to govern the form.[598]

It should be noted that *Goldschmidt* differentiates between three aspects to be determined when answering the question of the law governing the form. The first step is to determine which law is going to establish the formal requirements; the second, which law governs the implementation of the form imposed, and lastly, the law establishing the formal requirements shall determine the equivalence of the form chosen with the form required by law.[599]

The principle of *locus regit actum* applies whenever contracts are entered into between parties that are in the presence of each other (*inter praesentes*). However, the rule is abandoned for contracts entered into *inter absentes* (Section 1181 Argentine Civil Code).[600] There are two different scenarios concerning

---

[596] *Santos Cifuentes,* in: Belluscio / Zannoni (Eds.), Código Civil, Volume 4, 2001, Section 973, pp. 457-465; *Cabanellas,* Diccionario de Derecho Usual, Volume II, 1974, s.v. "Forma".

[597] *Goldschmidt,* Derecho Internacional Privado, 2002, p. 265.

[598] *Boggiano,* Derecho Internacional Privado, Volume II, 2006, pp. 213-214; *Feldstein de Cárdenas,* Derecho Internacional Privado – Parte Especial, 2000, pp. 262-263 and 280.

[599] *Goldschmidt,* Derecho Internacional Privado, 2002, p.266. This theory has been recognized by the Argentine Supreme Court of Justice in the case Méndez Valles vs. Pescio S.C.A., December 26, 1995, Fallos 318:2639; *Feldstein de Cárdenas,* Derecho Internacional Privado – Parte Especial, 2000, pp. 283-284. The ruling is also well-known for modifying previous case law and establishing that the interpretation of international treaties always involves a federal matter for an extraordinary appeal (*recurso extraordinario*) before the Supreme Court.

[600] *Smith,* in: Belluscio / Zannoni (Eds.), Código Civil, Volume 5, 2002, Section 1181, pp. 817-821; *Mosset Iturraspe,* in: Bueres / Highton (Eds.), Código Civil, Volume 3B, 2005, Section 1181, pp. 661-663.

contracts entered into between absent parties (Section 1181 Argentine Civil Code). The first one is when the contract is signed in a private instrument by one of the parties. In that case the formal validity of the contract is governed by the law of the place indicated in the instrument. The second scenario is a contract entered into through several private instruments signed in several places. Here the law most favorable to the formal validity of the contract applies.[601] The Argentine Civil Code does not specify the laws among which it is to be decided which one the most favorable is. Nevertheless, only those laws with an objective and real link to the contract will most likely be the ones taken into account.

In the case of electronic contracts, when dealing with the situation described in the second scenario, that is, a contract signed in several places, it has to be analyzed which electronic signature legislation is most favorable to the formal validity of the contract. In this analysis the formal requirements imposed by each law shall be taken into account. If one law does not impose formal requirements, then that law will most likely be the one most favorable to the contract. In the event that all laws require the written form and a signature, the electronic signature statues shall be compared.

III. Applicable law

1. Party autonomy

Parties to an international contract have the power to choose the law applicable to the contract.[602] This principle is not expressly stated in norms of national character but it is contained in international treaties to which Argentina is a party. Also, the principle has been recognized by case law[603] and legal scholars.[604] Therefore, the norms of the Argentine Civil Code determining the

---

[601] *Spota*, Instituciones de Derecho Civil – Contratos, Volume III, 1975, pp. 171-172.
[602] Nevertheless, the freedom of the parties to choose the applicable law is subject to certain restraints. See *Feldstein de Cárdenas*, Derecho Internacional Privado – Parte Especial, 2000, pp. 349-352; La Buenos Aires Cía. de seguros vs. Capitán y/o Arm. y/o Prop. Buque Gladiator, Argentine Supreme Court of Justice, August 25, 1998, Fallos 321:2297. Argentine law does not only recognize the power of the parties to choose an applicable law but also to draft their own material provisions, see *Boggiano*, Derecho Internacional Privado, Volume II, 2006, pp. 176-187; La Buenos Aires Cía de Seguros vs. Capitán y/o Arm. y/o Prop. Buque Gladiator, Argentine Supreme Court of Justice, August 25, 1998, La Ley 1998-F, 16.
[603] Tactician Int. Corp. y otros vs. Dirección Gral. de Fabricaciones Militares, Argentine Supreme Court of Justice, March 15, 1994, Fallos 317:182; Méndez Valles, Fernando vs. Pescio, A., Argentine Supreme Court of Justice, December 26, 1995, Fallos 318:2639.
[604] *Boggiano*, Derecho Internacional Privado, Volume II, 2006, pp. 172-176; *Goldschmidt*, Derecho Internacional Privado, 2002, pp. 191-202; *Weinberg*, Contratos internacionales, La Ley 1984-C, 915.

proper law of the contract are applicable only when the parties have not made a choice of law.[605]

Under Argentine law party autonomy is recognized in objective international contracts.[606] This means that the parties may not subject a domestic contract to a foreign law and, consequently, the choice of a foreign law requires the preexistence of an objective international contract.

2.   Absence of a choice of law

In case the parties do not make a choice of law, the Argentine Civil Code follows fixed points of connection to determine the applicable law to a contract. The rules of the Argentine Civil Code apply to all type of contracts regardless of whether they were executed electronically or not.[607] Section 1205 of the Argentine Civil Code states that contracts executed abroad are to be governed by the law of the place of execution. On the other hand, Section 1209 of the Argentine Civil Code applies Argentine law to contracts to be performed in Argentina regardless of the place where they have been executed. Therefore, despite the rule of Section 1205 establishing the application of the law of the place of execution, if a contract is performed in Argentina, it is subject to Argentine law even if executed abroad. In turn, Section 1210 of the Argentine Civil Code determines applicable the law of the place of performance in the case of contracts executed in Argentina but to be performed abroad. Again, the law of the place of performance prevails. Therefore, Section 1205 applies the connecting point of the place of execution and Sections 1209 and 1210 follow the connecting point of the place of performance.

In order to construe these three sections coherently, legal scholars distinguish between contracts with and without Argentine contacts.[608] When a contract does not have contacts with Argentina the law of the place of execution applies –

---

[605] Transportes Mabellini, S. A. vs. Expofrut, S. R. L., Commercial First Instance Court No. 13, July 29, 1977, La Ley 1980-B, 378.

[606] *Goldschmidt*, Derecho Internacional Privado, 2002, p. 393; *Feldstein de Cárdenas*, Derecho Internacional Privado – Parte Especial, 2000, p. 350; *Boggiano*, Derecho Internacional Privado, Volume I, 2006, p. 437 and Volume II , 2006, p. 175.

[607] *Marzorati*, Reflexiones sobre jurisdicción y ley aplicable en internet, in: Kleinheisterkamp / Lorenzo Idiarte (Eds.), Avances del Derecho Internacional Privado en América Latina, 2002, pp. 322-324.

[608] *Smith*, in: Belluscio / Zannoni (Eds.), Código Civil, Volume 5, 2002, Section 1205, pp. 1018-1019 and Sections 1215 and 1216, pp. 1033-1034; *Goldschmidt*, Derecho Internacional Privado, 2002, pp. 393-394; *Boggiano*, Derecho Internacional Privado, Volume II, 2006, p. 195; *Feldstein de Cárdenas*, Derecho Internacional Privado – Parte Especial, 2000, pp. 359-360; *Weinberg*, Contratos internacionales, La Ley 1984-C, 915; *Kaller de Orchansky*, in: Bueres / Highton (Eds.), Código Civil, Volume 3C, 2005, Sections 1205 to 1210, pp. 73-74.

regardless of where the place of performance is. Thus, a contract executed abroad to be performed either in that same country or in another foreign country is governed by the law of the place of execution (Section 1205).[609] Consequently, in order to determine the applicable law to contracts which lack contacts with Argentina it is not relevant whether the foreign contract is domestic or international. Contrarily, for contracts with Argentine contacts the law of the place of performance governs. Sections 1209 and 1210 reflect this principle from two different angles: when the contract is to be performed in Argentina (Section 1209) and when the contract is to be performed in a foreign country (Section 1210). The nationality of the parties is of no relevance for the determination of the applicable law (Sections 1209 and 1210).

The application of different rules to contracts with and without contacts with Argentina is also sustained by the wording of Sections 1209 and 1210 of the Argentine Civil Code. Section 1209, determining the law applicable to contracts to be performed in Argentina, expressly refers to contracts executed in or outside the Argentine Republic. Therefore, all contracts to be performed in Argentina are governed by Argentine law regardless of their place of execution. In turn, Section 1210, dealing with contracts to be performed outside Argentina, embraces only contracts entered into in Argentina excluding from its scope contracts entered into abroad to be performed abroad, which are governed by Section 1205.[610]

Sections 1209 and 1210 of the Argentine Civil Code indicate that *Story* is their main source;[611] however, the Argentine Civil Code deviates from the theory of *Story* and introduces different rules depending on the country where the contract was executed and performed. The majority of Argentine legal scholars construe this approach in the need to find a middle point between *Savigny's* ideas – subjecting the contract to the law of the place of performance because this is the

---

[609] *Smith*, in: Belluscio / Zannoni (Eds.), Código Civil, Volume 5, 2002, Section 1205, pp. 1018-1019 (Contracts executed abroad and with incidental performance in Argentina also fall, according to the author, within the scope of Section 1205.).

[610] Contracts governed by a foreign law which are deemed immoral or against the rights and interests of the nation are not to be recognized (Section 1206 Argentine Civil Code). Likewise, contracts entered into in one country that infringe the law of another country are not valid (Sections 1207 and 1208 Argentine Civil Code). Therefore, contracts entered into in Argentina that infringe laws of another country and contracts entered into abroad that infringe the laws of Argentina have no value even when valid in the place where executed.

[611] The wording of Sections 1206 to 1209, as indicated by their footnotes, are inspired in the work of *Story*, see *Story*, Commentaries on the Conflict of Laws, 2007, pp. 203 *et seq.*

place where it has its main seat,[612] and *Story's* ideas – applying the law of the place of execution of the contract[613].[614]

3. Place of performance

International contracts with contacts to Argentina are governed by the law of the place of performance (Sections 1209 and 1210 of the Argentine Civil Code). The Argentine Civil Code follows *Savigny's* ideas concerning the determination of the place of performance.[615] The place of performance of a contract is determined, in the first place, based on what is stated in the contract (Section 1212 Argentine Civil Code). When a contract determines the place of performance that is the clearest evidence of where the contract is going to be performed.

Another element to elucidate the place of performance is the nature of the contractual obligations (Section 1212 Argentine Civil Code).[616] If not possible to determine the place of performance based on these two criteria, the law deems that the place of performance is the place where the contract was entered into as long as it coincides with the domicile of the debtor (Section 1212 Argentine Civil Code). In case the contract was entered into at a place that was not the domicile of the debtor, then the current domicile of the debtor is considered the place of performance even if it is not the same he or she had at the time the contract was entered into (Section 1213 Argentine Civil Code).[617]

However, in a contract with bilateral obligations it is necessary to determine which obligation and which debtor Sections 1212 and 1213 are referring to.

---

[612] *von Savigny*, System des heutigen deutschen Recht, Volume 8, 1974, pp. 200 *et seq.*

[613] However, Story clarifies that the principle of *locus regit actum* is applicable when execution and performance take place in the same place; therefore, when the place of execution and performance are different the law of the place of performance may be applicable, see *Story*, Commentaries on the Conflict of Laws, 2007, pp. 233.

[614] *Feldstein de Cárdenas*, Derecho Internacional Privado – Parte Especial, 2000, p. 360; *Goldschmidt*, Derecho Internacional Privado, 2002, p. 394. According to *Boggiano* the private international norms contained in the Argentine Civil Code follow the ideas of *Savigny* and only exceptionally follow *Story*, see *Boggiano*, Derecho Internacional Privado, Volume I, 2006, p. 41.

[615] *von Savigny*, System des heutigen deutschen Recht, Volume 8, 1974, p. 247.

[616] For example, services that must be provided in a certain place or the sale of real property, see *Kaller de Orchansky*, in: Bueres / Highton (Eds.), Código Civil, Volume 3C, 2005, Sections 1212 and 1213, p. 75.

[617] *Kaller de Orchansky*, in: Bueres / Highton (Eds.), Código Civil, Volume 3C, 2005, Sections 1212 and 1213, pp. 74-76.

Case law[618] and legal scholars[619] have followed the concept of the most characteristic performance.[620] The characteristic performance approach is also used in the Rome Convention, which determines the applicable law to the contract based on the domicile of the characteristic performer at the time of the execution of the contract. However, under Argentine law the determination of the applicable law is based on the place where the characteristic performance takes place. If it is not possible to determine it, only then the connecting factor of the domicile of the party with the most characteristic performance is applied.[621]

The mentioned rules apply to contracts between present parties. For contracts entered into between absent parties (the Argentine Civil Code refers to contracts signed in different places, through agents or by post), the contract is governed by the place of performance if that place is determined (Section 1214 Argentine Civil Code).[622] When the place of performance is not designated, the contract is governed with respect to each party by the law of his or her domicile (Section 1214 Argentine Civil Code).[623] This approach has been criticized because of the inconvenience of having different laws instead of one law applicable to the contract.[624]

---

[618] *Feldstein de Cárdenas*, Derecho Internacional Privado – Parte Especial, 2000, pp. 362-364 (The author mentions several judicial decisions where this principle was applied.).

[619] *Boggiano*, Derecho Internacional Privado, Volume II, 2006, pp. 193-194.

[620] The determination of the place of performance for jurisdictional purposes does not follow the same criterion. In order to determine the proper forum, the courts of any of the places of performance have jurisdiction to hear the case and not only the judge of the place of the characteristic performance, see Espósito e hijos SRL vs. Jocqueviel de Vieu, National Commercial Court of Appeals, La Ley 1986-D, 49; *Goldschmidt*, Jurisdicción internacional en contratos internacionales, La Ley 1986-D, 46 (The author comments the judicial decision and states that when determining the applicable law, the idea is to find one law applicable to the contract. Contrarily, when determining jurisdiction the idea is to have multiple options to guarantee the parties' access to courts.).

[621] *Kaller de Orchansky*, in: Bueres / Highton (Eds.), Código Civil, Volume 3C, 2005, Sections 1212 and 1213, pp. 75-76. However, it has been suggested that this latter approach shall be the predominant rule, see *Boggiano*, Derecho Internacional Privado, Volume II, 2006, pp. 193-194.

[622] *Kaller de Orchansky*, in: Bueres / Highton (Eds.), Código Civil, Volume 3C, 2005, Section 1214, p. 76; *Feldstein de Cárdenas*, Derecho Internacional Privado – Parte Especial, 2000, p. 353.

[623] *Kaller de Orchansky*, in: Bueres / Highton (Eds.), Código Civil, Volume 3C, 2005, Section 1214, p. 76; *Feldstein de Cárdenas*, Derecho Internacional Privado – Parte Especial, 2000, pp. 353-354.

[624] *Smith*, in: Belluscio / Zannoni (Eds.), Código Civil, Volume 5, 2002, Section 1214, pp. 1031-1032 (It is proposed that the solution of Section 42 Treaty on

4.   Jurisprudence

The following two judicial decisions deal with the issues of the internationality of a contract, applicable law and determination of the most characteristic performance.

In the case Transportes Mabellini vs Expofrut SRL[625] the first instance judge addresses the internationality of a contract and the determination of its applicable law.[626] The parties had entered into a contract for the transport of goods. The transport company sued for payment and the defendant introduced the statute of limitation defense alleging that the claim was time barred because the one-year limitation period had run (Section 855 paragraph 1 Argentine Commercial Code). The plaintiff in turn alleged that the two-year limitation period applied because the transport contract was international (Section 855, paragraph 2 Argentine Commercial Code). The first instance judge ruled that the contract was international, that Argentine law governed the contract and, therefore, that the two-year statute of limitations applied. Thus, the defendant was ordered to pay for the transport.

In order to reach this decision, the first question the judge addressed was whether the contract was international. The contract was entered into FOB Uruguayana (Brazil). Consequently, the contract was deemed international because it was entered into in Argentina and performed in Brazil. The defendant unsuccessfully alleged that the stop in Brazil had been only a technical stop for the delivery of the goods and that, therefore, it did not render the contract international.

The second issue to determine was the law applicable to the contract. The parties had not made a choice of law, which as the court held would have been possible and recognized due to the international nature of the contract. The first instance judge applied Section 1210 of the Argentine Civil Code to determine the applicable law, according to which the law of the place of performance is the applicable law. The judge had already decided in the issue of the internationality of the contract that the place of performance was in Brazil. However, the judge distinguished between the place of performance for determining the internationality of the contract, on the one hand, and the applicable law, on the other; consequently, the court concluded on the basis of the following reasoning that Argentine law was the applicable law.

International Civil Law of Montevideo is adopted according to which the law of the country where the offer was accepted governs.).
[625] Transportes Mabellini, S. A. vs. Expofrut, S. R. L., National Commercial First Instance Court No. 13, July 29, 1977, La Ley 1980-B, 378.
[626] The judge in this case was *Antonio Boggiano*, a specialist in Private International Law and later appointed judge of the Argentine Supreme Court of Justice.

The parties had not designated the place of performance; therefore, Sections 1212 and 1213 of the Argentine Civil Code apply. According to them, when the place of performance has not been designated or cannot be inferred from the nature of the obligation, the place of performance is deemed to be the domicile of the debtor. If the contract is made where the debtor is domiciled, the domicile of the debtor at the time the contract is made will be considered (Section 1212). If in turn, place of contracting and domicile do not coincide, then the current domicile of the debtor is the relevant one (Section 1213). The provisions do not establish though the domicile of which debtor determines the applicable law. The judge concluded that it had to be the domicile of the debtor with the most characteristic performance. The reasoning for choosing the party with the most characteristic performance is the wording of Section 1212, which refers to the nature of the obligation. In the case of a transport contract the transporter is deemed the party with the most characteristic performance. Therefore, as the transporter was domiciled in Argentina the contract was governed by Argentine law. In any event the judgment clarified that even if Brazilian law had been chosen as the applicable law, the Argentine statute of limitations would have applied because it is a special norm that preempted the application of the statute of limitation periods of the foreign law.[627]

In another case, Sagemüller Francisco G. vs Sagemüller de Hinz, Liesse L., an Argentine court had to answer the question of the law applicable to a contract entered into in Frankfurt for the sale of shares of an Argentine company. In this case, the sellers were domiciled in Germany but with a special domicile for the purpose of the contract in Argentina; the buyer was domiciled in Argentina; the price was to be paid in a Swiss bank in Switzerland, and the transfer of the shares was to take place in Buenos Aires.[628] The claim dealt with the application of the impracticability theory to international contracts. The purchaser invoked Section 1198 of the Argentine Civil Code due to the Argentine currency devaluation before the US dollar.

The first issue addressed was the internationality of the contract. The contract was qualified as international based on the theory of the economic function of the contract. Then, there followed the issue of the law applicable to the contract. The parties had made no choice of law; however, the parties had agreed to the

---

[627] *Goldschmidt*, Transporte internacional, La Ley 1980-B, 375 (The author also considers that the contract is to be governed by Argentine law but based on the ground that the transport is national. Consequently, the one-year limitation period applies and the plaintiff's action should have been dismissed. In any event, the author reaches the conclusion that if the contract had been qualified as international, it would have been also governed by Argentine law.).

[628] Sagemüller, Francisco G. vs. Sagemüller de Hinz, Liesse L. y otro, Second Civil and Commercial Court of Appeals of Parana, August 10, 1988, La Ley 1989-E, 192.

jurisdiction of the courts of the city of Paraná, Province of Entre Ríos, Argentina. The choice of a jurisdiction meant also the choice of the forum's private international law because the forum judge applies its own private international law. As a result, Argentine private international law led to the application of Argentine substantive law. This conclusion was based on the application of sections 1209, 1210 and 1212 of the Argentine Civil Code. When contracts have different places of execution and performance (and one of those is in Argentina) the law of the place of performance will govern the contract. In bilateral contracts there are two performances but the performance to be taken into account in order to determine the applicable law is the most characteristic one. In the case of a sales contract the delivery of the goods is considered the most characteristic performance. However, the Appellate Court did not conclude the analysis there. The deciding argument was not so much where the shares were going to be transferred but what the shares were transferring. Therefore, the most characteristic performance was determined to be that of the seller based on the fact that the shares belonged to an Argentine company with domicile and place of business in Argentina

IV.   Contracts between absent and present parties

The Argentine rules of private international law apply different connecting factors for contracts entered into between absent and present parties. That is the case in the determination of the place of performance for the purposes of establishing the applicable law (Section 1214 Argentine Civil Code) and in the determination of the law that will govern the formal validity of a contract (Section 1181 Argentine Civil Code).

Traditionally, a contract is entered into between present parties when the parties are physically present in the same place and able to communicate without a lapse of time. When the parties are in the presence of each other and the negotiations of the contract take place verbally, if the parties reach an agreement, that is the moment and place of execution of the agreement.[629] In turn, in a contract between absent parties the parties are in distant places and this entails a time period in between the communication of the parties.

However, the simultaneous existence of distance and lack of immediate communication started to blur with the appearance of the telephone.[630] Moreover, today's means of communication allow people not only to talk but to see each other. Therefore, geographical distance does not any longer equal lack of instant communication between the parties. Then, the question is whether electronic contracts are contracts between present parties or contracts between

---

[629] According to Section 1151 of the Argentine Civil Code a verbal offer shall be accepted immediately.
[630] *Lorenzetti*, Comercio Electrónico, 2001, pp. 191-193 and 195-198.

absent parties. In this respect there are two issues to be distinguished and which need to be addressed separately: one is the moment of execution of the contract; the other is the place of execution of the contract.

Concerning the moment of execution of a contract the relevant factor is whether the electronic medium allows instant communication between the parties or not.[631] In the first case, the contract is deemed executed between present parties and in the second, between absent parties. Therefore, even if there is geographical distance between the parties as long as there is immediacy in the communication, the contract is deemed executed between present parties. On the contrary, if the electronic medium does not allow immediate communication between the parties, the contract is considered executed between absent parties.[632] Therefore, with today's means of communication the focus is not so much on where the parties are but on how they communicate.

In case a contract entered into through electronic means is deemed a contract between absent parties, there are different criteria to determine the moment of execution of a contract.[633] The predominant criteria are two. One is that the contract is executed when the acceptance is sent to the offeror. That is, in general terms, the solution adopted by Argentine law (Section 1154 Argentine Civil Code).[634] This is also the rule adopted in the common law legal system.[635]

---

[631] *Lavalle Cobo*, in: Belluscio / Zannoni (Eds.), Código Civil, Volume 5, 2002, Section 1147, pp. 757-758; *Mosset Iturraspe*, in: Bueres / Highton (Eds.), Código Civil, Volume 3B, 2005, Section 1147, p. 558; *Lorenzetti*, Tratado de los Contratos – Parte General, 2004, pp. 274-278. For approaches in other jurisdictions, especially in the European Union, see *Vibes / Delupí*, El comercio electrónico frente al derecho positivo argentino, La Ley 2000-E, 1079.

[632] *Lorenzetti*, Tratado de los Contratos – Parte General, 2004, pp. 276-277; Sprayette S.A. vs. Ciudad de Buenos Aires, Administrative and Tax Court of Appeals of the City of Buenos Aires, December 2, 2004, RCyS 2005-III, 75 (The judge ruled that a contract entered into over the phone is a contract between present parties because it allows the immediate acceptance of the offer.). Also foreign literature follows the same approach, see *Bachman*, Internet und IPR, in: Lehman, (Ed.), Internet- und Multimediarecht (Cyberlaw), 1997, p. 173.

[633] Namely, the information, acceptance, reception and declaration theories, see *Feldstein de Cárdenas*, Derecho Internacional Privado – Parte Especial, 2000, p. 353; *Spota*, Instituciones de Derecho Civil – Contratos, Volume I, 1975, pp. 289-294; *Borda*, Tratado de Derecho Civil – Obligaciones, 1989, pp. 170-171; *Lavalle Cobo*, in: Belluscio / Zannoni (Eds.), Código Civil, Volume 5, 2002, Section 1154, pp. 769-771; *Lorenzetti*, Comercio Electrónico, 2001, pp. 193-194; *Lorenzetti*, Tratado de los Contratos – Parte General, 2004, pp. 271-272.

[634] *Lorenzetti*, Tratado de los Contratos – Parte General, 2004, pp. 273-274; *Borda*, Tratado de Derecho Civil – Obligaciones, 1989, p. 172; *Lavalle Cobo*, in: Belluscio / Zannoni (Eds.), Código Civil, Volume 5, 2002, Section 1154, pp. 771-773; *Banaparte*, Enciclopedia Jurídica Omeba, Volume IV, 1956 s.v. "Contratos entre ausentes". However, the different criteria are normally combined and thus it

The second criterion is when the offer is received by the offeror.[636] CISG follows this latter rule (Article 23).

With respect to the determination of the place of execution of a contract, an electronic contract is considered executed between absent parties.[637] Consequently, the determination of its formal validity as well as the place of performance for establishing the applicable law is made according to the rules established for contracts between absent parties.

B. German law

The German legal system has incorporated the Rome Convention into its national conflict of law rules, which are contained in the Introduction Law to the Civil Code (*Einführungsgesetz zum Bürgerlichen Gesetzbuch* – EGBGB).[638] Therefore, the issues of the internationality of the contract, the formal validity and the law applicable to the contract follow the principles of said convention.

I.   International contracts

According to Section 3(1) EGBGB, the rules of private international law apply where the facts of a case are linked to a foreign legal system (*Sachverhalten mit Auslandsberührung*).[639] Consequently, a contract is subject to private international law if its elements have links with the legal system of a foreign country. Under German law it is sufficient that the connection with a foreign

---

is possible to revoke acceptance before it was received, see *Spota*, Instituciones de Derecho Civil – Contratos, Volume I, 1975, p. 294. See the application to a concrete case in: Arlan SCA vs. Revestimientos La Europea S.A., National Civil Court of Appeals, La Ley 1993-D, 417 and its comment by *Caivano,* La formación del consentimiento entre ausentes en nuestro derecho positivo, La Ley 1993-D, 415.

[635] For further issues concerning the application of the mail-box rule, the rules contained in the UCC and CISG for the formation of contracts, as well as the terms the contract is governed by – known as the battle of forms, see *Gillette / Walt*, Sales Law – Domestic and International, 1999, pp. 53-74.

[636] Enciclopedia Jurídica Omeba, Volume IV, 1956, s.v. "Contrato entre ausentes".

[637] The analysis is sometimes conducted for contracts executed over the telephone but the conclusions are applicable to other means of communication, see *Spota*, Instituciones de Derecho Civil – Contratos, Volume I, 1975, pp. 287-288; *Lavalle Cobo,* in: Belluscio / Zannoni (Eds.), Código Civil, Volume 5, 2002, Sections 1147 and 1151, pp. 757 and 766; *Lorenzetti*, Tratado de los Contratos, Volume III, 2000, pp. 850-851; *Mosset Iturraspe*, Contratos, 1984, p. 108.

[638] *Spellenberg*, in: Münchener Kommentar zum Bürgerlichen Gesetzbuch, 4th Edition, 2006, Section 11 EGBGB, marginal number 5.

[639] *Heldrich*, in: Palandt, Bürgerliches Gesetzbuch, 68th Edition, 2009, Section 3 EGBGB, marginal number 2; *Hohloch*, in: Erman, Bürgerliches Gesetzbuch, 12th Edition, 2008, Section 3 EGBGB, marginal number 2.

country is triggered by the choice of a foreign law.[640] In this case the contract is not objectively international because the choice of law clause is the only connecting factor between the contract and the foreign legal system; consequently, the choice of law is subject to additional limitations not existing for objective international contracts (Section 27(3) EGBGB).

II. Formal validity

Section 11 EGBGB, which contains the rules to determine the laws that will govern the formal validity of contracts, is based on Article 9 of the Rome Convention.[641] Contracts are formally valid if they comply with the formal requirements established by the law governing the contract (*lex causae*) (Sections 11(1) and 11(2) EGBGB).[642]

Additionally, a contract is formally valid if it complies with the law of any of the places where the contracting parties (or their agents)[643] are at the time of issuing the offer or acceptance (Sections 11(1) and 11(2) EGBGB).[644] The place where

---

[640] *Heldrich*, in: Palandt, Bürgerliches Gesetzbuch, 68th Edition, 2009, Section 3 EGBGB, marginal number 2; *Hohloch*, in: Erman, Bürgerliches Gesetzbuch, 12th Edition, 2008, Section 3 EGBGB, marginal number 2; *Hausmann*, in: Staudinger, Kommentar zum Bürgerlichen Gesetzbuch, New Edition, 2003, Section 3 EGBGB, marginal number 6.

[641] *Spellenberg*, in: Münchener Kommentar zum Bürgerlichen Gesetzbuch, 4th Edition, 2006, Section 11 EGBGB, marginal number 5; *Heldrich*, in: Palandt, Bürgerliches Gesetzbuch, 67th Edition, 2008, Section 11 EGBGB, marginal number 1.

[642] *Spellenberg*, in: Münchener Kommentar zum Bürgerlichen Gesetzbuch, 4th Edition, 2006, Section 11 EGBGB, marginal number 52; *Heldrich*, in: Palandt, Bürgerliches Gesetzbuch, 68th Edition, 2009, Section 11 EGBGB, marginal numbers 2 and 5. Section 11(1) EGBGB encompasses all types of legal acts; therefore, it is not limited to contracts, see: *Heldrich*, in: Palandt, Bürgerliches Gesetzbuch, 68th Edition, 2009, Section 11 EGBGB, marginal number 3; *Spellenberg*, in: Münchener Kommentar zum Bürgerlichen Gesetzbuch, 4th Edition, 2006, Section 11 EGBGB, marginal numbers 5 and 11-12. In turn, Section 11(1) addresses the formal validity of one specific type of contract, the distant contract, see: *Spellenberg*, in: Münchener Kommentar zum Bürgerlichen Gesetzbuch, 4th Edition, 2006, Section 11 EGBGB, marginal numbers 6 and 11-12.

[643] Section 11(3) EGBGB, see *Heldrich*, in: Palandt, Bürgerliches Gesetzbuch, 68th Edition, 2009, Section 11 EGBGB, marginal number 19; *Mäsch*, in: Bamberger / Roth (Eds.), Beck'scher Online-Kommentar, 14th Edition, 2009, Section 11 EGBGB, marginal number 52; *Spellenberg*, in: Münchener Kommentar zum Bürgerlichen Gesetzbuch, 4th Edition, 2006, Section 11 EGBGB, marginal number 101.

[644] *Spellenberg*, in: Münchener Kommentar zum Bürgerlichen Gesetzbuch, 4th Edition, 2006, Section 11 EGBGB, marginal numbers 1 and 81; *Mäsch*, in: Bamberger / Roth (Eds.), Beck'scher Online-Kommentar, 14th Edition, 2009,

the parties are located does not refer to the domicile or place of business but the place from which the offer or acceptance is issued.[645] The different wording of Section 11(1) EGBGB referring to the place of the execution and Section 11(2) EGBGB referring to the location of the parties is to be construed as referring in both cases to the place from which the offer or acceptance is made.[646] The place where the offer or acceptance is received by the counterparty is irrelevant.[647] In the case of electronic contracts it refers to the place where a contracting party is when the offer or acceptance is sent electronically, that is, the place of the mouse click.[648]

At the time of sending the offer or acceptance the parties may be in a same country or in different ones (the latter case is a distant contract – *Distanzverträge*). If the parties are in the same country, the formal validity of the contract is governed by the law of that country (Section 11(1) EGBGB). In the case contracting parties are in different countries, the application of the law of any of those countries determines the formal validity of the contract (Section 11(2) EGBGB).[649] Consequently, the formal validity of distant contracts is

---

Section 11 EGBGB, marginal number 42; *Heldrich*, in: Palandt, Bürgerliches Gesetzbuch, 68th Edition, 2009, Section 11 EGBGB, marginal numbers 2 and 11.

[645] *Mäsch*, in: Bamberger / Roth (Eds.), Beck'scher Online-Kommentar, 14th Edition, 2009, Section 11 EGBGB, marginal numbers 43 and 50; *Spellenberg*, in: Münchener Kommentar zum Bürgerlichen Gesetzbuch, 4th Edition, 2006, Section 11 EGBGB, marginal number 87; *Heldrich*, in: Palandt, Bürgerliches Gesetzbuch, 68th Edition, 2009, Section 11 EGBGB, marginal number 15 (Even if the party is only temporarily at the place where the offer or acceptance is issued.).

[646] *Spellenberg*, in: Münchener Kommentar zum Bürgerlichen Gesetzbuch, 4th Edition, 2006, Section 11 EGBGB, marginal number 87; *Mäsch*, in: Bamberger / Roth (Eds.), Beck'scher Online-Kommentar, 14th Edition, 2009, Section 11 EGBGB, marginal number 50; *von Mohrenfels,* in: Staudinger, Kommentar zum Bürgerlichen Gesetzbuch, New Edition, 2007, Section 11 EGBGB, marginal number 223.

[647] *Spellenberg*, in: Münchener Kommentar zum Bürgerlichen Gesetzbuch, 4th Edition, 2006, Section 11 EGBGB, marginal number 88; *von Mohrenfels,* in: Staudinger, Kommentar zum Bürgerlichen Gesetzbuch, New Edition, 2007, Section 11 EGBGB, marginal number 224.

[648] *Spellenberg*, in: Münchener Kommentar zum Bürgerlichen Gesetzbuch, 4th Edition, 2006, Section 11 EGBGB, marginal number 93; *Mäsch*, in: Bamberger / Roth (Eds.), Beck'scher Online-Kommentar, 14th Edition, 2009, Section 11 EGBGB, marginal number 43; *Geis*, Die digitale Signatur, NJW 1997, 3000. Other authors consider relevant the place of location of the server, see *von Mohrenfels,* in: Staudinger, Kommentar zum Bürgerlichen Gesetzbuch, New Edition, 2007, Section 11 EGBGB, marginal number 161.

[649] *Spellenberg*, in: Münchener Kommentar zum Bürgerlichen Gesetzbuch, 4th Edition, 2006, Section 11 EGBGB, marginal numbers 1, 4, 6, 44, 97; *Mäsch*, in: Bamberger / Roth (Eds.), Beck'scher Online-Kommentar, 14th Edition, 2009,

subject to either the legal system of the place where the offeror issued the offer or of the place where the acceptance was sent.[650] Any of those laws governs the formal validity of the entire contract instead of subjecting the acceptance and offer to different laws, namely, each to the law of the place where issued.[651] Therefore, in the case of a contract with two contracting parties in different countries the contract may be formally valid if it complies with the law of any of the three laws available to the parties: the law governing the contract or the law of the country where either party was located when issuing the offer or acceptance.[652]

Consequently, under German law there are several possible laws to govern the formal validity of a contract. They are all alternative laws and none of them has priority over the other.[653] Therefore, it is sufficient that the contract is formally valid according to one of those laws.

The above mentioned rules do not apply to consumer contracts falling within Section 29(1) EGBGB[654] (Section 29(3) EGBGB). The formal validity of consumer contracts falling within Section 29(1) EGBGB is governed by the law of the place where the consumer has his or her habitual residence (Section 29(3) EGBGB).[655]

Section 11 EGBGB, marginal number 49; *Heldrich*, in: Palandt, Bürgerliches Gesetzbuch, 68th Edition, 2009, Section 11 EGBGB, marginal number 18.

[650] *Spellenberg*, in: Münchener Kommentar zum Bürgerlichen Gesetzbuch, 4th Edition, 2006, Section 11 EGBGB, marginal number 6.

[651] *Spellenberg*, in: Münchener Kommentar zum Bürgerlichen Gesetzbuch, 4th Edition, 2006, Section 11 EGBGB, marginal numbers 6, 44, 48, 97.

[652] *Heldrich*, in: Palandt, Bürgerliches Gesetzbuch, 68th Edition, 2009, Section 11 EGBGB, marginal number 18; *Mäsch*, in: Bamberger / Roth (Eds.), Beck'scher Online-Kommentar, 14th Edition, 2009, Section 11 EGBGB, marginal number 49.

[653] *Spellenberg*, in: Münchener Kommentar zum Bürgerlichen Gesetzbuch, 4th Edition, 2006, Section 11 EGBGB, marginal numbers 1, 81; *Mäsch*, in: Bamberger / Roth (Eds.), Beck'scher Online-Kommentar, 14th Edition, 2009, Section 11 EGBGB, marginal number 1; *Heldrich*, in: Palandt, Bürgerliches Gesetzbuch, 68th Edition, 2009, Section 11 EGBGB, marginal number 2.

[654] The three situations described in Section 29(1) EGBGB are consistent with Article 5.2 of the Rome Convention, see *Hohloch*, in: Erman, Bürgerliches Gesetzbuch, 12th Edition, 2008, Section 29 EGBGB, marginal numbers 1 and 11-14; *Martiny*, in: Münchener Kommentar zum Bürgerlichen Gesetzbuch, 4th Edition, 2006, Section 29 EGBGB, marginal numbers 34-44; *Thorn*, in: Palandt, Bürgerliches Gesetzbuch, 68th Edition, 2009, Section 29 EGBGB, marginal number 6.

[655] *Thorn*, in: Palandt, Bürgerliches Gesetzbuch, 68th Edition, 2009, Section 29 EGBGB, marginal number 10; *Spellenberg*, in: Münchener Kommentar zum Bürgerlichen Gesetzbuch, 4th Edition, 2006, Section 27 EGBGB, marginal number 45; *Martiny*, in: Münchener Kommentar zum Bürgerlichen Gesetzbuch, 4th Edition, 2006, Section 29 EGBGB, marginal number 74; *Hohloch*, in: Erman,

III. Applicable law

The rules to determine the law applicable to contracts are contained in Sections 27 *et seq.* of the EGBGB.

Under German law the parties to an international contract are able to choose the law applicable to their contract (Section 27(1)1 EGBGB).[656] However, if a contract subject to a foreign law has – except for the choice of law clause – only contacts to one country, the mandatory provisions of that country apply (Section 27(3) EGBGB).[657]

In case a contract does not contain a choice of law provision – either express (Section 27(1)2 EGBGB)[658] or tacit (Section 27(1)2 EGBGB)[659] – the contract is governed by the law of the country with which the contract has its closest connections (Section 28(1)1 EGBGB).[660] It is presumed that a contract is most closely connected to the country where the party with the characteristic performance has his or her domicile at the time the contract is executed (Section 28(2)1 EGBGB).[661] This presumption applies also to contracts executed

---

Bürgerliches Gesetzbuch, 12th Edition, 2008, Section 29 EGBGB, marginal number 21.

[656] *Thorn*, in: Palandt, Bürgerliches Gesetzbuch, 68th Edition, 2009, Section 27 EGBGB, marginal numbers 1 and 3; *Martiny*, in: Münchener Kommentar zum Bürgerlichen Gesetzbuch, 4th Edition, 2006, Section 27 EGBGB, marginal numbers 1, 2 and 8; *Hohloch*, in: Erman, Bürgerliches Gesetzbuch, 12th Edition, 2008, Section 27 EGBGB, marginal number 7.

[657] *Thorn*, in: Palandt, Bürgerliches Gesetzbuch, 68th Edition, 2009, Section 27 EGBGB, marginal number 4; *Magnus*, in: Staudinger, Kommentar zum Bürgerlichen Gesetzbuch, 13th Edition, 2002, Section 27 EGBGB, marginal number 27; *Hohloch*, in: Erman, Bürgerliches Gesetzbuch, 12th Edition, 2008, Section 27 EGBGB, marginal number 25.

[658] *Martiny*, in: Münchener Kommentar zum Bürgerlichen Gesetzbuch, 4th Edition, 2006, Section 11 EGBGB, marginal numbers 42-43; *Magnus*, in: Staudinger, Kommentar zum Bürgerlichen Gesetzbuch, 13th Edition, 2002, Section 27 EGBGB, marginal numbers 52-58; *Hohloch*, in: Erman, Bürgerliches Gesetzbuch, 12th Edition, 2008, Section 27 EGBGB, marginal number 12.

[659] *Thorn*, in: Palandt, Bürgerliches Gesetzbuch, 68th Edition, 2009, Section 27 EGBGB, marginal number 5; *Martiny*, in: Münchener Kommentar zum Bürgerlichen Gesetzbuch, 4th Edition, 2006, Section 27 EGBGB, marginal numbers 45-47 (The tacit choice of law shall not be confused with a presumed choice of law.); *Magnus*, in: Staudinger, Kommentar zum Bürgerlichen Gesetzbuch, 13th Edition, 2002, Section 27 EGBGB, marginal numbers 59-89; *Hohloch*, in: Erman, Bürgerliches Gesetzbuch, 12th Edition, 2008, Section 27 EGBGB, marginal number 13; BGH, NJW-RR 2005, 206, 208.

[660] *Thorn*, in: Palandt, Bürgerliches Gesetzbuch, 68th Edition, 2009, Section 28 EGBGB, marginal numbers 1-2.

[661] *Thorn*, in: Palandt, Bürgerliches Gesetzbuch, 68th Edition, 2009, Section 28 EGBGB, marginal number 3; *Magnus*, in: Staudinger, Kommentar zum

electronically.[662] In this type of contracts the location of the server is not decisive.[663]

It is also possible for the parties to choose and for a judge to determine – however, in the latter case only exceptionally – that different laws govern different parts of the contract (Sections 27(1)3 and 28(1)2 EGBGB).[664]

In the case of consumer contracts (as defined by Section 29(1) EGBGB), and following Article 9.3 of the Rome Convention, the parties are free to choose the applicable law but the mandatory provisions of the legal system of the consumer's habitual residence apply (Section 29(1) EGBGB).[665] Absent a choice of law by the parties, the law of the consumer's habitual residence is applicable to the contract (Section 29(2) EGBGB).[666]

Bürgerlichen Gesetzbuch, 13th Edition, 2002, Section 28 EGBGB, marginal number 63. However, the presumption is rebuttable and a court may consider that the contract has closer links with another country (Section 28(5) EGBGB).

[662] *Magnus*, in: Staudinger, Kommentar zum Bürgerlichen Gesetzbuch, 13th Edition, 2002, Section 28 EGBGB, marginal number 63; *Hohloch*, in: Erman, Bürgerliches Gesetzbuch, 12th Edition, 2008, Section 28 EGBGB, marginal number 11; *Martiny*, in: Münchener Kommentar zum Bürgerlichen Gesetzbuch, 4th Edition, 2006, Section 28 EGBGB, marginal number 47.

[663] *Magnus*, in: Staudinger, Kommentar zum Bürgerlichen Gesetzbuch, 13th Edition, 2002, Section 28 EGBGB, marginal number 78; *Martiny*, in: Münchener Kommentar zum Bürgerlichen Gesetzbuch, 4th Edition, 2006, Section 28 EGBGB, marginal number 47.

[664] *Magnus*, in: Staudinger, Kommentar zum Bürgerlichen Gesetzbuch, 13th Edition, 2002, Section 27 EGBGB, marginal numbers 90 and 93 and Section 28 EGBGB, marginal number 55; *Martiny*, in: Münchener Kommentar zum Bürgerlichen Gesetzbuch, 4th Edition, 2006, Section 27 EGBGB, marginal number 70 and Section 28, marginal number 24; *Hohloch*, in: Erman, Bürgerliches Gesetzbuch, 12th Edition, 2008, Section 27, marginal number 19 and Section 28 EGBGB, marginal number 19.

[665] *Thorn*, in: Palandt, Bürgerliches Gesetzbuch, 68th Edition, 2009, Section 29 EGBGB, marginal numbers 5-6; *Martiny*, in: Münchener Kommentar zum Bürgerlichen Gesetzbuch, 4th Edition, 2006, Section 29 EGBGB, marginal numbers 54, 56 and 59; *Hohloch*, in: Erman, Bürgerliches Gesetzbuch, 12th Edition, 2008, Section 29 EGBGB, marginal number 8.

[666] *Thorn*, in: Palandt, Bürgerliches Gesetzbuch, 68th Edition, 2009, Section 29 EGBGB, marginal number 9; *Martiny*, in: Münchener Kommentar zum Bürgerlichen Gesetzbuch, 4th Edition, 2006, Section 29 EGBGB, marginal number 62; *Hohloch*, in: Erman, Bürgerliches Gesetzbuch, 12th Edition, 2008, Section 29 EGBGB, marginal numbers 19-20.

C.　US law

I.　International contracts

According to Section 1-301 of the UCC a transaction is deemed international if it bears a reasonable relation to a foreign country. Several factors are taken into account to consider whether a contract has connections with a foreign country, such as, the place of negotiation, the place of contracting, the nationality of the parties or the nature of the transaction.[667]

II.　Formal validity

Under US law, a contract is formally valid if it complies with the law of the place where entered into or with the law governing the contract.[668] Therefore, a contract may comply with the formal requirements either of the *lex causae* or of the *lex loci contractus*.

III.　Applicable law

The law applicable to the contract is the law chosen by the parties[669] and, absent a choice, the law with the most significant relationship to the transaction.[670] The power to choose the law applicable to the contract has a long tradition in the United States of America.[671] However, it is subject to certain restrictions. In the first place, the law chosen shall bear a substantial relationship to the parties or the contract or, absent a substantial relationship, then a reasonable basis must exist for the parties' choice of that law.[672] In the second place, the chosen law shall not affect the public policy of the forum judge.[673]

---

[667] *Delaume*, What is an international contract? An American and a Gallic Dilemma, The International and Comparative Law Quarterly, Volume 28, 1979, 258-279.

[668] Restatement (Second) of Conflict of Laws, Section 199.

[669] Restatement (Second) of Conflict of Laws, Sections 186 and 187; *Lando*, The Conflict of Laws on Contracts – General Principles, 1985, pp. 272-278; *Fresnedo de Aguirre*, La autonomía de la voluntad en la contratación internacional, 1991, pp. 27-34.

[670] Restatement (Second) of Conflict of Laws, Sections 186 and 188. For an evolution of the different standards to determine the law applicable to the contract absent a choice by the parties, see *Lando*, The Conflict of Laws on Contracts – General Principles, 1985, pp. 346-358.

[671] *Scoles / Hay / Borchers / Symeonides*, Conflict of Laws, 2000, pp. 860-861.

[672] Restatement (Second) of Conflict of Laws, Section 187(2)(a), comment (f) *Scoles / Hay / Borchers / Symeonides*, Conflict of Laws, 2000, pp. 860-862 and 870-877 (However, the state of New York admits that contracts without a substantial contact be nonetheless subject to New York law if the contracts exceed a certain

For determining the proper law of the contract absent a choice of law by the parties, the conflict of law rules seek to elucidate the law which has the most significant relationship to the contract.[674] A law is considered to have the most significant contacts if it is the law of the place of execution, negotiation, performance or location of the subject matter of the contract, or the law of the domicile or nationality of the parties.[675] In case the negotiations were conducted in the same place where the contract is performed, the law of that place is the applicable law.[676] However, some courts – arguably only a minority – continue to apply the rule of the *locus regit actum,* which used to be the connecting factor traditionally applied to determine the law applicable to contracts.[677]

The UCC has its own rules for determining the law applicable to contracts falling within its scope.[678] Section 1-301 UCC governs the determination of the law applicable only to transactions governed by the UCC and as long as no other conflict of law provision contained in the UCC is applicable.[679] The parties to an international contract may subject the contract to the law of a foreign country whereas in a domestic contract they do not have this power; therefore, the freedom to choose a foreign law exists only when the contract is international.[680] The foreign law chosen does not have to be related to the contract (Section 1-301(c)(2) UCC), except in the case of consumer contracts (Section 1-301(e)(1) UCC).[681] Section 1-301 replaces former Section 1-105, which required a reasonable relationship between the contract and the country whose law is chosen.[682]

---

value, see p. 872); *van Cutsem / Viggria / Güth,* E-Commerce in the World, 2003, p. 323.

[673] Restatement (Second) of Conflict of Laws, Section 187(2)(b), comment (g).

[674] Restatement (Second) of Conflict of Laws, Section 188(1).

[675] Restatement (Second) of Conflict of Laws, Section 188(2)(a)-(e), comment (e).

[676] Restatement (Second) of Conflict of Laws, Section 188(3), comment (f).

[677] *Scoles / Hay / Borchers / Symeonides,* Conflict of Laws, 2000, pp. 892-895.

[678] UCC, Section 1-301, Official Comment 1.

[679] UCC, Section 1-301, Official Comment 1.

[680] On the contrary, in case the contract is domestic, the parties have to limit their choice to the law of the states of the United States of America, not being able to choose the law of a foreign country (Section 1-301(c)(1) UCC and Official Comments 4 and 5).

[681] Moreover, the consumer enjoys the protections granted by the law of the country where the consumer has his or her principal residence and, in the case of a contract for the sale of goods, of the country where the contract is executed and the goods are delivered (Section 1-301(e)(2) UCC).

[682] *Scoles / Hay / Borchers / Symeonides,* Conflict of Laws, 2000, pp. 877-880.

D. Conclusions

The formal validity of a contract is fundamental for the contracting parties because a contract which does not comply with the formal requirements may be void or unenforceable. In an international contract multiple possible laws may determine the question of the formal validity. Each legal system follows its own rules; however, all three jurisdictions analyzed recognize the formal validity of a contract that complies with the formal requirements of the law of the place of execution or of the law governing the substance of the contract. For contracts where the parties are in several places even a more flexible approach is adopted. German law assesses the formal validity of the contract under any of the laws where any of the parties is located when issuing the relevant declaration. Argentine law applies the law most favorable to the formal validity of the contract.

Concerning the *lex causae*, party autonomy is recognized in all three jurisdictions; consequently, contracting parties may not only choose the law that will govern the substance of the contract but may also apply that law to the formal validity of the contract. Party autonomy is normally dependent on the existence of an international contract. Domestic law adopts a flexible approach towards the characterization of a contract as international. However, party autonomy has also been recognized in domestic contracts but the law chosen is subject to important limitations.

In conclusion, in the national laws examined, when the parties follow the formal requirements of the law applicable to the contract or of the law of the place of execution, the contract is going to be considered formally valid by the courts in the other jurisdictions (absent the application of special provisions like, for example, in consumer contracts).

Chapter 10: The interaction of electronic signature legislation

Once the law that will govern the formal validity of a contract has been determined it is known which electronic signature statute will establish the signature requirements, if any, because whether a signature is required and which type of signature is required depends on the formal requirements imposed by that national law.

Different connecting points may lead to the designation of Argentine, German or US law as the legal system determining the formal validity of an international contract. For example, one of those jurisdictions may be the place where the contract was entered into, the place where one of the parties is or the country whose law governs the substance of the contract. However, in an international contract electronic signatures may have been created following the electronic signature legislation of a law other than the one determining the formal validity of the contract. The different legal approaches adopted by legal systems concerning the concept and validity of electronic signatures require that the parties be aware of the electronic signature requirements in other jurisdictions. Contracting parties shall verify whether the electronic signatures which will be used to sign the contract will be recognized as valid under the law governing the formal requirements of the contract. Thus, it has to be analyzed how the interaction of the Argentine Digital Signature Act with the German Electronic Signatures Act and the statutes in the United States of America, UETA[683] and E-Sign, impacts on the formal validity of international contracts.

A. Argentine law governing the form

If the formal validity of a contract is subject to Argentine law, the first issue to determine is which requirements the contract has to comply with, if any at all. The Argentine Digital Signature Act is applicable only in the case the written form is required.

I. Formal requirements under Argentine law

Under Argentine law the principle of freedom of forms is the rule.[684] This means that no special form is required to carry out a transaction and that the parties

---

[683] Not every state in the United States of America enacted legislation following UETA but a large majority did, see National Conference of State Legislators, Uniform Electronic Transactions Act, <http://www.ncsl.org/programs/lis/CIP/ueta-statutes.htm>.

[684] Section 974 Argentine Civil Code. See *Borda*, Tratado de Derecho Civil – Parte general, Volume II, 1991, pp. 165-166; *Santos Cifuentes*, in: Belluscio / Zannoni (Eds.), Código Civil, Volume 4, 2001, Section 974, pp. 465-466; *Rivera*, Instituciones de Derecho Civil – Parte General, Volume II, 1993, pp. 625-626.

may choose the form they deem most convenient. Accordingly, the parties may voluntarily decide to draft their agreement in writing.

However, there are exceptions to the principle of freedom of forms and in certain cases the law requires a specific formal requirement. In most cases, formal requirements are needed in order to prove the act (ad probationem).[685] This means that if the act does not comply with the forms established by law, the enforcement of the contract is at stake because when the law imposes a certain form an act has to be proved only by those means.[686] The act, however, is valid even if not executed according to the legal requirements.[687] Only exceptionally is the form required ad solemnitatem, that is, for the act to be valid.[688] In these cases, the non-compliance with the formal requirements renders the act void.

---

[685] Spota, Instituciones de Derecho Civil – Contratos, Volume III, 1975, pp. 108-113; Borda, Tratado de Derecho Civil – Obligaciones, Volume II, 1989, pp. 145-146; Santos Cifuentes, in: Belluscio / Zannoni (Eds.), Código Civil, Volume 4, 2001, Section 974, pp. 466-469 (As this author explains, there are also more classifications of the acts according to their formal requirements. One classification distinguishes between acts with absolute and relative formal requirements. Acts with absolute formal requirements are void and produce no effect unless in accordance with the legal forms. On the other hand, acts with relative formal requirements have effects inasmuch as a party can legally force the other to produce the act under the formal requirements established by law. One example of an act with relative formal requirements is the sale of real property. The Argentine Civil Code requires a special form for these contracts, namely the public deed. However, if the contract is drafted in a signed writing, the contract for the sale of real property is not executed but a valid contract with the obligation to produce the public deed is (Sections 1184 and 1185 Argentine Civil Code).).

[686] Section 1191 Argentine Civil Code. See Lavalle Cobo, in: Belluscio / Zannoni (Eds.), Código Civil, Volume 5, 2002, Section 1191, pp. 870-872; Mosset Iturraspe, in: Bueres / Highton (Eds.), Código Civil, Volume 3C, 2005, Section 1191, pp. 6-8.

[687] Rivera, Instituciones de Derecho Civil – Parte General, Volume II, 1993, p. 628. Examples of contracts where the formal requirements are required ad probationem are surety contracts (Section 2006 Argentine Civil Code) and deposit contracts for an amount above AR$ 200 (Section 2201 Argentine Civil Code). These contracts do not require special formal requirements but may only be proved by written evidence. See Lavalle Cobo, in: Belluscio / Zannoni (Eds.), Código Civil, Volume 5, 2002, Section 119, p. 877. Besides, Section 1193 of the Argentine Civil Code requires all contracts for a value exceeding AR$ 10.000 to be in writing, see Lavalle Cobo, in: Belluscio / Zannoni (Eds.), Código Civil, Volume 5, 2002, Sections 1193, pp. 877-879.

[688] For example, the donation of real property, see Spota, Instituciones de Derecho Civil – Contratos, Volume I, 1975, p. 192.

For certain acts Argentine law imposes the written form.[689] Under Argentine law there are two types of written instruments: public instruments and private instruments.[690] Public instruments involve the intervention of a public officer. The most common type of public instrument is the public deed. These types of instruments require special formal requirements not yet compatible with the use of the electronic form and, therefore, excluded from the scope of the Argentine Digital Signature Act (Section 4(d)). Thus, the analysis will focus on private instruments.

In the field of private instruments the freedom of the parties is the rule. According to Section 1020 of the Argentine Civil Code the parties may execute private instruments in the language they desire and following the formalities they deem most appropriate.[691] Therefore, it is not required that the private instrument be drafted on paper. Paper is the usual means but it is not mandated by law.[692] Despite the freedom of forms in private instruments, every private instrument requires a signature. Section 1012 of the Argentine Civil Code establishes that a signature is an essential condition for the existence of a private instrument.[693]

According to the Argentine Civil Code a signature is the habitual manner in which a person writes his or her name.[694] However, this simple concept deserves some attention because it does not appear so clearly from certain sections of the Argentine Civil Code. In fact, Section 1012 of the Argentine Civil Code expressly specifies that a signature cannot be replaced by signs or initials. Moreover, Section 1014 of the Argentine Civil Code states that if a document is signed with signs or initials, they only have the value of a signature if the

---

[689] Section 1184 of the Argentine Civil Code lists the contracts which have to be executed in a public deed.

[690] Based on the wording of Sections 978, 1181, 1185, 1186, 1188 and 1190 of the Argentine Civil Code some authors distinguish between particular and private instruments. A signed particular instrument is a private instrument, see *Rivera*, Instituciones de Derecho Civil – Parte General, Volume II, 1993, pp. 722-723.

[691] *Lagomarsino*, in: Belluscio / Zannoni (Eds.), Código Civil, Volume 4, 2001, Section 1020, pp. 657-658.

[692] As *Rivera* sustains, what is relevant is not the medium but its ability to transmit ideas, see *Rivera*, Instituciones de Derecho Civil – Parte General, Volume II, 1993, pp. 728-729. See also *Alegría*, Nuevas fronteras de la documentación, la forma y la prueba de las relaciones comerciales, La Ley 1985-E, 660.

[693] In bilateral acts the law also requires the contract to be drafted in as many copies as parties with different interests (Section 1021 Argentine Civil Code), see *Lagomarsino*, in: Belluscio / Zannoni (Eds.), Código Civil, Volume 4, 2001, Section 1021, pp. 658-659.

[694] *Rivera*, Instituciones de Derecho Civil – Parte General, Volume II, 1993, p. 733.

signatory voluntarily recognizes them.[695] In other words, the person who affixes the signs or initials cannot be forced to recognize them.

However, these provisions shall be read together with Section 3633 of the Argentine Civil Code where the concept of signature is further developed. This provision is located in the part devoted to wills and testaments but it is nevertheless applicable to other types of documents.[696] In its first sentence Section 3633 also contains a strict approach to the concept of signature; namely, a signature shall contain the person's full name and no letter can be missing. To make this clearer it is expressly stated that the last name or initials do not satisfy the signature requirement. Such a type of signatures is deemed irregular or incomplete. However, in the same section the Argentine Civil Code relaxes the signature requirements by determining that an irregular or incomplete signature will be admissible when this is the way a person is used to signing in public and private acts.[697] Therefore, the requirement of the full name, even though presented as the rule, is soon abandoned by a more flexible and realistic approach that considers how a person normally signs. In other words, what is relevant in a signature is the customary way in which a person writes his or her name. The footnote to Section 3639 reinforces the concept that the main feature in a signature is the habitual manner of signing. Thus, it might be the case that the signs or initials are the usual way in which a person signs.[698]

The prohibition to use signs or initials aims at protecting persons who do not know how to write and read from signing documents ignoring their content.[699] A common sign used in these cases is the fingerprint. Therefore, very often the validity of fingerprints is analyzed together with the ability of an illiterate to understand the act he or she is performing and expressing consent to. In Argentina, case law and legal scholars are divided concerning the validity of fingerprints.[700] Fingerprints allow the precise identification of a person; thus, as

---

[695] See *Lagomarsino*, in: Belluscio / Zannoni (Eds.), Código Civil, Volume 4, 2001, Section 1014, pp. 651-652.

[696] *Lagomarsino*, in: Belluscio / Zannoni (Eds.), Código Civil, Volume 4, 2001, Section 1012, pp. 646.

[697] However, according to *Borda* an unusual signature in a contract is valid if made with the intention to be bound by the act. Otherwise, it would be very easy to get out of contractual obligations. However, this criterion does not apply to testaments, see *Borda*, Tratado de Derecho Civil – Parte General, Volume II, 1991, pp. 168-169.

[698] *Borda*, Tratado de Derecho Civil – Parte general, Volume II, 1991, p. 169; *Lagomarsino*, in: Belluscio / Zannoni (Eds.), Código Civil, Volume 4, 2001, Section 1012, pp. 645-646; *Rivera*, Instituciones de Derecho Civil – Parte General, Volume II, 1993, pp. 731-732.

[699] *Borda*, Tratado de Derecho Civil – Parte General, Volume II, 1991, p. 169.

[700] *Hocsman*, Negocios en Internet, 2005, pp. 355-356; *Rivera*, Instituciones de Derecho Civil – Parte General, Volume II, 1993, pp. 734-736.

far as establishing the identity of a person is concerned, fingerprints are of higher reliability than handwritten signatures, which may be forged. However, when a fingerprint is used the concern resides in the voluntary nature of the act. The majority opinion does not regard fingerprints as equivalent to handwritten signatures. Some base their opinions on the lack of a handwritten signature and, therefore, the fact that the signature requirement is not fulfilled.[701] For others, the argument for dismissing the value of fingerprints is the lack of consent or will to perform the act.[702] In contrast, a minority recognizes that fingerprints may be valid if they serve not only the function to identify a person but also to express that person's consent.[703]

The Argentine Civil Code was written when the current means of communications were not even conceived. Therefore, in the Argentine Civil Code the concept of instrument and signature is tied to the notion of paper.[704]

---

[701] B., J. H. vs. Establecimiento Frigorífico Azul, National Civil Court of Appeals, April 28, 1997, La Ley 1998-C, 627; Huguet, Juanita B. vs. Martínez, Delia, Civil and Commercial Court of Appeals of Resistencia, October 11, 2001, La Ley Litoral 2002, 324; Orge Martínez, Jesús y otra vs. Martínez, María. suc., Supreme Court of Justice of the Province of Buenos Aires, October 19, 1993, La Ley 1994-D, 477; Pennesi, Teresa O. vs. Maldonado, Santos R., May 12, 1978, published in <www.laleyonline.com.ar>.

[702] Rivera, Instituciones de Derecho Civil – Parte General, Volume II, 1993, pp. 735-736; Sudar, Basilio vs. Subterráneos de Buenos Aires, National Commercial Court of Appeals, March 9, 1979, La Ley Online; Suárez, Francisco vs. Gomez, Carlos, Supreme Court of Justice of the Province of Buenos Aires, June 21, 1998, La Ley 1989-B, 605; Enciclopedia Jurídica Omeba, Volume XII, 1960, s.v. "Firma". However, some authors reckon that if the person is literate but is not able to sign for other reasons, the fingerprint has the same value as a handwritten signature, see *Borda*, Tratado de Derecho Civil – Parte General, Volume II, 1991, p. 172; *Rivera*, Instituciones de Derecho Civil – Parte General, Volume II, 1993, p. 736.

[703] De Souza Jorge vs. Jure, Jorge, National Civil Court of Appeals, July 30, 1981, La Ley 1982-A, 287 (The court held that, despite her illiteracy, the wife had validly given the consent required by Section 1277 of the Argentine Civil Code for the sale of property.); Saucedo, Ramona vs. Sued, Mario, Civil and Commercial Court of Appeals of San Isidro, September 30, 1997, La Ley Buenos Aires 1998, 539. (The court held that an illiterate person may sign a private document with a sign or fingerprint but the opposing party has to prove that the illiterate person voluntarily consented to be bound by that act. However, the court in this case found that the voluntary consent requirement was not met.); Orge Martínez, Jesús y otra vs. Martínez, María. suc., Supreme Court of Justice of the Province of Buenos Aires, October 10, 1993, Ley Ley, 1994-D, 477, dissenting opinion of Judge Negri – the dissenting opinion is shared by *Colerio*, ¿Es la firma privada un requisito esencial para la existencia de todo acto bajo forma privada?, La Ley 1994-D, 475; Neyra, José M. vs. Aspitia Hnos., Civil, Commercial, Criminal and Labor Court of Appeals of Cruz del Eje, April 8, 1983, La Ley Online.

[704] *Rivera*, Instituciones de Derecho Civil – Parte General, Volume II, 1993, p. 727.

Sections 1012 and 3633 were drafted taking into account handwritten signatures even though it is not stated therein that signatures are to be written with ink. With the passing of time the legislation started to recognize the implementation of technologies for signing. For example, Section 212 of the Business Companies Act 19.550 as amended authorizes shares to bear an impression as a means of ensuring their authenticity instead of the traditional handwriting signature. Also the Checks Act 24.452 as amended accepts the signing of checks by electronic means.[705] Finally, Argentine law did not fall behind the trend of enacting a legal framework for electronic and digital signatures.

A private instrument drafted on paper requires a handwritten signature and a private instrument in electronic form requires an electronic signature. The Argentine Digital Signature Act requires a digital signature to comply with the legal requirement of a signature. That is, if the law requires the written form the document has to bear a signature. However, if the law does not require the written form, the parties may agree that the contract has to be executed in writing. Therefore, absent a specific legal formal requirement the parties are free to choose the written form but once chosen, the document has to bear a signature.[706] However, in this scenario it may be argued that a digital signature is not necessary but that an electronic signature that complies with Section 5 of the Argentine Digital Signature Act is sufficient to meet the signature requirement. Section 3 of the Argentine Digital Signature Act requires a digital signature for legal acts where the law imposes the written requirement. Therefore, *a contrario sensu* it may be argued that when the law does not impose the written form an electronic signature may be used.

II.   The Argentine Digital Signature Act in international contracts

1.   Argentine and US law

If Argentine law has been determined as the one establishing the formal requirements of a contract and if according to Argentine law an electronic contract has to be in writing, then, provided that the contract is not excluded from its scope, the Argentine Digital Signature Act applies and sets forth the requirements for electronic signatures. Consequently, if an international electronic contract contains signatures in compliance with a statute in the United States of America, Argentine law will be the one determining whether the foreign electronic signatures are valid and whether they satisfy the legal requirements of a signature. In other words, foreign electronic signatures need to be recognized as valid signatures under Argentine law.

---

[705] Section 2.6 of the Checks Act (The Central Bank shall grant the authorization when the systems for reproducing signatures ensure reliability and authenticity.).

[706] *Rivera*, Instituciones de Derecho Civil – Parte General, Volume II, 1993, p. 724.

The Argentine Digital Signature Act and the US statutes, UETA and E-Sign, follow a different approach concerning the regulation and recognition of electronic signatures. The Argentine Digital Signature Act gives a predominant role to digital signatures. Contrarily, legislation in the United States of America does not require a special type of technology to comply with the legal requirement of a signature. Electronic signature legislation in the United States of America takes a very flexible and wide concept of electronic signature. It should be noted that even though electronic signature legislation in the United States of America is not uniform, most of the states have adopted a variant of UETA.[707]

The Argentine Digital Signature Act only contains provisions for the recognition of foreign digital certificates and there are no provisions determining the recognition of foreign electronic signatures not based on digital certificates. Section 16 of the Argentine Digital Signature Act establishes two ways to recognize foreign digital certificates. One way is that the foreign digital certificate complies with the same legal requirements as domestic digital certificates and that a reciprocity agreement between Argentina and the country of origin of the certificate is in force (Section 16(a)). It is not clear why if a foreign digital certificate meets the same legal requirements as a domestic one still a reciprocity agreement is needed.[708] The second option is that a licensed certifier in Argentina recognizes the validity of the foreign digital certificate and that, in turn, the application authority confirms the recognition (Section 16(b)).

If electronic signatures issued according to US law are not based on a certificate, there are no legal provisions addressing the validity of this type of foreign signatures. Therefore, it could be argued that foreign electronic signatures (as opposed to digital signatures) cannot be considered a valid signature under Argentine law and, as a consequence, that the formal requirements would not be fulfilled. However, if domestic electronic signatures are considered sufficient to comply with the legal requirements of a signature, foreign electronic signatures performing the same functions shall also be recognized. As previously argued, in contracts where no signature requirement is legally mandated a restrictive

---

[707] Forty-six of the fifty US states, the District of Columbia and the Virgin Islands enacted legislation following UETA, see National Conference of State Legislators, Uniform Electronic Transactions Act, <http://www.ncsl.org/programs/lis/CIP/ueta-statutes.htm>. The remaining four states (Georgia, Illinois, New York and Washington) also have electronic signature legislation, see McBride, Baker & Coles, Legislative Analysis Database for E-Commerce and Digital Signatures <http://www.mbc.com/ecommerce/legislative.asp>.

[708] Currently, there are no agreements between Argentina and the United States of America in this matter, see Digital Signature website of the Argentine Republic, <http://www.pki.gov.ar/index.php?option=com_content&task=view&id=95&Itemi d=10>.

interpretation of Section 3 of the Argentine Digital Signature Act, which determines the use of digital signatures to comply with the legal requirement of a signature, would allow contracting parties to use electronic signatures to enter into contracts. In other words, if Section 3 of the Argentine Digital Signature Act is limited to acts where the law imposes the written form, then it can be argued that for acts on which the law does not impose the signature requirement an electronic signature is sufficient. The lack of provisions concerning the recognition of foreign electronic signatures not based on digital certificates shall not be a restriction to their recognition.

Nevertheless, in the event that foreign electronic signatures (including also invalid digital signatures) are not recognized as valid for complying with the signature requirement it does not mean that the contract is invalid. As mentioned, under Argentine law the form is required mainly for evidentiary purposes (*ad probationem*). This means that the contract is not void but that it may not be enforceable in court because of lack of the required legal form. Contracts requiring a determined form by law may be proven only with the designated form (Section 1191 Argentine Civil Code). Notwithstanding this rule, a contract not complying with the legal forms may be proven by other means if there is a document from the counterparty that renders the claim at stake plausible (*principio de prueba por escrito*) (Sections 1191 and 1192 Argentine Civil Code.).[709] It should be noted that the document from the counterparty does not even need to be signed.[710] Therefore, in the event that the electronic signature is not considered to be a valid signature and to comply with the legal requirement of a signature the existence of a contract bearing an electronic signature opens the door for the contract to be proved by any other type of evidence.

Additionally, when the Argentine Civil Code addresses the issue of the signature requirement for private instruments it clearly states that the signature cannot be replaced by the signs or initials but, if recognized by the signatory, they are valid as a signature (Sections 1012 and 1014 Argentine Civil Code). This means that even when a signature complying with the legal requirement is not present, the

---

[709] *de Aguinis / Kleidermacher*, Nuevas formas de contratación. Contratación por ordenador, La Ley 1987-C, 892; *Lavalle Cobo*, in: Belluscio / Zannoni (Eds.), Código Civil, Volume 5, 2002, Sections 1191 and 1192, pp. 870-876; *Mosset Iturraspe*, in: Bueres / Highton (Eds.), Código Civil, Volume 3C, 2005, Sections 1191 and 1192, pp. 6-10.

[710] *Compagnucci de Caso*, Prueba de los contratos, La Ley 1996-D, 66. See also Leone, Jorge N. vs. Maquieira, Jorge S., National Civil Court of Appeals, August 11, 2005 and its comment by *Alterini*, Nuevamente sobre la prueba en el Derecho Informático, La Ley 2006-A, 13 (An e-mail was not considered sufficient to prove a loan contract because the authenticity of the e-mail was not established but it was admitted into evidence as a particular, unsigned instrument or as existence of minimum written evidence.).

voluntary recognition of the signatory of that he or she wrote with the intention to sign is deemed a signature. The same could be the case in electronic signatures. Therefore, a contracting party may voluntarily recognize the electronic signature not complying with the formal requirements of a signature.

To sum up, when the law imposes the written form foreign digital signatures have to comply with the requirements of Section 16 of the Argentine Digital Signature Act. Consequently, a contract signed with a foreign electronic signature that is not recognized by a licensed certifier is not considered validly signed and does not comply with the legal formal requirements. However, for contracts where no form is imposed it is possible to argue that an electronic signature is a valid signature. In any event, except otherwise established by law, the lack of compliance with the form does not mean that the contract is invalid but that its enforceability is at stake. Nevertheless, the electronic contract signed with an electronic signature is minimum written evidence (*principio de prueba por escrito*) and, therefore, allows the introduction of all type of evidence to prove the contract by all means available. The counterparty may also recognize the electronic signature in the contract and that shall cure the absence of a digital signature.

2.   Argentine and German law

An international electronic contract may trigger the interrelation between Argentine and German law. In a contract whose formal validity is governed by Argentine law, electronic signatures may have been created in compliance with the German Electronic Signatures Act. In this case, Argentine law will have to assess the validity of those foreign electronic signatures.

Argentine law requires a digital signature in order to comply with the legal requirement of a signature. Therefore, if an electronic contract has to be in writing, the parties need to sign it with digital signatures. If the foreign electronic signature was issued in accordance with the German law and is based on a digital certificate, the digital certificate has to comply with the requirements imposed by the Argentine Digital Signature Act and related norms; moreover, there needs to be a valid agreement between Argentina and Germany (Section 16(a)).[711] Alternatively, the foreign digital certificate needs to be recognized by an Argentine licensed certifier and by the application authority (Section 16(b)).

The Electronic Signatures Directive imposes the requirement that qualified electronic signatures be given the same value as handwritten signatures. Accordingly, the German law requires a qualified electronic signature when the

---

[711] So far there are none, see Digital Signature website of the Argentine Republic, <http://www.pki.gov.ar/index.phpoption=com_content&task=view&id=95&Itemi d=106>.

law mandates the written form (Section 126a BGB) and no other type of signature may be used to comply with the signature requirement when the signature is legally imposed. Even though neither the Electronic Signatures Directive nor German law use the term digital signature, it is considered that the requirements for qualified electronic signatures may currently only be complied with by using public key cryptography.[712] Based on this, it is likely that a certificate issued in accordance with the German Electronic Signatures Act is recognized by a licensed certifier domiciled in Argentina.[713]

However, when German law does not impose the written form any type of signature can be used unless agreement to the contrary by the parties (Section 127(3) BGB). A similar idea may be sustained under Argentine law. When Argentine law does not require a signature, a restrictive interpretation of Section 3 of the Argentine Digital Signature Act allows arguing that electronic signatures may be used for contracts not requiring the written form. Section 3 of the Argentine Digital Signature Act establishes the equivalence of digital signatures and handwritten signatures when the law requires a signature. Therefore, if Section 3 is limited to the cases where the law imposes the written form, electronic signatures may be used to sign contracts subject to no legal formal requirements.

Concerning the recognition of foreign electronic signatures the law has no special provisions but this shall not be an obstacle to their recognition. If domestic electronic signatures are considered valid, then foreign electronic signatures must be granted the same legal effects.

Moreover, a contract bearing an electronic signature (concept which according to the Argentine Digital Signature Act also embraces invalid digital signatures) is not void but unenforceable unless the written form is required *ad solemnitatem*. Therefore, what is at stake is the enforceability of the contract and not its validity. Furthermore, because the contract bearing an electronic signature provides evidence of a plausible claim then all types of evidence may

---

[712] International Chamber of Commerce, Electronic invoicing in and with the European Union, 2005, p. 9; *Blythe*, Digital Signature Law of the United Nations, European Union, United Kingdom and United States: Promotion of Growth in E-Commerce with Enhanced Security, Richmond Journal of Law and Technology, Volume IX, No. 2, 2005, 1, 9; Commission of the European Communities, Report from the Commission to the European Parliament and Council, Report of the operation of Directive 1999/93/EC on a Community framework for electronic signatures, 2006, p. 4.

[713] At the time this thesis was submitted there were no licensed certifiers in Argentina, see <http://www.pki.gov.ar/index.phpoption=com_content&task=view&id=95&Ite mid=10&lang=en> (no longer available). In the meantime, two certifiers have obtained a license, see <http://www.pki.gov.ar/index.php?option=com_content&ta sk=view&id=95&Itemid=106>.

be produced to prove the contract (Sections 1191 and 1192 Argentine Civil Code). Lastly, the signatory may recognize the electronic signature and in that case it should have the value of a proper signature (Sections 1012 and 1014 Argentine Civil Code).

III. The Argentine Digital Signature Act in domestic contracts

Parties to an Argentine domestic contract may consider the possibility of having a foreign law governing their contract. This may be sought for different reasons: because the foreign law is more familiar to both parties, because the foreign law is more beneficial to their business, or because a certain type of contract is better regulated under a foreign law. The question is whether a domestic contract – that is, one lacking any connecting factor with a foreign country – can be subject to a foreign law by choice of the parties. The answer under Argentine law is no.

Under Argentine law the freedom of the contracting parties to choose a foreign law to govern their contract is dependent upon the existence of an international contract.[714] Consequently, parties to a domestic contract may not choose the law applicable to their contract and, therefore, the contract is governed in its entirety by Argentine law. Also the formal validity is subject to Argentine law because there is no other legal system linked to the contract. The reason is that all connecting points link the contract to the same country; consequently, it is not possible to avoid the formal requirements imposed by Argentine law. As a result, whether the contract has to comply with any formal requirement, and if so, whether the formal requirements may be fulfilled electronically is to be answered by Argentine law. Thus, for electronic contracts the Argentine Digital Signature Act applies. In this case the following types of signatures are available to the parties: (i) digital signatures in the legal sense, (ii) digital signatures in the technical sense (electronic signatures), or (iii) electronic signatures.

1. Digital signatures in the legal sense

The Argentine Digital Signature Act recognizes the legal validity of digital signatures as equivalent to handwritten signatures. Contracts that under Argentine law have to be in writing and signed can, as long as not excluded by Article 4 of the Argentine Digital Signature Act, be drafted in electronic form and be digitally signed. In order to do so the contracting parties have to comply with the Argentine Digital Signature Act and related norms. One of the

---

[714] *Boggiano*, Derecho Internacional Privado,Volume II, 2006, p. 175; *Goldschmidt*, Derecho Internacional Privado, 2002, p. 393; *Feldstein de Cárdenas*, Derecho Internacional Privado – Parte Especial, 2000, p. 350. Neither may a domestic contract be subject to a foreign jurisdiction. According to Section 1 of the National Civil and Commercial Procedural Code only international cases may be submitted to a foreign jurisdiction.

requirements set out by the statute is that the digital certificates be issued by a licensed certifier; otherwise the digital signature, as well as the digital certificate, is not valid. However, for several years after the enactment of the Argentine Digital Signature Act there were no licensed certifiers and for this reason it was not possible for contracting parties to sign a contract using a valid digital signature.[715]

2.   Digital signatures in the technical sense (electronic signatures)

The parties may use electronic signatures based on public key cryptography where digital certificates have been issued by non-licensed certifiers. Such a signature is a digital signature in the technical sense but not in the legal sense. This means that the signature is based on the same technology and following the same procedures but it does not comply with one requirement of the Argentine Digital Signature Act: the issuance of the digital certificate by a certifier that holds a government-issued license.

The question that arises now is about the value of that signature and whether it complies with the legal requirement of a signature. A signature not based on a digital certificate issued by a licensed certifier is invalid in terms of Section 9 of the Argentine Digital Signature Act; it is considered an electronic signature in terms of Section 5 of the Argentine Digital Signature Act. Therefore, there is no doubt that according to the wording of the law such a signature does not satisfy the signature requirement.

The goal of having a licensing scheme is to control the functioning and reliability of the certifiers and the certificates they issue. To this end, the Argentine Digital Signature Act and related norms impose duties and obligations to ensure the proper performance of the system. According to these norms the requirements have to be in accordance with international standards. Therefore, the situation could then be that the parties´ digital certificate has been issued by certifiers complying with international standards and even with good reputation worldwide. On these grounds a court has the power to assess whether the non-licensed certifiers meet the requirements set out by the Argentine Digital Signature Act. It should be noted that form requirements are not ordered *per se* but as a means; therefore, if it is proven that the goals of the imposition of the form are achieved, a court might attach to that signature the same value as to a handwritten signature.

---

[715] For a long time the reason for the absence of licensed certifiers was the government´s failure to issue the relevant regulation. Said regulation was issued by means of the Administrative Decision 6/2007 (published in the Official Gazette on February 12, 2007). Currently, there are two licensed certifiers.

Nevertheless, in case signatures based on public key cryptography are not recognized because of the lack of a certificate issued by a licensed certifier it shall not be forgotten that the contract bears nonetheless an electronic signature. Therefore, the signatory may voluntarily recognize the electronic signature (Sections 1012 and 1014 Argentine Civil Code). Moreover, the existence of a writing allows the introduction of all means of evidence to prove the contract (Sections 1191 and 1192 Argentine Civil Code).

3.   Electronic signature

A contract may bear an electronic signature. In this case we consider only electronic signatures not based on public-key cryptography, that is, excluding invalid digital signatures. The use of electronic signatures may be feasible in contracts where there is no form mandated by law if Section 3 of the Argentine Digital Signature Act is construed restrictively. But even if this restrictive interpretation of Section 3 is not accepted, Sections 1012 and 1014 of the Argentine Civil Code concerning the voluntary recognition of signatures apply and according to Sections 1191 and 1192 Argentine Civil Code the existence of a writing allows the introduction of all means of evidence to prove the contract.

B.   German law governing the form

I.   Form requirements under German law

The Electronic Signatures Directive establishes the legal framework for electronic signatures in Europe. However, in principle, directives are not directly applicable and have to be transposed by each national legislative body. The implementation of the Electronic Signatures Directive in German law led to the amendment of Sections 126 and 127 BGB and to the introduction of Sections 126a and 126b BGB by means of the Form Adaptation Act.

Section 126(1) BGB establishes the signature requirement: whenever the law requires the written form, the document has to bear a handwritten signature or a notarized handwritten sign.[716] Under German law, however, the principle of

---

[716] *Hertel*, in: Staudinger, Kommentar zum Bürgerlichen Gesetzbuch, New Edition, 2004, Section 126, marginal number 2; *Palm*, in: Erman, Bürgerliches Gesetzbuch, 12th Edition, 2008, Section 126, marginal numbers 7 and 11; *Heinrichs / Ellenberger*, in: Palandt, Bürgerliches Gesetzbuch, 68th Edition, 2009, Section 126, marginal number 7; *Wendtland*, in: Bamberger / Roth, Bürgerliches Gesetzbuch, 2nd Edition, 2007, Section 126, marginal numbers 6 and 8.

freedom of forms is the rule and the compliance with formal requirements, the exception.[717]

In general, the requirement of the written form may be fulfilled by means of the electronic form (Section 126(3) BGB).[718] In this case, the electronic document must include the signer's name[719] and qualified electronic signature,[720] as defined by the German Electronic Signatures Act (Section 126a(1) BGB). Unlike Section 126(2), Section 126a does not establish the requirement of

---

[717] *Heinrichs / Ellenberger*, in: Palandt, Bürgerliches Gesetzbuch, 68th Edition, 2009, Section 125, marginal number 1; *Heydn*, Germany, in: Campbell (Ed), E-Commerce and the Law of Digital Signatures, 2005, pp. 235-239 (The author also analyzes the different types of formal requirements under German law.); *Hertel*, in: Staudinger, Kommentar zum Bürgerlichen Gesetzbuch, New Edition, 2004, Section 127, marginal number 8; *Miedbrodt*, Signaturregulierung im Rechtsvergleich, 2000, p. 39. Nevertheless, when the law does require a special formal requirement the legal act is void if it is not in compliance with it (Section 125 BGB), see *Heinrichs / Ellenberger*, in: Palandt, Bürgerliches Gesetzbuch, 68th Edition, 2009, Section 125, marginal number 12.

[718] *Hertel*, in: Staudinger, Kommentar zum Bürgerlichen Gesetzbuch, New Edition, 2004, Section 126, marginal number 3; *Palm*, in: Erman, Bürgerliches Gesetzbuch, 12th Edition, 2008, Section 126a, marginal number 2.

[719] *Palm*, in: Erman, Bürgerliches Gesetzbuch, 12th Edition, 2008, Section 126a, marginal number 4; *Hertel*, in: Staudinger, Kommentar zum Bürgerlichen Gesetzbuch, New Edition, 2004, Section 126a, marginal number 44; *Prütting / Wegen / Weinreich*, BGB Kommentar, 4th Edition, 2009, Section 126a, marginal number 4 (Initials are not sufficient; however, the complete name of the person is not required either, the last name being sufficient.); *Marly*, in: Soergel, Bürgerliches Gesetzbuch, 13th Edition, 2002, Section 126a, marginal number 22; *Heinrichs / Ellenberger*, in: Palandt, Bürgerliches Gesetzbuch, 68th Edition, 2009, Section 126a, marginal number 8; *Wendtland*, in: Bamberger / Roth, Bürgerliches Gesetzbuch, 2nd Edition, 2007, Section 126a, marginal number 4. In contrast to a handwritten signature (*Unterschrift*), the name does not have to be at the end of the document, see *Marly*, in: Soergel, Bürgerliches Gesetzbuch, 13th Edition, 2002, Section 126a, marginal number 23; *Heinrichs / Ellenberger*, in: Palandt, Bürgerliches Gesetzbuch, 68th Edition, 2009, Section 126a, marginal number 8; *Palm*, in: Erman, Bürgerliches Gesetzbuch, 12th Edition, 2008, Section 126a, marginal number 4; *Hertel*, in: Staudinger, Kommentar zum Bürgerlichen Gesetzbuch, New Edition, 2004, Section 126a, marginal number 44.

[720] *Heinrichs / Ellenberger*, in: Palandt, Bürgerliches Gesetzbuch, 68th Edition, 2009, Section 126a, marginal number 9; *Palm*, in: Erman, Bürgerliches Gesetzbuch, 12th Edition, 2008, Section 126a, marginal number 5; *Wendtland*, in: Bamberger / Roth, Bürgerliches Gesetzbuch, 2nd Edition, 2007, Section 126a, marginal number 5. The qualified electronic signature fulfills the same requirements as the handwritten signature, see *Heinrichs / Ellenberger*, in: Palandt, Bürgerliches Gesetzbuch, 68th Edition, 2009, Section 126a, marginal number 5.

signing only one document.[721] Therefore, concerning electronic contracts it is sufficient that each contracting party includes his or her name and his or her qualified signature in separate, but nonetheless identical, electronic documents (Section 126(2) BGB).[722] Of course, the parties are not hindered from signing the same electronic document.[723]

The possibility to use the electronic form instead of the written form always exists unless otherwise established by the law (Section 126(3) BGB).[724] In fact, in several provisions the German law expressly excludes the use of the electronic form.[725] The exclusions are based on different grounds. One of the reasons is that electronic signatures are not considered to fulfill the warning function in all cases.[726] Therefore, persons may not act with the same care as

---

[721] *Palm*, in: Erman, Bürgerliches Gesetzbuch, 12th Edition, 2008, Section 126a, marginal number 7; *Hertel*, in: Staudinger, Kommentar zum Bürgerlichen Gesetzbuch, New Edition, 2004, Section 126a, marginal number 56; *Einsele*, in: Münchener Kommentar zum Bürgerlichen Gesetzbuch, 5th Edition, 2006, Section 126a, marginal number 26.

[722] *Palm*, in: Erman, Bürgerliches Gesetzbuch, 12th Edition, 2008, Section 126a, marginal number 7. Each party has to include its name and electronically sign the copy the other party is going to keep, see *Einsele*, in: Münchener Kommentar zum Bürgerlichen Gesetzbuch, 5th Edition, 2006, Section 126a, marginal number 26; *Heinrichs / Ellenberger*, in: Palandt, Bürgerliches Gesetzbuch, 68th Edition, 2009, Section 126a, marginal number 10.

[723] *Hertel*, in: Staudinger, Kommentar zum Bürgerlichen Gesetzbuch, New Edition, 2004, Section 126a, marginal number 56; *Palm*, in: Erman, Bürgerliches Gesetzbuch, 12th Edition, 2008, Section 126a, marginal number 7; *Einsele*, in: Münchener Kommentar zum Bürgerlichen Gesetzbuch, 5th Edition, 2006, Section 126a, marginal number 26.

[724] *Heinrichs / Ellenberger*, in: Palandt, Bürgerliches Gesetzbuch, 68th Edition, 2009, Section 126, marginal number 13 and Section 126a, marginal numbers 1-2; *Hertel*, in: Staudinger, Kommentar zum Bürgerlichen Gesetzbuch, New Edition, 2004, Section 126a, marginal number 30.

[725] *Heinrichs / Ellenberger*, in: Palandt, Bürgerliches Gesetzbuch, 68th Edition, 2009, Section 126a, marginal number 2; *Einsele*, in: Münchener Kommentar zum Bürgerlichen Gesetzbuch, 5th Edition, 2006, Section 126, marginal numbers 23-24; *Prütting / Wegen / Weinreich*, BGB Kommentar, 4th Edition, 2009, Section 126a, marginal number 2; *Hertel*, in: Staudinger, Kommentar zum Bürgerlichen Gesetzbuch, New Edition, 2004, Section 126a, marginal number 30; *Noack*, 2. Teil: Das Gesetz zur Anpassung der Formschriften des Privatrechts und anderer Vorschriften an den modernen Rechtsgeschäftsverkehr, in: Dauner-Lieb / Heidel / Rign (Eds.), Das Neue Schuldrecht – Ein Lehrbuch, 2002, pp. 444-445.

[726] *Einsele*, in: Münchener Kommentar zum Bürgerlichen Gesetzbuch, 5th Edition, 2006, Section 126a, marginal number 25; *Hertel*, in: Staudinger, Kommentar zum Bürgerlichen Gesetzbuch, New Edition, 2004, Section 126, marginal number 166 and Section 126a, marginal number 36; *Bettendorf*, Elektronische Dokumente und Formqualität, RNotZ 2005, 277, 285; *Hertel*, in: Staudinger, Kommentar zum Bürgerlichen Gesetzbuch, New Edition, 2004, Section 126a, marginal number 36.

when they sign a paper document.[727] Another reason for excluding the electronic form is that it might not be feasible to implement; for example, working certificates issued by employers at the end of the employee-employer relationship cannot be in electronic form because of the fear that the employee and public and private entities do not have the necessary equipment to read them.[728]

The requirement of a qualified electronic signature imposed by Section 126a BGB applies where the law requires the written form.[729] Otherwise, for acts where no formal requirements are imposed by law, the parties are free to choose the form they deem most appropriate. Therefore, the parties may choose the written form, the electronic form, the text form, or as a matter of fact, any other form. Moreover, the parties may establish the requirements they consider suitable for these forms not being limited by the legal requirements of those forms.[730] Therefore, if the parties choose the electronic form, they are not bound by Section 126(a)(1), which requires a qualified electronic signature. The parties may consider the signature requirement is complied with the use of a simple electronic signature or, on the contrary, require the use of a qualified electronic signature with provider accreditation.

In the case the parties have agreed on the electronic form without detailing the specific requirements they have to comply with, Sections 126, 126a and 126b BGB apply but Section 127 BGB simplifies their requirements.[731] Section 127 BGB relaxes the formal requirements when the law does not impose the written

---

[727] *Einsele*, in: Münchener Kommentar zum Bürgerlichen Gesetzbuch, 5th Edition, 2006, Section 126, marginal number 23 and Section 126a, marginal number 25; *Palm*, in: Erman, Bürgerliches Gesetzbuch, 12th Edition, 2008, Section 126a, marginal number 5; Begr. RegE zu §126a BGB, BT-Drucks. 14/4987, p. 17.

[728] *Einsele*, in: Münchener Kommentar zum Bürgerlichen Gesetzbuch, 5th Edition, 2006, Section 126, marginal number 24; Begr. RegE zu §126a BGB, BT-Drucks. 14/4987, p. 22.

[729] *Prütting / Wegen / Weinreich*, BGB Kommentar, 4th Edition, 2009, Section 126, marginal number 1; *Palm*, in: Erman, Bürgerliches Gesetzbuch, 12th Edition, 2008, Section 126, marginal number 1; *Wendtland*, in: Bamberger / Roth, Bürgerliches Gesetzbuch, 2nd Edition, 2007, Section 126, marginal number 1 and Section 126a, marginal number 1.

[730] *Einsele*, in: Münchener Kommentar zum Bürgerlichen Gesetzbuch, 5th Edition, 2006, Section 127, marginal numbers 2 and 6; *Heinrichs / Ellenberger*, in: Palandt, Bürgerliches Gesetzbuch, 68th Edition, 2009, Section 127, marginal number 1; *Palm*, in: Erman, Bürgerliches Gesetzbuch, 12th Edition, 2008, Section 127, marginal numbers 1 and 3; *Wendtland*, in: Bamberger / Roth, Bürgerliches Gesetzbuch, 2nd Edition, 2007, Section 127, marginal number 2.

[731] *Prütting / Wegen / Weinreich*, BGB Kommentar, 4th Edition, 2009, Section 127, marginal number 1; *Palm*, in: Erman, Bürgerliches Gesetzbuch, 12th Edition, 2008, Section 127, marginal numbers 6-7; *Steinbeck*, Die neuen Formvorschriften im BGB, DStR, 2004, 644, 647-648.

or the electronic form and the parties have not expressed in detail their will concerning the formal requirements of the contract. Therefore, if the parties agree on the electronic form, the law construes, absent an agreement of the parties to the contrary, that any type of electronic signature may be used (Section 127(3) BGB).[732] It is not necessary that the parties sign with a qualified electronic signature as established by Section 126a BGB. Therefore, when the law does not impose the written form and the parties have not agreed on a specific type of electronic signature all type of electronic signatures may be used.

Section 126b, which introduces the text form, is not subject to any simplifications because it is already the simplest form available.[733] The text form does not require a signature and that is why it is considered that it does not perform the same functions as the written form.[734]

II.   Written form required by law and the Argentine Digital Signature Act

According to German law a contract requiring the written form has to bear a qualified electronic signature as defined by the German Electronic Signatures Act (Section 126a BGB). If all electronic signatures in a contract meet that requirement, the contract is formally valid – as long as, of course, the law does not exclude the use of the electronic form for that type of contract. However, if a contract bears a signature based on a certificate issued by an Argentine certification-service-provider, German law has to assess the validity of that electronic signature (Section 23 German Electronic Signatures Act).

---

[732] *Heinrichs / Ellenberger*, in: Palandt, Bürgerliches Gesetzbuch, 68th Edition, 2009, Section 127, marginal number 5; *Prütting / Wegen / Weinreich*, BGB Kommentar, 4th Edition, 2009, Section 127, marginal number 5 (The parties can also waive the signature requirement.); *Einsele*, in: Münchener Kommentar zum Bürgerlichen Gesetzbuch, 5th Edition, 2006, Section 127, marginal number 13 (Also signatures outside the scope of the German Electronic Signatures Act may be used.); *Bettendorf*, Elektronische Dokumente und Formqualität, RNotZ 2005, 277, 282; *Hertel*, in: Staudinger, Kommentar zum Bürgerlichen Gesetzbuch, New Edition, 2004, Section 127, marginal number 78.

[733] *Prütting / Wegen / Weinreich*, BGB Kommentar, 4th Edition, 2009, Section 126b, marginal number 1; *Hertel*, in: Staudinger, Kommentar zum Bürgerlichen Gesetzbuch, New Edition, 2004, Section 126b, marginal number 1 and Section 127, marginal number 81; Begr. RegE zu §126a BGB, BT-Drucks. 14/4987, p. 21.

[734] *Heinrichs / Ellenberger*, in: Palandt, Bürgerliches Gesetzbuch, 68th Edition, 2009, Section 126b, marginal number 1; *Palm*, in: Erman, Bürgerliches Gesetzbuch, 12th Edition, 2008, Section 126b, marginal number 1; *Hertel*, in: Staudinger, Kommentar zum Bürgerlichen Gesetzbuch, New Edition, 2004, Section 126b, marginal number 10.

Under German law a certificate issued by an Argentine certification-service-provider is a foreign certificate because it has been issued by a certification-service-provider in a third country (Argentina is neither a member state nor an associate state of the European Union). Electronic signatures based on certificates are characterized as domestic or foreign depending on the location of the certification-service-provider issuing the certificate(Section 23(1) German Electronic Signatures Act).

Under German law, foreign electronic signatures are to be recognized when two requirements are met. First, the foreign certificate must be a qualified certificate and the foreign electronic signature, a qualified electronic signature, as defined by the German Electronic Signatures Act. Therefore, the foreign electronic signature and the foreign certificate on which the signature is based have to comply with the same requirements a German certificate and an electronic signature have to comply with. The second requirement involves the certification-service-provider. Even when the foreign certificate and electronic signature technically fulfill all the requirements set out by German law, they have not been issued by a certification-service-provider located in an EU member state or associate member state. Therefore, one of these three options needs to be present: (i) the foreign certification-service-provider is accredited in an EU member state, (ii) a certification-service-provider domiciled in a EU member state guarantees the certificate issued by the foreign certification-service-provider, or (iii) there is an agreement between on the one hand, the European Union and, on the other hand, the third state or an international organization for the recognition of the certificate or the certification-service-provider.

1.   Foreign certification-service-provider accredited in the European Union

One option for the recognition of foreign certificates and foreign qualified signatures (apart from the fact that they have to be in accordance with German law) is that the certification-service-provider issuing the certificate in Argentina complies with the requirements of the Electronic Signatures Directive and that it is accredited to a voluntary accreditation scheme in an EU member state (Section 23(1)1 German Electronic Signatures Act). This means that accreditation schemes are voluntary for certification-service-providers located in the European Union but mandatory for foreign certification-service-providers. It is not required that the foreign certification-service-provider be accredited to a voluntary accreditation scheme in Germany; it complies with the requirement by being accredited to a voluntary accreditation scheme pertaining to any of the other EU member states. As a result, the Argentine certification-service-provider, in addition to the legal requirements imposed by Argentine law, has to comply with the requirements imposed to a certification-service-provider located in the European Union.

2. Certification-service-provider domiciled in a EU member state guarantees the certificate

In this case a certification-service-provider already established in one of the member states of the European Union guarantees the certificate (Section 23(1)2). Unlike the previous case, the Argentine certification-service-provider issuing the certificate does not have to comply with any additional requirements. The intervention of a certification-service-provider located in the European Union turns any further action by the foreign certification-service-provider unnecessary. This situation might work out well in the case of international companies with offices in different countries. A certification-service-provider in the European Union may recognize the certificates issued by a branch located in Argentina.

3. Agreement recognizes the certificate or the certification-service-provider

The existence of agreements – either bilateral or multilateral – is certainly desirable in order to allow the contracting parties to know before entering into a contract that the foreign certificate is going to be recognized in Germany (Section 23(1)3 German Electronic Signatures Act).

However, in the other two scenarios the parties can know beforehand whether an electronic signature issued according to Argentine law will meet the requirements imposed by the German Electronic Signatures Act. The parties can verify whether the Argentine licensed certifier issuer of the certificate has complied with the requirements of the German Electronic Signatures Act and is registered in an accreditation scheme in the European Union. Otherwise, it is possible to check whether a certification-service-provider located in the European Union is willing to recognize the certificate issued in Argentina. Another option for the Argentine contracting party is to obtain a certificate from a certificate-service-provider located in the European Union or an associate state. All of these options avoid delaying the analysis of the formal validity of the signatures to the stage when the conflicts arise.

It should be noted that under Argentine law a digital certificate has to be issued by a licensed certifier. The fact that the digital certificate is issued by a licensed or non-licensed certifier is not relevant for its recognition under German law. Therefore, the certificate that is not considered valid to create valid digital signatures in Argentina may nonetheless comply with the requirements to be recognized as a valid signature under German law. The reasoning for this conclusion is that having a license is a requirement of domestic regulation. German law will conduct the analysis of whether the foreign certificate fulfills the requirements imposed by the German Electronic Signatures Act.

III. Written form not required by law

The German Electronic Signatures Act establishes the mechanism for the recognition of foreign signatures based on certificates (Section 23). The statute does not address the equivalence of other types of foreign electronic signatures. Therefore, when the parties use other types of signatures, such as a simple electronic signature, the statute does not establish how this type of foreign electronic signatures is to be recognized.

C. US law governing the form

I. Statute of Frauds

Under US law the requirement of a writing is encompassed in the legal provisions known as the Statute of Frauds.[735] The Statute of Frauds originated in an English Act named "An Act for the Prevention of Frauds and Prejudices" which dates from 1677. The name of the act reveals its goal: to prevent deceit in contracts.[736] The underlying idea is that the lack of a signed writing of the parties' agreement results in fraudulent conducts.[737] Therefore, certain contracts require a writing for the contract to be enforceable. Each US state has its own Statute of Frauds; however, normally five types of contracts fall under the Statute of Frauds: the contract of an executor or administrator to answer for a duty of his or her decedent; a contract to answer for the duty of another; a contract made upon consideration of marriage; a contract for the sale of an interest in land, and a contract that is not to be performed within one year from its making.[738] Besides, the Uniform Commercial Code contains in Section 2-201 a Statute of Frauds for the sale of goods for USD $500 or more.[739]

Whenever a contract falls under the Statute of Frauds, a signed writing is required in order to enforce the contract – the contract itself needs not be in writing.[740] The lack of this requirement does not affect the validity of the contract; however, the contract is unenforceable unless an exception to the

---

[735] The requirement of a writing and a signature is also present in other statutes, see *Smedinghoff*, The Legal Requirements for Creating Secure and Enforceable Electronic Transactions, 2002, p. 3.

[736] *Farnsworth*, Contracts, Volume II, 1990, pp. 82-87; *Fuller / Eisenberg*, Basic Contract Law, 2006, p. 1032-1035.

[737] *Fuller / Eisenberg*, Basic Contract Law, 2006, p. 1034.

[738] Restatement (Second) of Contracts, Section 110, see *Farnsworth*, Contracts, Volume II, 1990, pp. 87-126; *Fuller / Eisenberg*, Basic Contract Law, 2006, pp. 1038-1039 and 1045-1052.

[739] *Farnsworth*, Contracts, Volume II, 1990, pp. 126-130; *Fuller / Eisenberg*, Basic Contract Law, 2006, pp. 1038-1039.

[740] *Farnsworth*, Contracts, Volume II, 1990, p. 90, footnote 13.

application of the Statute of Frauds is triggered.[741] Case law has reduced the sphere of application of the Statute of Frauds by interpreting the concept of a signed writing and the exceptions to the Statute of Frauds broadly, as well as by construing narrowly the cases to which the Statute of Frauds applies.[742]

The Uniform Commercial Code contains a broad definition of the term signature which encompasses both handwritten and electronic signatures. What is relevant is not the form or type of the signature but the signer's intent to authenticate or to adopt what is being signed (Section 2-103(1)(p) UCC).[743] This is in line with the concept of electronic signature adopted by UETA and E-Sign.[744] Moreover, the UCC, based on the principles contained in UETA and E-Sign, expressly recognizes the non-discrimination against electronic signatures by establishing that the legal effects or enforceability of signatures may not depend exclusively on their electronic nature (Section 2-211(2) UCC).

II.   Electronic Signatures: Argentina and the United States of America

In the United States of America electronic signature legislation is predominantly technologically neutral. Therefore, in the United States of America the parties may use any type of electronic signature as long as it serves to prove the intent of the signatory. Neither UETA nor E-Sign contain rules directed to the recognition of foreign electronic signatures; therefore, foreign electronic signatures are subject to the same requirements as domestic electronic signatures.

When US law requires a writing this requirement may be fulfilled by the use of an electronic record and an electronic signature (provided no exception applies). The electronic signature does not need to be created in accordance with a special technology or to comply with additional requirements when the law imposes the

---

[741] The exceptions to the Statute of Frauds are contained in UCC Sections 2-201(2) (merchant's exception) and 2-201(3) (specially manufactured goods, admission or partial performance), see *Gillette / Walt*, Sales Law – Domestic and International, 1999, pp. 127-133.

[742] *Fuller / Eisenberg*, Basic Contract Law, 2006, pp. 1038 and 1053-1057. Courts held that telegrams, faxes, tape recordings, among others, comply with the writing requirement of the Statute of Frauds, see *Wright*, The law of Electronic Commerce, 1991, p. 280; *Greenstone*, An Introduction to the Uniform Electronic Transactions Act, 2001; *Farnsworth*, Contracts, Volume II, 1990, pp. 86 and 130 et. seq. Likewise, diverse types of signature such as a letterhead or a typed name have been regarded as sufficient to comply with the Statute of Frauds signature requirement, see *Farnsworth*, Contracts, Volume II, 1990, p. 145.

[743] *Wright*, The law of Electronic Commerce, 1991, pp. 282-283; *Smedinghoff*, The Legal Requirements for Creating Secure and Enforceable Electronic Transactions, 2002, pp. 11-12.

[744] *Fuller / Eisenberg*, Basic Contract Law, 2006, pp. 1057-1060.

requirement of a signature. The electronic signature statutes in the United States of America recognize one type of signature and this may be used whenever the law requires a signature as well as when it does not.

The principle of technology neutrality and the minimalist approach adopted by US legislation result in an ample freedom for the parties when it comes to decide which method to use to sign electronically.[745] An electronic signature, whatever its type, satisfies the legal requirement of a signature if it is affixed with the intent to sign and authenticate the contract. Therefore, a digital signature and an electronic signature issued in accordance with the Argentine Digital Signature comply with the requirements of an electronic signature under US law if those requirements are met. The type of signing method used is not relevant as long as the functions are performed.

D. Conclusions

Whether one legal system or another is designated as governing the formal validity of a contract impacts on its formal requirements. The first consequence is whether the legal system imposes a special formal requirement at all. The predominant principle in today's legal systems is the freedom of forms and, therefore, the requirement of a certain form is the exception.

The second consequence is whether a signature is required. A foreign electronic signature has to be recognized under the terms of the law governing the form. That means that the form requirements are assessed under the view of one law. If that law is Argentine law its provisions concerning recognition of foreign electronic signatures apply. The same is the case if the form is subject to German or US law. The divergence in the legal approaches to the regulation of electronic signatures is shown in different standards for the recognition of foreign electronic signatures.

An electronic signature issued under US law will not be considered to comply with the requirements of Argentine law unless based on a digital certificate; in other words, unless it is a digital signature. Likewise, also under German law when the signature is imposed by law the signature has to comply with strict requirements considered similar to those of digital signatures. US law has a broader approach which results in more flexibility towards the recognition of foreign electronic signatures; however, this flexibility may impinge on the recognition of electronic signatures based on US law because they might not be recognized under German and Argentine law for legal acts where the law requires a signature.

---

[745] Uniform Electronic Transactions Act with preparatory note and comments, 1999, pp. 9-10.

In case no written form is required by law, German law allows the parties to choose the type of signature. The parties have ample freedom and can demand stricter or softer conditions than the ones imposed by law. Moreover, absent an agreement by the parties the law construes that the signature requirement may be fulfilled with any type of electronic signature. This approach may also be applied to Argentine law. When Argentine law does not require a signature; that is, in terms of Section 3 of the Argentine Digital Signature Act, when it does not impose the obligation to sign, an electronic signature, instead of a digital signature, may be used. Therefore, the recognition of foreign electronic signatures seems to be easier when there is no legal requirement of a signature. US law does not distinguish between the cases where a signature is required by law and those where the parties can freely choose the form; rather, electronic signatures are always subject to the same analysis which focuses on the intent of the signer.

Final Conclusions

The Internet, EDI, and e-mail are new channels to enter into commercial agreements. The formal validity of these contracts is subject to the same rules applied to paper contracts; therefore, electronic contracts may need to be in writing and signed. For this reason it has been necessary to develop a functional equivalent to handwritten signatures to be used in electronic transactions.

The handwritten signature is a means of establishing the identity of a person and also the traditional means by which a person expresses his or her intention in written documents. The electronic world uses different methods (based on different technologies) to establish the identity of a person. When these methods are combined with the intention to sign the law recognizes the existence of a valid signature. The different methods to sign electronically offer dissimilar levels of reliability as well as of complexity. Some laws recognize only methods ensuring the highest authenticity security, which currently are those based on public key cryptography. Other laws do not address the technological issue recognizing all types of electronic signatures.

Due to the nature of electronic commerce it has been perceived that uniform standards for the recognition of electronic signatures would pave the way for the execution of online contracts. Nevertheless, right from the beginning the legal approach to the regulation of electronic signatures in different jurisdictions has been divergent. The first disagreement concerns what is understood under the term electronic signature. UETA and E-Sign present a single concept of electronic signature; the Electronic Signatures Directives and, consequently, the German Electronic Signatures Act contain three types of electronic signatures; the Argentine Digital Signature Act differentiates between electronic and digital signatures. Nevertheless, as far as the concept of the most simple type of electronic signature is concerned, there are no major differences between the different statutes.

The second disagreement refers to the lack of consensus among the different legal systems as to which type of electronic signature is considered legally valid for the execution of legal acts. The statutes analyzed in this work present different approaches ranging from flexible ones, as is the case of the legislation in the United States of America, which recognizes as valid all types of signatures falling within the single concept of electronic signature, to more restrictive ones, as is the case of Germany and Argentina, where only one type of signatures, among several, is admissible for the compliance with the legal requirement of a signature (at least when the signature requirement is imposed by law). Currently, in these latter jurisdictions, when the law requires a signature, electronic signatures have to be based on public key cryptography; therefore, public key cryptography remains predominant in several jurisdictions. Electronic signatures, especially digital signatures, are not as widely used as expected, at least for the execution of contracts and especially for those contracts where the law requires a signature. The reasons may be several: lack of familiarity with the new technology or its complex implementation, among others. Whether this might change in the near future is to be seen.

Efforts to achieve uniformity have been attempted through the work of international institutions. To this end, UNCITRAL prepared the Model Law on Electronic Commerce, the Model Law on Electronic Signatures and the Convention on the Use of Electronic Communications in International Contracts. Nevertheless, the reality is that today electronic signature legislation continues to be divergent. Harmonization requires time because it signifies finding a compromise among different legal systems, in particular between civil law and common law legal systems. In electronic signature legislation, civil law countries have in general adopted only secure techniques while common law countries are more open to the acceptance of all types of techniques to sign. Thus, the United States of America has in general followed a more flexible approach while the requirements are more stringent, at least when the law imposes the signature requirement, under German and Argentine law.

The different legal approaches to the regulation of electronic signatures impinges on the contract and the contracting parties. Parties to a contract shall be aware that in case the electronic transaction is international, the contract has contacts with different countries and, therefore, with different legal rules. This means that different laws may potentially govern the electronic signatures requirements. Nevertheless, the electronic signatures contained in the contract need to comply with the electronic signature statute in force in the country whose law determines the formal requirements of the contract. In all the statutes herein analyzed foreign electronic signatures need to comply with the same requirements as domestic electronic signatures do; however, the requirements of each legal system may differ substantially. This is specially the case in jurisdictions such as the United States of America on the one hand and Germany and Argentina on the other. While the United States of America adopted a technologically neutral approach to electronic signatures, Germany and Argentina, although with a different level of openness towards different technologies, an approach mainly based on public key cryptography.

Consequently, electronic signatures created according to US law may run the risk of not being recognized in jurisdictions like Argentina and Germany for cases where the law imposes the signature requirement. For cases where the freedom of the parties is the rule German law clearly accepts the use of all types of electronic signatures while Argentine law may be susceptible to that interpretation. The construction of the Argentine Digital Signature Act in this manner increases the sphere of application of electronic signatures and does not jeopardize the objectives of the lawmakers to admit the most secure type of electronic signature as equivalent to handwritten signature for acts where a signature is required by law. However, Argentine law has always been primarily based on digital signatures and the few decisions dealing with electronic documents or electronic signatures show the reluctance of courts to recognize documents not bearing digital signatures. In the case of German and Argentine law the dissimilarities are not so notorious. Basically, both require electronic signatures based on public key cryptography where the law imposes the written form.

When an electronic contract bears foreign electronic signatures the validity of domestic electronic signatures, if any, and of foreign electronic signatures is determined under one same law and this renders the divergence between the different statutes evident. However, the parties can minimize the consequences resulting from different legal approaches in the regulation of electronic signatures by establishing which law the formal validity of a contract will be subject to and complying with the requirements imposed by the electronic signature legislation of that legal system.

The formal validity of a contract is an issue that is of the highest importance to contracting parties because it may render the contract invalid or unenforceable. The rules of private international law establish the laws that may govern the formal validity of a contract. Again, each legal system follows its own rules; therefore, the laws designated as governing the formal requirements of a contract may not be the same under all legal systems. For example, in the European Union the law of the place where the contracting parties are at the time of issuing the offer or acceptance (even if just temporarily) may govern the formal validity of the whole contract. Other jurisdictions, on the contrary, may not accept as formally valid a contract complying with the formal requirements of that law. Nevertheless, it can be said that the basic principles are similar.

One of the laws that all legal systems herein analyzed recognize as valid for determining the formal validity of a contract is the law applicable to the substance of the contract. Moreover, party autonomy is recognized; therefore, the parties may choose the law applicable to the contract and subject the formal validity of the contract to that law. This means that if the parties make a choice of law and comply with the formal requirements imposed by that legal system, the contract will be considered formally valid in the other jurisdictions herein analyzed. In the case of an electronic contract it further signifies that the electronic signature statute of the law applicable to the contract will determine the requirements electronic signatures have to comply with. Likewise, the recognition of foreign electronic signatures will be determined according to that law. As a result, the formal requirements imposed by a legal system may be one of the aspects parties take into account when choosing the law applicable to the contract. For instance, there are laws that recognize all types of electronic signatures and this may be what the parties are looking for. On the other hand, maybe the law with higher security standards is preferable for transactions which have a significant monetary value.

Another law recognized by all jurisdiction as the one governing the formal requirements is the law of the place of contracting. Therefore, following the same criterion, the parties may subject the contract to the formal requirements of the law of the place of execution and the contract will be regarded as formally valid in the other jurisdictions covered in this work. That means, the contracting parties may comply with the requirements of the electronic signature statute in force in the country of the place of contracting.

Taking into account all of the above, when it comes to international electronic contracts the parties still have to conduct the same analysis as with paper transactions; that is, the law determining the formal validity of the contract has to be established. An electronic signature will be valid if in accordance with that law. Electronic signature legislation has helped the recognition of electronic signatures to the extent that electronic signatures are accepted as valid methods to sign contracts. However, when used in international contracts parties shall be aware of the different electronic signatures regulation. That means the parties shall know which law or possible laws the formal validity of an electronic contract may be subject to, and follow the requirements of the electronic signature statute of the relevant legal system, either by creating domestic signatures according to it or ensuring that foreign electronic signatures will be recognized as valid. In this manner, contracting parties may safely enter into valid and enforceable electronic contracts, so as to what electronic signatures is concerned, and reduce the impact of divergent electronic signature legislation.

Bibliography

Aalberts, Babette P. / van der Hof, Simone, Digital Signature Blindness – Analysis of legislative approaches toward electronic authentication, November 1999, <http://arno.uvt.nl/show.cgi?fid=4855>, pp. 1-72.

Alegría, Héctor, Nuevas fronteras de la documentación, la forma y la prueba de las relaciones comerciales, La Ley 1985-E, pp. 660.

Alterini, Juan Martín, Nuevamente sobre la prueba en el Derecho Informático, La Ley 2006-A, pp. 13.

American Bar Association, Digital Signature Guidelines, 1996, <http://www.aba net.org/scitech/ec/isc/dsg.pdf>, pp. 1-128.

Antecedentes Parlamentarios, La Ley Buenos Aires 2002, pp. 707-870.

Atreya, Mohan / Hammond, Benjamin / Paine, Stephen / Starrett, Paul / Wu, Stephen, Digital Signatures, New York 2002.

Audit, Bernard, Droit International Privé, 4th Edition, Paris 2006.

Bachman, Birgit, Internet und IPR, in: Lehman, Michael (Ed.), Internet- und Multimediarecht (Cyberlaw), Stuttgart 1997, pp. 169-183.

Baker, Stewart A. / Hurst, Paul R., The Limits of Trust – Cryptography, Governments, and Electronic Commerce, The Hague / London / Boston 1998.

Balestra, Ricardo R., Ley aplicable a los contratos de compraventa internacional de mercaderías, La Ley 1987-E, pp. 752.

Bamberger, Heinz Georg / Roth, Herbert (Eds.), Beck'scher Online-Kommentar, EGBGB, 14th Edition, 2009.

Bamberger, Heinz Georg / Roth, Herbert (Eds.), Bürgerliches Gesetzbuch, 2nd Edition, 2007.

Basedow, Jürgen, The Effects of Globalization on Private International Law, in: Basedow, Jürgen / Kono, Toshiyuki (Eds.), Legal aspects of globalization, The Hague / London / Boston 2000, pp. 1-10.

Batiffol, Henri / Lagarde, Paul, Droit International Privé, 7th Edition, Volume II, Paris 1983.

Baum, M., Electronic Contracting in the US: The Legal and Control Context, in: Walden, Ian (Ed.), EDI and the Law, London 1989, pp. 119-138.

Belluscio, Augusto C. / Zannoni, Eduardo A. (Eds.), Código Civil y leyes complementarias – Comentado Anotado y Concordado, Volume 4, Third Reprint, Buenos Aires 2001.

Belluscio, Augusto C. / Zannoni, Eduardo A. (Eds.), Código Civil y leyes complementarias – Comentado Anotado y Concordado, Volume 5, Third Reprint, Buenos Aires 2002.

Belluscio, Augusto C. / Zannoni, Eduardo A. (Eds.), Código Civil y leyes complementarias – Comentado Anotado y Concordado, Volume 9, Buenos Aires 2007.

Benabou, Valérie Laure, Should there be a minimum harmonization of the law?, in: Internet – International Law, International and European Studies and

Comments (International Colloquium 19-20 November 2001 Paris), Brussels 2005, pp. 167-178.

Bettendorf, Jörg, Elektronische Dokumente und Formqualität, RNotZ 2005, pp. 277-294.

Biddle, C. Bradford, Legislating Market Winners: Digital Signature Laws and the Electronic Commerce Market Place, San Diego Law Review, Volume 34, Number 3, pp. 1125-1246.

Bizer, Johann / Miedbrodt, Anja, Die digitale Signatur im elektronischen Rechtsverkehr – Deutsches Signaturgesetz und Entwurf der Europäischen Richtlinie, in: Kröger, Detlef / Gimmy, Marc A. (Eds.), Handbuch zum Internetrecht, Berlin / Heidelberg / New York 2000, pp. 135-163.

Black's Law Dictionary, 8th Edition, St. Paul, Minnesota 2004.

Blythe, Stephen E., Digital Signature Law of the United Nations, European Union, United Kingdom and United States: Promotion of Growth in E-Commerce with Enhanced Security, Richmond Journal of Law and Technology, Volume IX, Number 2, 2005, <http://law.richmond.edu/jolt/v11i 2/article6.pdf>, pp. 1-20.

Boggiano, Antonio, Contratos Internacionales – International Contracts, Buenos Aires 1995.

Boggiano, Antonio, Derecho Internacional Privado, Volumes I and II, 5th Edition Updated, Buenos Aires 2006.

Bonell, Michael Joachim, UNIDROIT Principles 2004 – The New Edition of the Principles of International Commercial Contracts adopted by the International Institute for the Unification of Private Law, Uniform Law Review, 2004, pp. 5-40.

Borda, Guillermo A., Tratado de Derecho Civil – Obligaciones, 6th Edition Updated, Buenos Aires 1989.

Borda, Guillermo A., Tratado de Derecho Civil – Parte General, 10th Edition Updated, Buenos Aires 1991.

Boyd, Colin / Mathuria, Anish, Protocols for Authentication and Key Establishment, Berlin / Heidelberg 2003.

Bradgate, Robert, Evidential issues of EDI, in: Walden, Ian (Ed.), EDI and the Law, London 1989, pp. 9-42.

Breslin, Adrienne J., Electronic Commerce: Will it ever truly realize its Global Potential?, Penn State International Law Review, Volume 20, Number 1, 2001-2002, pp. 275-300.

Bruen, Aiden A. / Forcinito, Mario A., Cryptography, Information Theory, and Error-Correction, Hoboken, NJ 2005.

Bueres, Alberto J. / Highton, Elena I. (Eds.), Código Civil y normas complementarias – Análisis doctrinal y jurisprudencial, Volumes 3B and 3C, Reprint, Buenos Aires 2005.

Burnstein, Matthew, A Global Network in a Compartmentalised Legal Environment, in: Boele-Woelki, Katharina / Kessedjian, Catherine (Eds.),

Internet – Which Court Decides? Which Law Applies?, Law and Electronic Commerce, Volume 5, The Hague / London / Boston 1998, pp. 23-34.

Cabanellas, Guillermo, Diccionario de Derecho Usual, 8th Edition, Volume II, Buenos Aires 1974.

Cabanellas, Guillermo, Diccionario Enciclopédico de Derecho Usual, Volume IV (F-I), 26th Edition Revised, Updated and Expanded by Luis Alcalá-Zamora y Castillo, Buenos Aires 1998.

Caivano, Roque J., La formación del consentimiento entre ausentes en nuestro derecho positivo, La Ley 1993-D, pp. 415.

Calvo Caravaca, Alfonso Luis / Carrascosa González, Javier, Conflictos de leyes y conflictos de jurisdicción en Internet, Madrid 2001.

Chissick, Michael, Electronic Commerce: Law and Practice, London 1999.

Clarkson, C. M. V., / Hill, Jonathan, Jaffey on Conflict of Laws, London 2002.

Colerio, Juan Pedro, ¿Es la firma privada un requisito esencial para la existencia de todo acto bajo forma privada?, La Ley 1994-D, pp. 475.

Commission of the European Communities, Report from the Commission to the European Parliament and Council, Report of the operation of Directive 1999/93/EC on a Community framework for electronic signatures, Brussels, 15.3.2006, COM(2006) 120 final, <http://ec.europa.eu/information_society/e europe/i2010/docs/single_info_space/com_electronic_signatures_report_en.p df>, pp. 1-10.

Commission of the European Communities, the Communication from the Commission to the Council, the European Parliament, the European Economic and Social Committee and the Committee of the Regions on the Action Plan on e-signatures and e-identification to facilitate the provision of cross-border public services in the Single Market, <http://eur-lex.europa.eu/L exUriServ/LexUriServ.do?uri=COM:2008:0798:FIN:EN:PDF>.

Compagnucci de Caso, Rubén H., Prueba de los contratos, La Ley 1996-D, pp. 66.

Creifelds, Carl / Weber, Klaus (Eds.), Rechtswörterbuch, 19th Edition, München 2007.

Cuniberti, Gilles, Is the CISG Benefiting Anybody?, Vanderbilt Journal of Transnational Law, Volume 39 Number 4, October 2006, pp. 1511-1550.

de Aguinis, Ana María / Kleidermacher, Arnoldo, Nuevas formas de contratación. Contratación por ordenador, La Ley 1987-C, pp. 892.

Delaume, G.R., What is an International Contract? An American and Gallic Dilemma, The International and Comparative Law Quarterly, Volume 28, Number 2, April 1979, pp. 258-279.

Deutsches Rechts-Lexikon, Band 3 (Q-Z), 3rd Edition, München 2001.

Devoto, Mauricio, Comercio Electrónico y Firma Digital – La Regulación del Ciberespacio y las Estrategias Globales, Buenos Aires 2001.

Diccionario de la lengua española, Real Academia Española, 22nd Edition, <http://www.rae.es/>.

Dickie, John, Internet and Electronic Commerce Law in the European Union, Portland, Oregon 1999.

Diffie, Whitfield / Hellman, Martin E., New Directions in Cryptography, 1976, <http://www.cs.tau.ac.il/~bchor/diffie-hellman.pdf>, pp. 29-40.

Drobnig, Ulrich, The use of the UNIDROIT Principles by National and Supranational Courts, in: Institute of International Business Law and Practice – International Chamber of Commerce, UNIDROIT Principles for International Commercial Contracts: A new lex mercatoria?, Paris 1995, pp. 223-229.

Dumortier, Jos, The European Regulatory Framework for Electronic Signatures: A Critical Evaluation, in: Nielson, Ruth / Jakobsen, Søren Sandfeld / Trzaskowski, Jan (Eds.), EU Electronic Commerce Law, Copenhagen 2004, pp. 69-93.

Enciclopedia Jurídica Omeba, Volume IV (Cons-Cost), Buenos Aires 1956, Volume XII (Fami-Gara), Buenos Aires 1960.

Erber-Faller, Sigrun, Elektronischer Rechtsverkehr und digitale Signaturen in Deutschland – Bisherige Entwicklung, internationale Bezüge und Zukunftsperspektiven aus notarieller Sicht, in: Geis, Ivo (Ed.), Rechtsaspekte des elektronischen Geschäftsverkehrs, Eschborn 1999, pp. 85-105.

Erman, Bürgerliches Gesetzbuch, Handkommentar, 12th Edition, Köln 2008.

Estrella Faria, José Angelo, Harmonizing the Law of International Electronic Contracting: Adjust the Rules but don't Rewrite Them, in: Schulz, Andrea (Ed.), Legal Aspects of an E-Commerce Transaction, München 2006, pp. 73-98.

Fallon, M. / Meeusen, J., Le commerce électronique, la directive 2000/31/EC et le droit international privé, Revue critique de droit international privé, July-September 2002, pp. 435-490.

Farnsworth, Allan E., Contracts, Volume II, Boston / Toronto / London 1990.

Farrés, Pablo, Firma Digital – Ley Comentada y Concordada – Decreto Reglamentario 2628/2002, Buenos Aires 2005.

Feldstein de Cárdenas, Sara L, Derecho Internacional Privado – Parte Especial, Buenos Aires 2000.

Ferguson, Niels / Schneier, Bruce, Practical Cryptography, Indianapolis 2003.

Fernández Delpech, Horacio, Internet: Su Problemática Jurídica, 2nd Edition Updated, Buenos Aires 2004.

Fischer-Dieskau, Stefanie / Hornung, Gerrit, Erste höchstrichterliche Entscheidung zur elektronischen Signatur, NJW 2007, pp. 2897-2899.

Fischer, Susanna Frederick, Saving Rosencrantz and Guildenstern in a Virtual World? A Comparative Look at Recent Global Electronic Signature

Legislation, Boston University Journal of Science & Technology Law, Volume 7, 2001, pp. 229-242.

Foelix, M., Traité du Droit International Privé ou du conflit des lois de différentes nations en matière de droit privé, 4th Edition Revised and Extended by Charles Demangeat, Paris 1866.

Ford, Warwick / Baum, Michael S., Secure Electronic Commerce, Upper Saddle River, New Jersey 1997.

Fresnedo de Aguirre, Cecila, La autonomía de la voluntad en la contratación internacional, Montevideo 1991.

Fry, Patricia Brumfield, Why Enact UETA? The Role of UETA After E-Sign, 2002, <http://www.nccusl.org/Update/Docs/Why20Enact%20UETA.asp>.

Fuller, Lon L. / Eisenberg, Melvin Aron, Basic Contract Law, 8th Edition, St. Paul, Minnesota 2006.

Garro, Alejandro M., La Convención de las Naciones Unidas sobre los contratos de compraventa internacional de mercaderías: su incorporación al orden jurídico argentino (Segunda parte), La Ley 1985-A, pp. 930.

Geis, Ivo, Die digitale Signatur, NJW 1997, pp. 3000.

Geis, Ivo, Die elektronische Signatur: Eine internationale Architektur der Identifizierung im E-Commerce, MMR 2000, pp. 667-674.

Gillette, Clayton P. / Walt, Steven D., Sales Law – Domestic and International, New York 1999.

Giuliano, Mario / Lagarde, Paul, Report on the Convention on the law applicable to contractual obligations, Journal officiel n° C 282 du 31/10/1980, <http://www.rome-convention.org/instruments/i_rep_ lagarde_en.htm>, pp. 1–50.

Goldschmidt, Werner, Derecho Internacional Privado, 9th Edition Reprint, Buenos Aires 2002.

Goldschmidt, Werner, Jurisdicción internacional en contratos internacionales, La Ley 1986-D, pp. 46.

Goldschmidt, Werner, Transporte internacional, La Ley 1980-B, pp. 375.

Greenstone, Richard J., An Introduction to the Uniform Electronic Transactions Act, 2001, <www.rjg.com/ueta.html>.

Griffiths, David Hugh / Harrison, Joel, European Union, in: Campbell, Dennis (Ed.), E-Commerce and the Law of Digital Signatures, Dobbs Ferry, New York 2005, pp. 733-762.

Gutmann, Daniel, Droit International Privé, 2nd Edition, Paris 2000.

Hall, Juan Andrés, El rol de la encriptación de datos en la despapelización, in: Palazzi, Pablo Andrés (Ed.), Derecho y nuevas tecnologías, Year 1, Number 0, Buenos Aires 2000, pp. 21-30.

Hartkamp, A.S., Principles of contract law, in: Grosheide, F. Willem / Hondius, Ewoud (Eds.), International Contract Law, Antwerp 2004, pp. 171-196.

Hartkamp, Arthur, The use of the UNIDROIT Principles of International Commercial Contracts by National and Supranational Courts, in: Institute of International Business Law and Practice – International Chamber of Commerce, UNIDROIT Principles for International Commercial Contracts: A new lex mercatoria?, Paris 1995, pp. 253-260.

Heydn, Truiken J., Germany, in: Campbell, Dennis (Ed), E-Commerce and the Law of Digital Signatures, Dobbs Ferry, New York 2005, pp. 221-268.

Hocsman, Heriberto Simón, Negocios en Internet, Buenos Aires 2005.

Holleaux, Dominique / Foyer, Jacques / La Pradelle, Géraud de Geouffre, Droit International Privé, Paris 1987.

Huet, Jérôme, The law applicable to digital networks, in: Internet – International Law, International and European Studies and Comments (International Colloquium 19-20 November 2001 Paris), Brussels 2005, pp. 73-80.

Hultmark, Christina, Interpretation of legal text in an electronic and international environment, in: Hohloch, Gerhard (Ed.), Recht und Internet, 6. "Deutsch-Schwedisches Juristentreffen" vom 31. März bis 2. April 2000, Baden-Baden 2001, pp. 45-57.

International Chamber of Commerce, A Global Action Plan for Electronic Business, 3rd Edition, 2002, <http://www.iccwbo.org/uploadedfiles/3EdGAP. pdf?terms=GUIDEC+I>, pp. 1-83.

International Chamber of Commerce, Electronic invoicing in and with the European Union, Policy Statement, prepared by the Commission on Commercial Law and Practice, Document n° 460/592, 2005, <http://www.icc wbo.org/uploadedFiles/ICC/policy/clp/Statements/Electronic_invoicing_in_a nd_with_EU.pdf>, pp. 1-13.

International Chamber of Commerce, GUIDEC II – General Usage for International Digitally Ensured Commerce (version II), Paris 2001.

International Chamber of Commerce, ICC eTerms 2004, <http://www.iccwbo.or g/policy/law/id279/index.html>.

International Chamber of Commerce, ICC Guide for eContracting, <http://www. iccwbo.org/policy/law/id3670/index.html>.

Internet Law & Public Forum (ILPF), An Analysis of International Electronic and Digital Signature Implementation Initiatives, A Study Prepared for the ILPF by Kuner, Chris / Barcelo, Rosa / Baker, Stewart / Greenwald, Eric, September 2000, <http://www.ilpf.org/groups/analysis_IEDSII.htm>.

Jacquet, Jean-Michel, Le contrat international, 2nd Edition, Paris 1999.

Kania, Edward D., The ABA´s Digital Signature Guidelines: An Imperfect Solution to Digital Signatures on the Internet, CommLaw Conspectus: Journal of Communications Law and Policy, Volume 7, 1999, pp. 297-313.

Kaufman, Charlie / Perlman, Radia / Speciner, Mike, Network Security – Private Communication in a Public World, 2nd Edition, Upper Saddle River, New Jersey 2002.

Kiran, Shahi / Lareau, Patricia / Lloyd, Steve, PKI Basics – A Technical Perspective, PKI Forum, November 2002, <http://www.oasis-pki.org/pdfs/PK I_Basics-A_technical_perspective.pdf>, pp. 1-12.

Kronke, Herbert, Applicable law in Torts and Contracts in Cyberspace, in: Boele-Woelki, Katharina / Kessedjian, Catherine (Eds.), Internet – Which Court Decides? Which Law Applies?, Law and Electronic Commerce, Volume 5, The Hague / London / Boston 1998, pp. 65-87.

Kuechler, William / Grupe, Fritz H., Digital Signatures: A Business View, Information Systems Management, Volume 20, Number 1, Winter 2003, pp. 19-28.

Lando, Ole, The Conflict of Laws on Contracts – General Principles, Extract from the Recueil des cours, Volume 189, Dordrecht / Boston / London 1985.

Lillie, Stephanie, Will E-Sign force states to adopt UETA?, Jurimetrics, The Journal of Law, Science, and Technology, Volume 42, 2001, pp. 21-30.

Lincoln, Anda, Electronic Signature Laws and the Need for Uniformity in the Global Market, The Journal of Small and Emerging Business Law, Volume 8, 2004, pp. 67-86.

Lord Mance, The Future of Private International Law, Journal of Private International Law, Volume 1, Number 2, October 1995, pp. 185-195.

Lorenzetti, Ricardo L., Comercio Electrónico, Buenos Aires 2001.

Lorenzetti, Ricardo Luis, Tratado de los Contratos – Parte General, Buenos Aires 2004.

Lorenzetti, Ricardo Luis, Tratado de los Contratos, Volume III, Buenos Aires 2000.

Lorenzo Idiarte, Gonzalo A., ¿Cuándo un contrato es internacional? Análisis desde una perspectiva regional, in: Kleinheitsterkamp, Jan / Lorenzo Idiarte, Gonzalo A. (Eds.), Avances del Derecho Internacional Privado en América Latina, 1st Edition, Montevideo 2002, pp. 105-132.

Loussouarn, Yvon / Bourel, Pierre / de Vareilles-Sommières, Pascal, Droit International Privé, Paris 2004.

Lui-Kwan, Kalama M., Recent Developments in Digital Signature Legislation and Electronic Commerce, Berkeley Technology Law Journal, 1990, Volume 14, pp. 463-481.

Luz Clara, Bibiana, Ley de Firma Digital Comentada, Rosario 2006.

Mann, Ronald J. / Winn, Jane, Electronic Commerce, 2nd Edition, New York 2005.

Marella, Fabrizio, Choice of Law in Third-Millennium Arbitrations: The Relevance of the UNIDROIT Principles of International Commercial

Contracts, Vanderbilt Journal of Transnational Law, Volume 36, May 2003, pp. 1137-1188.

Marquess, Kate, Sign on the Dot-Com Line, ABA Journal, October 2000, pp. 74-76.

Marzorati, Osvaldo J., Derecho de los negocios internacionales, 3ʳᵈ Edition Updated and Extended, Buenos Aires 2003.

Marzorati, Osvaldo J., Reflexiones sobre jurisdicción y ley aplicable en internet, in: Kleinheisterkamp, Jan / Lorenzo Idiarte, Gonzalo A. (Eds.), Avances del Derecho Internacional Privado en América Latina, Montevideo 2002, pp. 301-324.

Marzorati, Osvaldo, Derecho de los negocios internacionales o Derecho Internacional de los negocios, La Ley 2005-E, pp. 1418.

Marzorati, Osvaldo, Jurisdicción competente y la ley aplicable en las relaciones jurídicas formalizadas en el ciberespacio, La Ley 2004-D, pp. 1373.

Mason, Stephen, Electronic Signatures in Practice, Journal of High Technology Law, Volume VI, Number 2, 2006, pp. 148-164.

Mayer, Pierre / Heuzé, Vincent, Droit international privé, 8ᵗʰ Edition, Paris 2004.

Mayss, Abla J., Principles of Conflict of Laws, London / Sydney 1996.

Mendez, Tiffany A., Adopting the Digital Signature Guidelines in Implementing Public Key Infrastructure for Federal Procurement of Electronic Commerce, Public Contract Law Journal, Volume 29, Winter 2000, pp. 285-307.

Menicocci, Alejandro A., Compraventa internacional de mercaderías y derecho aplicable al pago del precio, La Ley Impuestos 2006-11, pp. 1443.

Menicocci, Alejandro A., Prueba del contrato y ley aplicable al pago del precio de la compraventa internacional de mercaderías, La Ley 2006-C, pp. 776.

Merriam Webster Online Dictionary, <http://www.m-w.com/dictionary/>.

Miedbrodt, Anja, Signaturregulierung im Rechtsvergleich – Ein Vergleich der Regulierungskonzepte in Deutschland, Europa und in den Vereinigten Staaten von Amerika, Frankfurt 2000.

Morris J.H.C. / McClean, David, The Conflict of Laws, 5ᵗʰ Edition, London 2000.

Mosset Iturraspe, Jorge, Contratos, Buenos Aires 1984.

Münchener Kommentar zum Bürgerlichen Gesetzbuch, Volume 1, (Allgemeiner Teil, 1. Halbband: §§1-240), 5ᵗʰ Edition, München 2006.

Münchener Kommentar zum Bürgerlichen Gesetzbuch, Volume 10, (Einführungsgesetz zum Bürgerlichen Gesetzbuche, Art. 1-46), 4ᵗʰ Edition, München 2006.

Nimmer, Raymond T., The legal landscape of E-Commerce: Redefining Contract Law in an Information Era, Journal of Contract Law, Volume 23, Numbers 1 and 2, April 2007, pp. 10-31.

Noack, Ulrich, 2. Teil: Das Gesetz zur Anpassung der Formschriften des Privatrechts und anderer Vorschriften an den modernen Rechtsgeschäftsverkehr, in:

Dauner-Lieb, Barbara / Heidel, Thomas / Rign, Gerhard (Eds.), Das Neue
Schuldrecht – Ein Lehrbuch, Heidelberg 2002, pp. 441-461.

Nödler, Jens M., Legal Framework of Electronic Signatures in the European
Union and Germany, Seminar in Network Security, Institute of Computer
Science, Georg-August-Universität Göttingen, 2006, <http://noedler.de/artikel
/legal-framework-of-electronic-signatures.pdf>, pp. 1-19.

Organization for economic co-operation and development, Electronic
Commerce – Opportunities and Challenges for Government, Paris 1997.

Palandt, Bürgerliches Gesetztbuch, 68th Edition Revised, München 2009.

Pommier, Jean-Christophe, Principe d'Autonomie et Loi du Contrat en Droit
International Privé Conventionnel, Paris 1992.

Prütting, Hanns / Wegen, Gerhard / Weinreich Gerd (Eds.), BGB Kommentar,
4th Edition revised and extended, Neuwied 2009.

Rainey, John S. "Chip", United States, in: Kinsella, N. Stephan / Simpson,
Andrew F. (Eds.), Online Contract Formation, 1st Edition, Dobbs Ferry, New
York 2004, pp. 309-336.

Reed, Chris, Internet law, 2nd Edition, Cambridge 2004.

Rehse, Steven, Der Vertragsschluss auf elektronischem Wege in Deutschland
und England, Berlin 2005.

Reyes Krafft, Alfredo Alejandro, La firma electrónica y las entidades de
certificación, 1st Edition, Mexico 2003.

Rivera, Julio Cesar, Instituciones de Derecho Civil – Parte General, Volume II,
Buenos Aires 1993.

Rosner, Norel, International Jurisdiction in European Union E-Commerce
Contracts, in: Kisella, N. Stephan / Simpson, Andrew F. (Eds.), Online
Contract Formation, 1st Edition, Dobbs Ferry, New York 2004, pp. 481-495.

Roßnagel, Alexander, Die Ausgabe sicherer Signaturerstellungseinheiten, MMR
2006, pp. 441-446.

Roßnagel, Alexander, Die europäische Richtlinie für elektronische Signaturen
und ihre Umsetzung im neuen Signaturgesetz, in: Lehman, Michael (Ed.),
Electronic Business in Europa – Internationales, europäisches und deutsches
Online-Recht, München 2002, pp. 131-160.

Roßnagel, Alexander, Die fortgeschrittene elektronische Signatur, MMR Issue 3,
2003, pp. 164-170.

Roßnagel, Alexander, Elektronische Signaturen mit der Bankkarte? – Das Erste
Gesetz zur Änderung des Signaturgesetzes, NJW 2005, pp. 385-388.

Roßnagel, Alexander, Rechtliche Unterschiede von Signaturverfahren, MMR
2002, pp. 215-222.

Schaub, Martien, European Legal Aspects of E-Commerce, Groningen 2004.

Schellekens, M.H.M., Electronic Signatures – Authentication Technology from a Legal Perspective, Information Technology & Law Series, Number 5, The Hague 2004.

Schlechter, Richard, Ein europäischer Rahmen für elektronische Signaturen, in: Geis, Ivo (Ed.), Rechtsaspekte des elektronischen Geschäftsverkehrs, 1999, pp. 107-125.

Scoles, Eugene F. / Hay, Peter / Borchers, Patrick J. / Symeonides, Symeon C., Conflicts of Laws, 3rd Edition, St. Paul 2000.

Scoville, Adam White, Clear Signatures, Obscure Signs, Cardozo Arts & Entertainment Law Journal, Volume 17, 1999, pp. 345-416.

Shenk, Maury D. / Baker, Stewart A. / Chang, Winnie, Cryptography and Electronic Signatures, in: Campbell, Dennis / Bán, Chrysta (Eds.), Legal Issues in the Global Information Society, Dobbs Ferry, New York 2005, pp. 377-399.

Smart, Adam R., E-Sign Versus State Electronic Signature Laws: The Electronic Statutory Battleground, North Carolina Banking Institute, Volume 5, 2001, pp. 485-522.

Smedinghoff, Thomas J., The Legal Requirements for Creating Secure and Enforceable Electronic Transactions, 2002, <http://www.imf.org/external/np/l eg/sem/2002/cdmfl/eng/smedin.pdf>, pp. 1-30.

Smedinghoff, Thomas J./ Bro, Ruth Hill, Electronic Signature Legislation, 1999, <http://library.findlaw.com/1999/Jan/1/241481.html>.

Soergel, Hans Theodor (Founder) / *Wolf, Manfred* (Ed.), Bürgerliches Gesetzbuch mit Einführungsgesetz und Nebengesetzen, Band 2a, 13th Edition, 2002.

Sorge, Christoph, Softwareagenten – Vertragsschluss, Vertragsstrafe, Reugeld, Karlsruhe 2006.

Sorieul, Renaud, The UNCITRAL'S Model Law on Electronic Signatures, in: Internet – International Law, International and European Studies and Comments, Brussels 2005, pp. 299-397.

Spota, Alberto G., Instituciones de Derecho Civil – Contratos, Volume I, Reprint, Buenos Aires 1975.

Spota, Alberto G., Instituciones de Derecho Civil – Contratos, Volume III, Buenos Aires 1975.

Staudingers, J., Kommentar zum Bürgerlichen Gesetzbuch mit Einführung und Nebengesetzen, Buch 1, Allgemeiner Teil, New Edition, Berlin 2004.

Staudingers, J., Kommentar zum Bürgerlichen Gesetzbuch mit Einführung und Nebengesetzen, Einführungsgesetz zum Bürgerlichen Gesetzbuch/IPR, New Edition, Berlin 2007.

Staudingers, J., Kommentar zum Bürgerlichen Gesetzbuch mit Einführung und Nebengesetzen, Einführungsgesetz zum Bürgerlichen Gesetzbuch/IPR, New Edition, Berlin 2003.

Staudingers, J., Kommentar zum Bürgerlichen Gesetzbuch mit Einführung und Nebengesetzen, Einführungsgesetz zum Bürgerlichen Gesetzbuch/IPR, 13th Edition, Berlin 2002.

Steinbeck, Anja, Die neuen Formvorschriften in BGB, DStR, 2003, pp. 644-650.

Stern, Jonathan E., The Electronic Signatures in Global and National Commerce Act, Berkeley Technology Law Journal, Volume 16, 2001, pp. 391-414.

Story, Joseph, Commentaries on Conflicts of laws, Reprint of the Edition Berlin 1834, Stockstadt 2007.

Tilburg University, Digital Signature Law Survey, <https://dsls.rechten.uvt.nl/>.

U.S. Department of Commerce, National Telecommunications and Information Administration, Electronic Signatures: A Review of the Exceptions to the Electronic Signature in Global and National Commerce Act, 2003, <http://usi nfo.state.gov/infousa/economy/technology/docs/esignfinal.pdf>, pp. 1-76.

UNCITRAL, Commentary on the draft Convention on the International Sale of Goods, March 17, 1976, Yearbook of the United Nations Commission on International Trade Law, Volume VII, 1976, (A/CN.9/116, annex II), <http:// www.uncitral.org/pdf/english/yearbooks/yb-1976-e/vol7-p96-142-e.pdf>, pp. 96-142.

UNCITRAL, Digest of case law on the United Nations Convention on the International Sale of Goods, Article 1, (A/CN.9/SER.C/DIGEST/CISG/1), <http://daccessdds.un.org/doc/UNDOC/GEN/V04/547/19/PDF/V0454719.pdf ?OpenElement>, pp. 1-16.

UNCITRAL, Digest of case law on the United Nations Convention on the International Sale of Goods, Article 11, (A/CN.9/SER.C/DIGEST/CISG/11), <http://daccessdds.un.org/doc/UNDOC/GEN/V04/548/25/PDF/V0454825.pdf ?OpenElement>, pp. 1-4.

UNCITRAL, Explanatory note by the UNCITRAL secretariat on the United Nations Convention on the Use of Electronic Communications in International Contracts, in: United Nations Convention on the Use of Electronic Communications in International Contracts, 2007, <http://www.un citral.org/pdf/english/texts/electcom/0657452_Ebook.pdf>, pp. 1-100.

UNCITRAL, Final Act of the United Nations Conference on Contracts for the International Sale of Goods (Vienna 10 March – 11 April, 1980), Yearbook of the United Nations Commission on International Trade Law, Volume XI, 1980, (A/CONF.97/18), <http://www.uncitral.org/pdf/english/yearbooks/yb-1980-e/vol11-p149-150-e.pdf>, pp. 149-150.

UNCITRAL, General Assembly, Resolution 56/80, (A/RES/56/80), <http://dacc essdds.un.org/doc/UNDOC/GEN/N01/490/26/PDF/N0149026.pdf?OpenElem ent>, pp. 1-7.

UNCITRAL, Legal aspects of automatic data processing: report of the Secretary General, Yearbook of the United Nations Commission on International Trade Law, Volume XV, 1984, (A/CN.9/254), <http://daccessdds.un.org/doc/U NDOC/GEN/NL8/401/39/PDF/NL840139.pdf?OpenElement>, pp. 328-331.

UNCITRAL, Legal Aspects of automatic trade data interchange, October 21, 1982, presented by the delegations of Denmark, Finland, Norway and Sweden, in: Note by the secretariat: legal aspects of automatic data processing (A/CN.9/238), Yearbook of the United Nations Commission on International Trade Law, Volume XIV, 1983, (TRADE/WP.4/R.185/Rev.1), <http://dacces sdds.un.org/doc/UNDOC/GEN/NL8/303/25/PDF/NL830325.pdf?OpenEleme nt>, pp. 176-188.

UNCITRAL, Legal value of computer records: report of the Secretary General, Yearbook of the United Nations Commission on International Trade Law, Volume XVI, 1985, (A/CN.9/265), <http://daccessdds.un.org/doc/UNDOC/G EN/NL8/501/41/PDF/NL850141.pdf?OpenElement>, pp. 351-365.

UNCITRAL, Model Law on Electronic Commerce with Guide to Enactment 1996 with additional article 5bis as adopted in 1998, New York 1999, <http:// www.uncitral.org/pdf/english/texts/electcom/05-89450_Ebook.pdf>, pp. 1-75.

UNCITRAL, Model Law on Electronic Signatures with Guide to Enactment (2001), New York 2002, <http://www.uncitral.org/pdf/english/texts/electcom/ ml-elecsig-e.pdf>, pp. 1-72.

UNCITRAL, Note by the secretariat: legal aspects of automatic data processing, Yearbook of the United Nations Commission on International Trade Law, Volume XI, 1983, (A/CN.9/238), <http://daccessdds.un.org/doc/UNDOC/GE N/NL8/303/25/PDF/NL830325.pdf?OpenElement>, pp. 174-178.

UNCITRAL, Recommendation regarding the interpretation of article II, paragraph 2, and article VII, paragraph 1, of the Convention on the Recognition and Enforcement of Foreign Arbitral Awards, done in New York, 10 June 1958, adopted by the United Nations Commission on International Trade Law on 7 July 2006 at its thirty-ninth session, (A/6/17), <http://www.uncitral.org/p df/english/texts/arbitration/NY-conv/A2E.pdf>, pp. 61-62.

UNCITRAL, Report of the Secretary-General: Analysis of comments by Governments and international organizations on the draft Convention on the international sale of goods as adopted by the Working Group on the international sale of goods, April 7, 1977, Yearbook of the United Nations Commission on International Trade Law, Volume VIII, (A/CN.9/126), <http://www.uncitral.org/pdf/english/yearbooks/yb-1977-e/vol8-p142-163-e.p df>, pp. 142-163.

UNCITRAL, Report of the Secretary-General: Electronic Funds Transfer, Yearbook of the United Nations Commission on International Trade Law, Volume XIII, 1982, (A/CN.9/221 ** and Corr. 1 – French only), <http://dacce ssdds.un.org/doc/UNDOC/GEN/NL8/205/33/PDF/NL820533.pdf?OpenElem ent>, pp. 272-285.

UNCITRAL, Report of the United Nations Commission on International Trade Law and the work of its seventeenth session (New York 25 June-10 July, 1984), Yearbook of the United Nations Commission on International Trade Law, Volume XV, 1984, (A/39/17), <http://www.uncitral.org/pdf/english/trav aux/arbitration/ml-arb/a-39-17-e.pdf>, pp. 3-22.

UNCITRAL, Report of the United Nations Commission on International Trade Law on the work of its eighteenth session (Vienna, 3-21 June, 1985), Yearbook of the United Nations Commission on International Trade Law, Volume XVI, 1985, (A/40/17), <http://www.uncitral.org/pdf/english/yearboo ks/yb-1985-e/vol16-p3-46-e.pdf>, pp. 3-46.

UNCITRAL, Report of the United Nations Commission on International Trade Law on the work of its eleventh session (New York 20 May – 16 June, 1978), Yearbook of the United Nations Commission on International Trade Law, Volume IX, 1978, (A/33/17), <http://www.uncitral.org/pdf_english/yearbooks /yb-1978-e/vol9-p11-45-e.pdf>, pp. 11-45.

UNCITRAL, Report of the United Nations Commission on International Trade Law on the work of its fifteenth Session (New York, 26 July – 6 August, 1982), (A/37/17), <http://daccessdds.un.org/doc/UNDOC/GEN/NL8/205/42/ PDF/NL820542.pdf?OpenElement>, pp. 3-20.

UNCITRAL, Report of the United Nations Commission on International Trade Law on the work of its second session (1969), Yearbook of the United Nations Commission on International Trade Law, Volume I, 1970, (A/7618), <http://www.uncitral.org/pdf/english/travaux/sales/limit/a7618-e.pdf>, pp. 94-128.

UNCITRAL, Report of the United Nations Commission on International Trade Law on the work of its thirty-first session (New York from 1-12 June 1998), General Assembly, Official Records, Fifty-third Session, Supplement No. 17, (A/53/17), <http://daccessdds.un.org/doc/UNDOC/GEN/V98/549/82/PDF/V9 854982.pdf?OpenElement>, pp. 1-34.

UNCITRAL, Report of the United Nations Commission on International Trade Law on the work of its twenty-fifth session, (New York, 4-22 May, 1992), (A/47/17), Yearbook of the United Nations Commission on International Trade Law, Volume XXIII, 1992, <http://www.uncitral.org/pdf/english/yearb ooks/yb-1992-e/vol23-p3-24-e.pdf>, pp. 3-24.

UNCITRAL, Report of the United Nations Commission on International Trade Law on the work of its twenty-ninth session (New York, 28 May – 14 June, 1996), General Assembly, Official Records, Fifty-first Session Supplement No. 17, (A/51/17), <http://daccessdds.un.org/doc/UNDOC/GEN/N96/206/41/ PDF/N9620641.pdf?OpenElement>, pp. 1-79.

UNCITRAL, Report of the United Nations Commission on International Trade Law on the work of its thirtieth session (Vienna, 12-30 May, 1997), General Assembly, Official Records, Fifty-first Session Supplement No. 17, (A/52/ 17), <http://daccessdds.un.org/doc/UNDOC/GEN/V97/251/88/PDF/V972518 8.pdf?OpenElement>, pp. 1-79.

UNCITRAL, Report of the Working Group on Electronic Commerce on the work of its thirty-first session (New York, February 18-28, 1997), (A/CN.9/437), <http://daccessdds.un.org/doc/UNDOC/GEN/V97/214/90/PDF/V9721490.pdf ?OpenElement>, pp. 1-45.

UNCITRAL, Report of the Working Group on the International Sale of Goods, First session, Yearbook of the United Nations Commission on International Trade Law, Volume I, 1970, (A/CN.9/35).

UNCITRAL, Report of the Working Group on the international sale of goods on the work of its first session (January 5-16, 1970), Yearbook of the United Nations Commission on International Trade Law, 1970, Volume I, (A/CN.9/35), <http://daccessdds.un.org/doc/UNDOC/GEN/NL7/001/02/PDF/NL700102.pdf?OpenElement>, pp. 176.

UNCITRAL, Report of the Working Group on the International Sale of Goods on the work of its ninth session (Geneva, September 19-30, 1977), Yearbook of the United Nations Commission on International Trade Law, 1978, Volume IX, (A/CN.9/142), <http://www.uncitral.org/pdf/english/ yearbooks/y b-1978-e/vol9-p61-85-e.pdf>, pp. 61-85.

UNCITRAL, The First Session (1968), Yearbook of the United Nations Commission on International Trade Law, Volume I, 1970, (A/7216), <http:// www.uncitral.org/pdf/english/travaux/sales/limit/a7216-e.pdf>, pp. 71-93.

UNCITRAL, Thirty-first session (New York, 1-12 June 1998), Report of the Working Group on Electronic Commerce on the Work of its Thirty-second Session (Vienna, 19-30 January 1998), February 11, 1998, (A/CN.9/446), <http://daccessdds.un.org/doc/UNDOC/GEN/V98/508/91/PDF/V9850891.pd f?OpenElement>, pp. 1-62.

UNCITRAL, Thirty-fourth session (Vienna, 25 June-13 July 2001), Report of the Working Group on Electronic Commerce on its thirty-eighth session (New York, 12-23 March 2001), April 24, 2001, (A/CN.9/484), <http://dacces sdds.un.org/doc/UNDOC/GEN/V01/829/54/PDF/V0182954.pdf?OpenEleme nt>, pp. 1-26.

UNCITRAL, Thirty-fourth session, 25 June-13 July 2001, Report of the Working Group on Electronic Commerce on the work of its thirty-seventh session (Vienna 18-19 September 2000), October 6, 2000, (A/CN.9/483), <htt p://daccessdds.un.org/doc/UNDOC/GEN/V01/829/54/PDF/V0182954.pdf?O penElement>, pp. 1-43.

UNCITRAL, Thirty-second session (17 May-4 June 1999), Report of the Working Group on Electronic Commerce on the work of its thirty-third session (New York, 29 June – 10 July 1998) August 21, 1998, (A/CN.9/454), <http://daccessdds.un.org/doc/UNDOC/GEN/V98/554/38/PDF/V9855438.pdf ?OpenElement>, pp. 1-50.

UNCITRAL, Thirty-second session (Vienna 17 May-4 June 1999), Report of the Working Group on Electronic Commerce on the work of its thirty-fourth session (Vienna 8-9 February 1999), February 25, 1999, (A/CN.9/457), <http: //daccessdds.un.org/doc/UNDOC/GEN/V99/813/56/ PDF/V9981356.pdf?Ope nElement>, pp. 1-30.

UNCITRAL, Thirty-third session (New York, 12 June-7 July 2000), Report of the Working Group on Electronic Commerce on the Work of its Thirty-fifth session (Vienna, 6-17 September 1999), 23 September 1999, (A/CN.9/465),

<http://daccessdds.un.org/doc/UNDOC/GEN/V99/881/17/PDF/V9988117.pdf
?OpenElement>, pp. 1-42.

UNCITRAL, Thirty-third session (New York, 12 June-7 July 2000), Report of the Working Group on Electronic Commerce on the work of its thirty-sixth session (New York, 14-25 February 2000), April 5, 2000, (A/CN.9/467), <http://daccessdds.un.org/doc/UNDOC/GEN/V00/528/84/PDF/V0052884.pdf ?OpenElement>, pp. 1-36.

UNCITRAL, Working Group IV (Electronic Commerce), Thirty-ninth session (11-15 March 2002, New York), Legal aspects of electronic commerce – Electronic contracting: provisions for a draft convention, Note by the Secretariat, September 20, 2001, (A/CN.9/WG.IV/WP.95), <http://daccessdd s.un.org/doc/UNDOC/LTD/V01/872/66/PDF/V0187266.pdf?OpenElement>, pp. 1-39.

UNCITRAL, Working Group on Electronic Commerce Thirty-fifth session, (Vienna 6-17 September 1999), Draft Uniform Rules on Electronic Signatures, Note by the Secretariat, June 29, 1999, (A/CN.9/WG.IV/WP.82), <http://daccessdds.un.org/doc/UNDOC/LTD/V99/856/56/PDF/V9985656.pdf ?OpenElement>, pp. 1-39.

UNCITRAL, Working Group on Electronic Commerce Thirty-fourth session, (8-19 February 1999), Draft Uniform Rules on Electronic Signatures, Note by the Secretariat, November 23, 1998, (A/CN.9/WG.IV/WP.79), <http://www.u ncitral.org/pdf/english/workinggroups/ wg_ec/wp-79.pdf>, pp. 1-32.

UNCITRAL, Working Group on Electronic Commerce Thirty-fourth session, (8-19 February 1999), Electronic Signatures, Note by the Secretariat, December 15, 1998, (A/CN.9/WG.IV/WP.80), <http://www.uncitral.org/pdf/e nglish/workinggroups/wg_ec/wp-80.pdf>, pp. 1-9.

UNCITRAL, Working Group on Electronic Commerce Thirty-second session (Vienna 19-30 January 1998), Draft Uniform Rules on Electronic Signatures, Note by the Secretariat, December 12, 1997, (A/CN.9/WG.IV/WP.73), <http:/ /www.uncitral.org/pdf/english/workinggroups/ wg_ec/wp-73.pdf>, pp. 1-37.

UNCITRAL, Working Group on Electronic Commerce Thirty-sixth session (New York, 14-25 February 2000), Draft Uniform Rules on Electronic Signatures, Note by the Secretariat, December 8, 1999, (A/CN.9/WP.84), <http://daccessdds.un.org/doc/UNDOC/LTD/V99/906/15/PDF/V9990615.pdf ?OpenElement>, pp. 1-46.

UNCITRAL, Working Group on Electronic Commerce, Thirty-first session (New York, 18-28 February 1997), Planning of future work on electronic commerce: digital signatures, certification authorities and related legal issues, Note by the Secretariat, December 31, 1996, (A/CN.9/WG.IV/WP.71), <http: //www.uncitral.org/pdf/english/workinggroups/ wg_ec/wp-71.pdf>, pp. 1-30.

UNCITRAL, Working Group on the International Sale of Goods, Report on the work of the Second Session (7-18 December 1970), Yearbook of the United Nations Commission on International Trade Law, 1971, Volume Π, (A/CN.9/ 52), <http://daccessdds.un.org/doc/UNDOC/GEN/NL7/100/14/PDF/NL71001

246 Bibliography

4.pdf?OpenElement>, pp. 50-65.

UNCTITRAL, Comments by Governments and international organizations on the draft convention on the international sale of goods, March 22, 1977, Yearbook of the United Nations Commission on International Trade Law, 1977, Volume VIII, (A/CN.9/125 and A/CN.9/125/Add. 1 to 3), <http://www.uncitral.org/pdf/english/yearbooks/yb-1977-e/vol8-p109-142-e.pdf>, pp. 109-142.

UNCTRAL, Report of the Secretary-General: pending questions with respect to the revised text of a uniform law on the international sale of goods, February 18, 1975, Yearbook of the United Nations Commission on International Trade Law, 1975, Volume VI, (A/CN.9/100, annex III), <http://www.uncitral.org/pdf/english/yearbooks/yb-1975-e/vol6-p88- 110-e.pdf>, pp. 88-110.

UNIDROIT, Principles of International Commercial Contracts, 2004,<http://www.unidroit.org/english/principles/contracts/main.htm>.

Uniform Electronic Transactions Act with preparatory note and comments, 1999, <http://www.law.upenn.edu/bll/archives/ulc/fnact99/1990s/ueta99.htm>, pp. 1-62.

United Nations General Assembly, General Resolution 33/93, Official Records of the General Assembly, Twenty-third session, <http://daccessdds.un.org/doc/RESOLUTION/GEN/NR0/361/11/IMG/NR036111.pdf?OpenElement>, pp. 217-218.

United Nations General Assembly, Resolution 60/21, <http://daccessdds.un.org/doc/UNDOC/GEN/N05/488/80/PDF/N0548880.pdf?OpenElement>.

United Nations, General Assembly Resolution 2205 (XXI), December 17, 1966, Report of the Sixth Committee, General Assembly – Twenty-first Session, <http://daccessdds.un.org/doc/RESOLUTION/GEN/NR0/005/08/IMG/NR000508.pdf?OpenElement>, pp. 99-100.

Vacca, John R., Practical Internet Security, Pomeroy, Ohio 2007.

Valenzi, Kathleen D., Digital Signatures: An Important "Sign" of the Future of E-Government, virginia.edu, Volume IV, Number 2, Fall 2000, <http://www.itc.virginia.edu/virginia.edu/fall00/digsigs> (no longer available).

van Cutsem, Jean-Pierre / Viggria, Arnaud / Güth, Oliver (Eds.), E-Commerce in the World, Brussels 2003.

van der Hof, Simone, Party autonomy and International Online Business-to-Business Contracts in Europe and the United States, in: Schulz, Andrea (Ed.), Legal Aspects of an E-Commerce Transaction, München 2006, pp. 123-134.

van Tilborg, Henk C.A. (Ed.), Encyclopedia of Cryptography and Security, United States of America 2005.

Vibes Federico P. / Delupí, Javier Eduardo, El comercio electrónico frente al derecho positivo argentino, La Ley 2000-E, pp. 1079.

von Savigny, Friedrich Carl, System des heutigen Römischen Recht, Volume 8, Reprint of the Edition Berlin 1849, Darmstadt 1974.

Webster New College Dictionary, 3rd Edition, Boston / New York 2005.

Weinberg, Inés M., Contratos internacionales, La Ley 1984-C, pp. 915.

Weiser, Steven M., United States, in: Campbell, Dennis (Ed.), E-Commerce and the Law of Digital Signatures, Dobbs Ferry, New York 2005.

Wright, Winn, The law of Electronic Commerce, Boston / Toronto / London 1991.

Internationaler Verlag der Wissenschaften

Peter Lang

Harriet Eidam

Typische Risiken des elektronischen Rechtsgeschäftsverkehrs

Frankfurt am Main, Berlin, Bern, Bruxelles, New York, Oxford, Wien, 2005.
265 S.
Schriften zum Wirtschafts- und Medienrecht, Steuerrecht und Zivilprozeßrecht.
Herausgegeben von Jürgen Costede und Gerald Spindler. Bd. 20
ISBN 978-3-631-54146-3 · br. € 48,70*

E-Commerce, M-Commerce, elektronische Marktplätze, automatisierte Willenserklärungen, Anbieterpflichten und Verbraucherschutz: Diese Arbeit befasst sich mit ausgewählten Problemen des elektronischen Rechtsgeschäftsverkehrs. Anhand der klassischen Problemkreise der Rechtsgeschäftslehre wird zunächst untersucht, ob sich die neuen Mittel und Wege zu kommunizieren und Verträge zu schließen, mit den Regeln des allgemeinen Teils des BGB lösen lassen oder ob hierfür ein neues Recht geschaffen werden muss. Anschließend werden die im allgemeinen Teil des Schuldrechts angesiedelten, aber ebenfalls die Rechtsgeschäftslehre betreffenden Vorschriften zur Einbeziehung von allgemeinen Geschäfts.bedingungen, zum Widerrufsrecht bei Fernabsatzgeschäften sowie die Vorgaben der E-Commerce-Richtlinie der EU und deren Umsetzung und Sanktionierung im deutschen Recht eingehend behandelt.

Aus dem Inhalt: Zurechnung elektronischer Willenserklärungen, Anfechtbarkeit, Abgabe und Zugang · Widerrufsrecht bei Fernabsatzgeschäften · Angebot und Annahme: Websites, Auktionen, Marktplätze, EDI, WAP, Commerce-Bots · Einbeziehung allgemeiner Geschäftsbedingungen · Anbieterpflichten gemäß § 312e BGB

Frankfurt am Main · Berlin · Bern · Bruxelles · New York · Oxford · Wien
Auslieferung: Verlag Peter Lang AG
Moosstr. 1, CH-2542 Pieterlen
Telefax 0041(0)32/3761727

*inklusive der in Deutschland gültigen Mehrwertsteuer
Preisänderungen vorbehalten
Homepage http://www.peterlang.de